ALL NEW 100 MATHS LESSONS

Licence

Please check front pocket for CD

YEAR 2

Caroline Clissold

Contents

Acknowledgements
Extracts from the National Numeracy Strategy Framework for Teaching Mathematics © Crown copyright. Reproduced under the terms of HMSO Guidance Note 8
The Royal Mint for the use of photographs of coins of the realm © Crown copyright

Every effort has been made to trace copyright holders for the works reproduced in this book, and the publishers apologise for any inadvertent omissions.

Designed using Adobe Inc. InDesign™ v2.0.1

British Library Cataloguing-in-Publication Data
A catalogue record for this book is available from the British Library.
ISBN 0-439-98468-8; 978-0439-98468-3

The right of Ann Montague-Smith to be identified as the Author of this work has been asserted by her in accordance with the Copyright, Designs and Patents Act 1988.

Published by
Scholastic Ltd
Villiers House
Clarendon Avenue
Leamington Spa
Warks. CV32 5PR

© Scholastic Ltd, 2005
Text © Caroline Clissold, 2005

Printed by Bell & Bain
3456789 5678901234

Series Consultant
Ann Montague-Smith

Author
Caroline Clissold

Editors
Nancy Candlin, Joel Lane
and Jo Kemp

Assistant Editor
Aileen Lalor

Series Designer
Joy Monkhouse

Designers
Catherine Mason, Micky
Pledge and Andrea Lewis

Illustrations
Debbie Clark and
Jennie Tulip
(Beehive Illustration)

CD development
CD developed in association
with Footmark Media Ltd

Visit our website at
www.scholastic.co.uk

About the series

100 Maths Lessons is designed to enable you to provide clear teaching, with follow-up activities that are, in the main, practical activities for pairs of children to work on together. These activities are designed to encourage the children to use the mental strategies that they are learning and to check each other's calculations. Many of the activities are games that they will enjoy playing, and that encourage learning.

About the book

This book is divided into three termly sections. Each term begins with a **Medium-term plan** ('Termly planning grid') based on the National Numeracy Strategy's *Medium-term plans* and *Framework for teaching mathematics*. Each term's work is divided into a number of units of differentiated lessons on a specific subject.

Note: Because the units in this book follow the structure of the National Numeracy Strategy's *Framework for teaching mathematics*, the units in each term jump from Unit 6 to Unit 8. The Strategy suggests you put aside the time for Unit 7 for Assess and review.

Finding your way around the lesson units

Each term is comprised of 11 to 12 units. Each unit contains:
- a short-term planning grid
- three to five lesson plans
- photocopiable activity sheets.

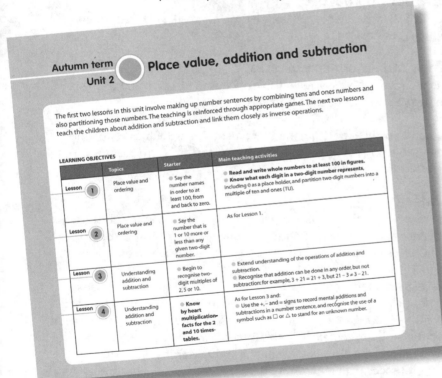

Short-term planning grids

The short-term planning grids ('Learning objectives') provide an overview of the objectives for each unit. The objectives come from the Medium-term plan and support clear progression through the year. Key objectives are shown in bold, as in the Yearly Teaching Programme in the NNS *Framework for teaching mathematics*.

Lesson plans

The lessons are structured on the basis of a daily maths lesson following the NNS's three-part lesson format: a ten-minute **Starter** of oral work and mental maths, a **Main teaching activities** session with interactive teaching time and/or group/individual work and a **Plenary** round-up including **Assessment** opportunities. In some lessons, differentiated tasks are supplied for more able and less able pupils.

However, this structure has not been rigidly applied. Where it is appropriate to concentrate on whole-class teaching, for example, the lesson plan may not include a group-work session at all. The overall organisation of the lesson plan varies from unit to unit depending on the lesson content. In some units all the plans are separate, though they provide different levels of detail. Elsewhere you may find a bank of activities that you can set up as a 'circus', or instruction and support for an extended investigation, either of which the children will work through over the course of several days.

Most units of work are supported with activity pages provided in the book, which can also be found on the accompanying CD. In addition to these core activity sheets, the CD contains differentiated versions for less able and more able ability levels. Some are available as blank templates, to allow you to make your own further differentiated versions.

How ICT is used

Ideas for using ICT are suggested wherever appropriate in *100 Maths Lessons*. We have assumed that you will have access to basic office applications, such as word-processing, and can email and research using the Internet. The QCA's *ICT Scheme of Work for Key Stages 1 and 2* has been used as an indicator of the skills the children will be developing formally from Year 1 and their progression in the primary years.

While some lessons use dataloggers or floor robots, we have avoided suggesting specific software, except for the games and interactive teaching programs (ITPs) provided by the NNS. If you do not already have them, these can be downloaded from the NNS website at: http://www.standards.dfes.gov.uk/numeracy

How to use the CD-ROM

System requirements
Minimum specification:
- PC with a CD-ROM drive and at least 32 MB RAM
- Pentium 166 MHz processor
- Microsoft Windows 98, NT, 2000 or XP
- SVGA screen display with at least 64K colours at a screen resolution of 800 x 600 pixels

100 Maths Lessons CD-ROMs are for PC use only.

Setting up your computer for optimal use
On opening, the CD will alert you if changes are needed in order to operate the CD at its optimal use. There are two changes you may be advised to make:

Viewing resources at their maximum screen size
To see images at their maximum screen size, your screen display needs to be set to 800 x 600 pixels. In order to adjust your screen size you will first need to **Quit** the program.

If using a PC, select **Settings**, then **Control Panel** from the **Start** menu. Next, double click on the **Display** icon and then click on the **Settings** tab. Finally, adjust the **Screen area** scroll bar to 800 x 600 pixels. Click **OK** and then restart the program.

Adobe® Acrobat® Reader®
Acrobat® Reader® is required to view Portable Document Format (PDF) files. All of the unit resources are PDF files. It is not necessary to install **Acrobat® Reader®** on your PC. If you do not have it installed, the application will use a 'run-time' version for the CD, i.e. one which only works with the 100 Maths Lessons application.
However if you would like to install **Acrobat® Reader®**, the latest version (6) can be downloaded from the CD-ROM*. To do this, right-click on the **Start** menu on your desktop and choose **Explore**. Click on the + sign to the left of the CD drive entitled '100 Maths Lessons' and open the folder called **Acrobat Reader Installer.** Run the program contained in this folder to install **Acrobat® Reader®.** If you experience any difficulties viewing the PDF files, try changing your **Acrobat® Reader®** preferences. Select **Edit**, then **Preferences**, within **Acrobat® Reader®**. You will then be able to change your viewing options.
(*Please note that **Acrobat® Reader®** version 6 is not compatible with some versions of Windows 98. To download version 5 or for further information about Adobe Acrobat Reader, visit the Adobe website at www.adobe.com.)

Getting started
The *100 Maths Lessons CD-ROM* program should auto run when you insert the CD-ROM into your CD drive. If it does not, use **My Computer** to browse the contents of the CD-ROM and click on the '100 Maths Lessons' icon.
From the start up screen there are three options: Click on **Credits** to view a list of acknowledgements. You must then read the **Terms and conditions**. If you agree to these terms then click **Next** to continue. **Continue** on the start up screen allows you to move to the Main menu.

Main menu

Each *100 Maths Lessons* CD contains:
- core activity sheets – with answers, where appropriate, that can be toggled by pressing the 'on' and 'off' buttons on the left of the screen
- differentiated activity sheets for more and less able pupils (though not necessarily both more and less able sheets in every instance)
- blank core activity sheets for selected core activity sheets – these allow you to make your own differentiated sheets by printing and annotating.
- general resource sheets designed to support a number of activities.

You can access the printable pages on the CD by clicking:
- the chosen term ('Autumn','Spring' or 'Summer')
- the unit required (for example,'Unit 2: Place value and ordering')
- the requisite activity page (for example,'Numbers to 10';'Less able').

To help you manage the vast bank of printable pages on each CD, there is also an 'Assessment record sheet' provided on the CD that you can use to record which children have tackled which pages. This could be particularly useful if you would like less able children to work through two or three of the differentiated pages for a lesson or topic. The termly planning grids found on pages 6-7, 76-77 and 142-143 have also been supplied on the CD in both **PDF** and **Microsoft Word** formats to enable you to incorporate the 'All New 100 Maths Lessons' units into your planning or to adapt them as required.

CD navigation

Back: click to return to the previous screen. Continue to move to the **Menu** or start up screens.

Quit: click **Quit** to close the menu program. You are then provided with options to return to the start up menu or to exit the CD.

Help: provides general background information and basic technical support. Click on the **Help** button to access. Click **Back** to return to the previous screen.

Alternative levels: after you have accessed a CD page, you will see a small menu screen on the left-hand side of the screen. This allows you to access differentiated or template versions of the same activity.

Printing

There are two print options:
- The **Print** button on the bottom left of each activity screen allows you to print directly from the CD program.
- If you press the **View** button above the **Print** option, the sheet will open as a read-only page in **Acrobat® Reader®**. To print the selected resource from **Acrobat® Reader®**, select **File** and then **Print**. Once you have printed the resource, minimise or close the **Adobe®** screen using _ or **x** in the top right-hand corner of the screen.

Viewing on an interactive whiteboard or data projector

The sheets can be viewed directly from the CD. To make viewing easier for a whole class, use a large monitor, data projector or interactive whiteboard.

About Year 2

Much of the work in Year 2 focuses on the progression from informal calculating methods to more formal standard methods. The Year 2 programme is designed to give step-by-step guidance through these methods and includes a number of practice activities for reinforcement and assessment. There are also a variety of games and puzzles to encourage children to learn and apply mental calculation strategies to ensure that the learning process is both challenging and fun. It is important at this stage that children are able to make informed and appropriate choices about the methods and strategies they use and there are a number of opportunities in the book for practising this. There is an emphasis on problem solving in many units, allowing for application of what the children have learnt to 'real life' situations including money. In the oral and mental starters you will find the rehearsal of areas that don't come up often in the framework and are notorious as 'trouble spots' for example time and fractions.

EVERY DAY: Practise and develop oral and mental skills (e.g. counting, mental strategies, rapid recall of +, – and × facts)			

Say the number names in order to at least 100, from and back to zero.
Describe and extend simple number sequences: count on or back in ones or tens, starting from any two-digit number.
Count in hundreds from and back to zero.
Read and write whole numbers to at least 100 in figures and words.
Say the number that is 1 or 10 more or less than any given two-digit number.
Begin to recognise two-digit multiples of 2, 5 or 10.
Know by heart multiplication facts for the 2 and 10 times-tables.
Know by heart addition and subtraction facts for each number to at least 10.
Know by heart doubles of all numbers to 10 and the corresponding halves.
Use the mathematical names for common 3-D and 2-D shapes.
Sort shapes and describe their features.

Units	Days	Topics	Objectives
1	3	Counting, properties of numbers and number sequences	• Count reliably up to 100 objects by grouping them in tens. • Describe and extend simple number sequences: count on or back in ones or tens, starting from any two-digit number. • Begin to recognise two-digit multiples of 2, 5 or 10.
2–4	15	Place value and ordering	• **Read and write whole numbers to at least 100 in figures.** • **Know what each digit in a two-digit number represents,** including 0 as a place holder, and partition two-digit numbers into a multiple of ten and ones (TU).
		Understanding addition and subtraction	• Extend understanding of the operations of addition and subtraction. • Recognise that addition can be done in any order, but not subtraction: for example, 3 + 21 = 21 + 3, but 21 – 3 ≠ 3 – 21. • Use the +, – and = signs to record mental additions and subtractions in a number sentence, and recognise the use of a symbol such as □ or △ to stand for an unknown number.
		Mental calculation strategies (+ and –)	• **Use knowledge that addition can be done in any order to do mental calculations more efficiently.** For example: – put the larger number first and count on in tens or ones – add/subtract 9 or 11: add/subtract 10 and adjust by 1 – identify near doubles, using doubles already known (e.g. 8 + 9, 40 + 41)
		Making decisions	• **Choose and use appropriate operations and efficient calculation strategies** (e.g. mental, mental with jottings) **to solve problems**.
		Problems involving 'real life', money or measures	• Recognise all coins and begin to use £.p notation for money (for example, know that £4.65 indicates £4 and 65p). • Find totals, give change, and work out which coins to pay.
		Checking results of calculations	• Repeat addition in a different order.
5–6	8	Measures	• Use and begin to read the vocabulary related to length. • **Estimate, measure and compare lengths, using standard units** (m, cm); **suggest suitable units and equipment for such measurements.** • Use and begin to read the vocabulary related to time. • Suggest suitable units to estimate or measure time. • Use units of time and know the relationships between them (second, minute, hour, day, week).
		Shape and space	• **Use the mathematical names for common 3-D and 2-D shapes,** including the pyramid, cylinder, pentagon, hexagon, octagon. • **Sort shapes and describe some of their features.** • Make and describe shapes. • **Use mathematical vocabulary to describe position, direction and movement:** e.g. example, describe, place, tick, draw or visualise objects in given positions.
		Reasoning about numbers or shapes	• Investigate a general statement about familiar shapes by finding examples that satisfy it.
7		Assess and review	

EVERY DAY: Practise and develop oral and mental skills (e.g. counting, mental strategies, rapid recall of +, – and × facts)

Read and write whole numbers to at least 100 in figures and words.
Describe and extend simple number sequences: count in hundreds from and back to zero.
Know by heart doubles of all numbers to 10 and the corresponding halves.
Begin to recognise two-digit multiples of 2, 5 and 10; Identify near doubles using doubles already known (e.g. 8 + 9, 40 + 41).
Know by heart all addition facts for each number to at least 10; Know by heart all pairs of numbers with a total of 20 (e.g. 13 + 7, 6 + 14).
Add/subtract 9 or 11: add/subtract 10 and adjust by 1.
Order whole numbers to at least 100 and position them on a 100 square.
Know by heart multiplication facts for the 2 and 10 times-tables; Derive quickly division facts corresponding to the 2 and 10 times-tables.
Read the time to the hour, half hour or quarter hour on an analogue clock and a 12-hour digital clock; Order months of the year.

Units	Days	Topics	Objectives
8	5	Counting, properties of numbers and sequences	• **Describe and extend simple number sequences:** – **count on or back in ones or tens, starting from any two-digit number.** – count on or back in twos. – recognise odd and even numbers to at least 30. • Begin to recognise two-digit multiples of 2.
		Reasoning about numbers or shapes	• Investigate a general statement about familiar numbers by finding examples. • **Solve mathematical problems or puzzles.** • **Suggest extensions by asking 'What if…?' or 'What could I try next?'**
9	5	Place value and ordering	• Use and begin to read the vocabulary of comparing and ordering numbers, including ordinal numbers to 100.
		Understanding +/ –	• Extend understanding of the operations of addition and subtraction. Use and begin to read the related vocabulary.
		Mental calculation strategies (+ / –)	• Use patterns of similar calculations. • Find a small difference by counting up from the smaller to the larger number (e.g. 42 – 39).
		Problems involving 'real life'	• Recognise all coins and begin to use £.p notation for money. • Find totals, give change and work out which coins to pay.
		Making decisions	• **Choose and use appropriate operations and efficient calculation strategies** (e.g. mental, mental with jottings) **to solve problems**.
10–11	10	Understanding ×/÷	• **Understand the operation of multiplication as repeated addition or as describing an array,** and begin to understand division as grouping or sharing. • Use and read the related vocabulary. • Use the ×, ÷ and = signs to record mental calculations in a number sentence, and recognise the use of a symbol such as □ or Δ to stand for an unknown number.
		Mental calculation strategies (×/÷)	• Use known number facts and place value to carry out simple multiplications and divisions.
		Problems involving 'real life'	• Use mental addition and subtraction, simple multiplication and division, to solve simple word problems, using one or two steps. • Explain how the problem was solved.
		Making decisions	• **Choose and use appropriate operations and efficient calculation strategies** (e.g. mental, mental with jottings) to solve problems.
		Fractions	• Begin to recognise and find one half and one quarter of shapes and small numbers of objects. • Begin to recognise that two halves or four quarters make one whole and that two quarters and one half are equivalent.
12–13	10	Measures	• **Read a simple scale to the nearest labelled division, including using a ruler to draw and measure lines to the nearest centimetre.** • Order the months of the year. • Read the time to the hour, half hour or quarter hour.
		Reasoning about numbers or shapes	• Solve mathematical problems or puzzles, recognise simple patterns and relationships, generalise and predict. • Suggest extensions by asking 'What if…?' or 'What could I try next?'
		Organising and using data	• Solve a given problem by sorting, classifying and organising information in simple ways. • Discuss and explain results.
14		Assess and review	

Numbers up to 100

This unit deals with estimating and then counting reliably up to 100 objects by grouping them in tens and, where appropriate, twos and fives, describing and extending number sequences and recognising multiples of 2, 5 and 10. Activities to reinforce the teaching include games and number line work.

LEARNING OBJECTIVES

		Topics	Starter	Main teaching activity
Lesson	1	Counting, properties of numbers and number sequences	● Say the number names in order to at least 100, from and back to zero. ● **Describe and extend simple number sequences: count on or back in ones or tens, starting from any two-digit number.**	● Count reliably up to 100 objects by grouping them in tens.
Lesson	2	Counting, properties of numbers and number sequences	As for Lesson 1.	● **Describe and extend simple number sequences: count on or back in ones or tens, starting from any two-digit number.**
Lesson	3	Counting, properties of numbers and number sequences	● **Describe and extend simple number sequences: count on or back in ones or tens, starting from any two-digit number.** ● Count in hundreds from and back to zero.	● Begin to recognise two-digit multiples of 2, 5 or 10.

Lessons   overview

Preparation
Make a pendulum by threading three Unifix or Multilink cubes onto a string about 1m long. Make up sets of 'Elephant estimating game' cards by copying onto card, cutting out and laminating.

Learning objectives
Starter
● Say the number names in order to at least 100, from and back to zero.
● **Describe and extend simple number sequences: count on or back in ones or tens, starting from any two-digit number.**
● Count in hundreds from and back to zero.
Main teaching activities
● Count reliably up to 100 objects by grouping them in tens.
● **Describe and extend simple number sequences: count on or back in ones or tens, starting from any two-digit number.**
● Begin to recognise two-digit multiples of 2, 5 or 10.

Vocabulary
number, zero, one hundred, two hundred… one thousand, count on (from, to), count back (from, to), count in ones, count in tens, multiple of, sequence, continue, predict

You will need:
Photocopiable pages
A copy of 'Circle grid for multiples of 2, 5 and 10' (page 11) for each child.

CD pages
A set of '0–100 number cards', a set of 'Elephant estimating game' cards and a set of 'Blank number lines' for each pair of children, an enlarged teacher set of 'Elephant estimating game' cards (see General resources).

Equipment
Unifix or Multilink cubes; 1m length of string; counting stick marked in tens; OHP; plastic cup; counters; whiteboard.

Lesson

Starter

Tell the children to count on in ones in time to the swing of the pendulum, starting from the number you call out. When you stop swinging the pendulum, say *Backwards* to start the children counting back from that number. Begin with single-digit numbers, then use numbers such as 23, 56, 67 and 72. Now use a counting stick marked in tens to help the children count on and back in tens from numbers such as 46, 12 and 9. Ask questions such as: *If 12 is at this end, what number will be at the third mark?* (42) … *the sixth mark?* (72) … *two more on from here?* (92)

Main teaching activities

Whole class: Explain to the children that today they will be learning to estimate how many objects there are in a collection, and then finding out how many there actually are by counting them. Place ten cubes on an OHP in twos. Quickly switch the OHP on and off. Ask: *How many cubes did you see? Make an estimate.* Turn on the OHP again: *How could we count the cubes?* Encourage counting in twos. Repeat this with different numbers of cubes less than 30. Group them in different ways to encourage a variety of counting techniques. For example: group 24 as two tens and two twos; group 18 in three fives and three ones. Encourage the children to estimate before counting.

Paired work: Give each pair a plastic cup containing up to 30 counters, and give each child an Elephant card, a pen and paper (or an individual whiteboard). Ask them to take turns to drop a handful of counters on the table. As quickly as possible, both children write down their estimates of how many have been dropped. The first child then counts them in groups onto an Elephant card, grouping them in different ways (not counting them singly).

Differentiation

Less able: This group can use up to 20 counters.
More able: Give this group up to 40 counters and ask them to drop a minimum of 20; encourage them to explore different ways of counting.

Plenary & assessment

Drop ten cubes onto the OHP and ask the children to suggest different ways of counting them. Drop on another ten and ask: *How many are there now? How could we count them easily?* Keep adding various numbers of cubes and asking how the total can be counted quickly; discourage counting them all singly. Ask: *If we count in ones or count in tens, will the answer be the same?* Through questioning, check that each child can count by grouping in tens.

Lesson

Starter

Repeat the Starter from Lesson 1, but with the children counting on and back in twos and tens from given numbers.

Main teaching activities

Whole class: Place a shuffled pack of number cards 0–50 face down. Invite someone to pick a card and write the number on the board. Write up the next five counting numbers and ask the children to tell you about the sequence. Focus initially on the way the units numbers go up in ones. Invite another child to pick a card and ask others to make a sequence as you did.

Draw a number line with ten divisions. Ask a child to pick a card and write the number in the middle of the line. Invite other children to complete the line and to say whether the numbers get bigger or smaller in each direction. Repeat this a few times.

Paired work: Give each pair CD page 'Blank number lines' and some number cards. They can take turns to pick a card and write the number in the middle of a number line, with the other child completing the line to make a sequence of numbers going up and down by five numbers in ones.

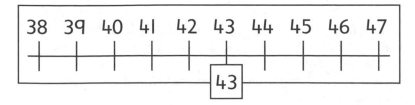

38 39 40 41 42 43 44 45 46 47

43

Differentiation

Less able: This group can use number cards to 20.
More able: This group can use number cards to 100.

Plenary & assessment

Invite a few pairs to draw one of their number lines on the board and show how they wrote in the numbers.

Draw a number line with the numbers going down from left to right. Put up three out of six numbers, for example:

| 23 | 22 | | | | 18 |

Ask the children what the missing numbers are. Ask them how they knew, and what clues they used to help them. Repeat this with tens. For example:

| 60 | | 40 | | 20 | |

Lesson ③

Starter

Repeat the counting stick part of the Starter from Lesson 1. Now ask the children what number comes after 99. Tell them that they are going to count in steps of 100. Count together up to 900, then ask whether anyone knows what comes next. Count back to zero.

Main teaching activities

Whole class: Explain that today the children will be learning to recognise numbers in the counting patterns of 2, 5 and 10. Say these patterns together. Explain that these numbers are called the 'multiples' of 2, 5 and 10. Write the twos 0–20, the fives 0–50 and the tens 0–100 on the board. What can the children tell you about these sequences? Focus on the units digits.

Using a set of number cards 0–50, hold up one card at a time and ask the children to tell you whether it shows a multiple of 2, 5, 10, a mixture or none. Record like this:

24 → 2   30 → 2, 5, 10   17 → none

Group work: Give each group a shuffled set of 0–100 cards and ask them to repeat the above activity.

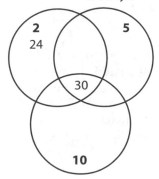

Differentiation

Less able: This group can use number cards to 20.
More able: Demonstrate the 'circle grid' method of recording (see illustration). Give the children the 'Circle grid for multiples of 2, 5 and 10' sheet to record on.

Plenary & assessment

Ask the more able group to explain the way of recording they used. Draw the circle grid on the board, hold up number cards and invite children to write each number in the appropriate place.

Name   Date

Circle grid for multiples of 2, 5 and 10

Use this grid to sort numbers.

Are they multiples of 2, 5 or 10?
Are they multiples of all three numbers?

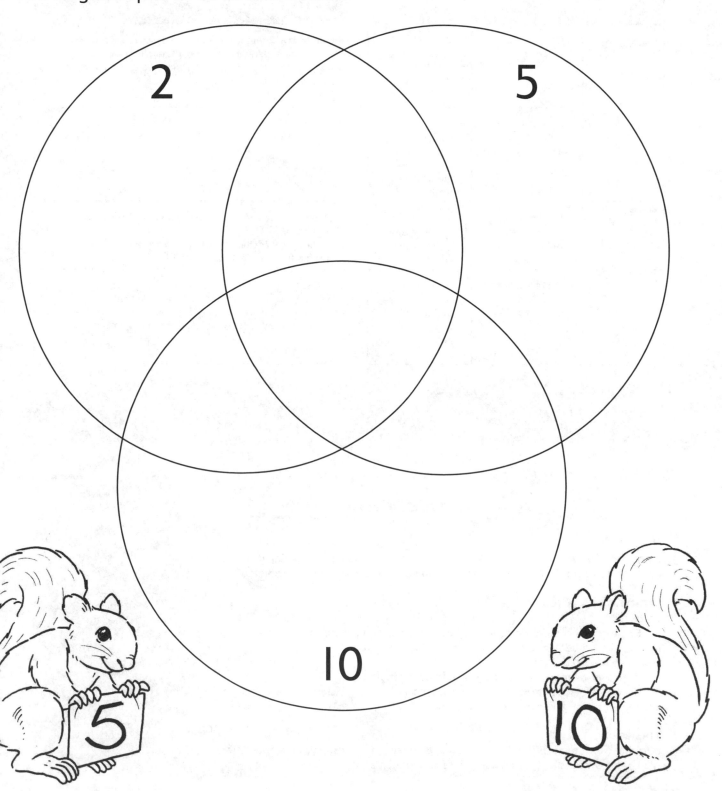

The first two lessons in this unit involve making up number sentences by combining tens and ones numbers and also partitioning those numbers. The teaching is reinforced through appropriate games. The next two lessons teach the children about addition and subtraction and link them closely as inverse operations.

LEARNING OBJECTIVES

	Topics	Starter	Main teaching activities
Lesson 1	Place value and ordering	● Say the number names in order to at least 100, from and back to zero.	● **Read and write whole numbers to at least 100 in figures.** ● **Know what each digit in a two-digit number represents**, including 0 as a place holder, and partition two-digit numbers into a multiple of ten and ones (TU).
Lesson 2	Place value and ordering	● Say the number that is 1 or 10 more or less than any given two-digit number.	As for Lesson 1.
Lesson 3	Understanding addition and subtraction	● Begin to recognise two-digit multiples of 2, 5 or 10.	● Extend understanding of the operations of addition and subtraction. ● Recognise that addition can be done in any order, but not subtraction: for example, $3 + 21 = 21 + 3$, but $21 - 3 \neq 3 - 21$.
Lesson 4	Understanding addition and subtraction	● **Know by heart multiplication facts for the 2 and 10 times-tables.**	As for Lesson 3 and: ● Use the +, – and = signs to record mental additions and subtractions in a number sentence, and recognise the use of a symbol such as □ or △ to stand for an unknown number.

Lessons   overview

Preparation
Prepare a set of number cards 10–100 from CD page '0–100 number cards'. Copy and enlarge a set of 'Arrow cards'. Copy the 'Up the mountain gameboard' onto card and laminate.

Learning objectives
Starter
● Say the number names in order to at least 100, from and back to zero.
● Say the number that is 1 or 10 more or less than any given two-digit number.
Main teaching activities
● **Read and write whole numbers to at least 100 in figures**.
● Know what each number in a two-digit number represents, including 0 as a place holder, and partition two-digit numbers into a multiple of ten and ones (TU).

Vocabulary
zero, one, two… to twenty and beyond, units, ones, tens, hundreds, digit, one-, two- or three-digit number, rule, place, place value, stands for, represents

You will need:
CD pages
'0–100 number cards', a class set of enlarged 'Arrow cards', 'Up the mountain 1' and 'Up the mountain gameboard' for each group (see General resources).

Equipment
An individual whiteboard and pen for each child; counters; a class 100 square.

Lesson 1

Starter
Quickly count together in ones from zero to 20 and back, then from any number below 20 for another 20 (for example, 16 to 36). Ask individuals to pick a number from the 10–100 number cards. Say: *Count on until I clap, then start counting backwards.* Clap after every few counts, so the children keep changing direction. Make sure the count crosses the tens boundaries often and encourage counting beyond 100.

Main teaching activities
Whole class: Explain that today the children will be revising how to make numbers over 10 by combining tens and ones. Make sure the children can read the enlarged 'ones' arrow cards, then the 'tens'. Now hold up one of each (for example, 20 and 5) and ask: *What number can we make if we put these two together?* Show 25. Repeat. Invite two children to come to the front and choose a 'tens' and a 'ones' card respectively. Ask the class to read each card and then say what the number is when the two cards are combined. Ask the two children to demonstrate. Repeat.

Hold up a 'ones' and a 'tens' card and ask the children to write down what number will be made when the cards are combined. Repeat several times. Show the children how to record this using a number sentence, for example 30 + 6 = 36. Invite some children to write one combination each on the board, then ask everyone to write several combinations on their whiteboards.
Group work: Model the instructions for the Lesson 1 version of the 'Up the mountain' game, then let the children play in groups.

Differentiation
Mixed-ability groups would be best for this game so the more able pupils can support the less able.

Plenary & assessment
Invite four or five children to select a 'ones' and a 'tens' card, combine them and say what their new number is. Ask the class to order these children from the lowest number to the highest. Write the order on the board. Repeat.

Lesson 2

Starter
Quickly count in tens from zero to 100 and back, then from any number below 100 for ten counts (for example, 37 to 137) and back. Ask the children to choose a number that fits certain criteria, such as a two-digit odd number between 30 and 40. Take a suggestion and ask another child to write it on the board. Ask: *What is one more… one less… ten more…ten less?* Use the class 100 square to help if needed.

Main teaching activities
Whole class: Pick a two-digit number card and ask the children to tell you what each digit represents – for example, in 46 the digits represent 4 tens and 6 ones. Demonstrate using the enlarged arrow cards: show the whole number and then reveal the zero of the 40 hidden under the 6. Explain the role of zero as a place holder. Write a number sentence: 46 = 40 + 6. Repeat.
Group work: Model the instructions for the Lesson 2 version of the 'Up the mountain' game, then let the children play in groups.

Differentiation
Model the instructions for the differentiated versions of the 'Up the mountain' game (shown on the Lesson 2 Instructions), then let the children play in groups.

Plenary & assessment

Hold up two-digit number cards and ask the children to partition them about eight times, writing the numbers on the board. Show another number and ask which of the eight is the closest (in number terms) to the one you are holding and which is the furthest away. Draw a number line and write the number you are holding in the middle, then invite volunteers to write the other numbers in the correct places on the line.

Lessons   overview

Preparation

Prepare a set of number cards 0–100 from '0–100 number cards' sheet, and a set of 0–9 number cards for each child. Cut out and laminate a character from 'Characters for a number line'. Draw a large number line 0–30 and place it where the children can move the character along it. Copy the relevant 'Add and subtract', and 'Arrow sentences' sheets according to ability, one for each child.

Learning objectives

Starter
- Begin to recognise two-digit multiples of 2, 5 or 10.
- Know by heart multiplication facts for the 2 and 10 times-tables.

Main teaching activities
- Extend understanding of the operations of addition and subtraction.
- Recognise that addition can be done in any order, but not subtraction: for example, $3 + 21 = 21 + 3$, but $21 - 3 \neq 3 - 21$.
- Use the +, – and = signs to record mental additions and subtractions in a number sentence, and recognise the use of a symbol such as $\square$ or $\triangle$ to stand for an unknown number.

Vocabulary

multiple of, odd, even, add, addition, more, plus, +, sum, make, total, altogether, subtract, take away, –, minus, leave, how many are left/left over?, how many less is… than…?, subtraction, lots of

You will need:

Photocopiable pages
One copy of 'Add and subtract' (page 16) and 'Arrow sentences' (page 17) for each child.

CD pages
'Add and subtract', less able, more able and template, 'Arrow sentences', less able, more able and blank versions (Autumn term, Unit 2), one set of '0–100 number cards' and a set of 0–9 number cards for each child, a cartoon character from 'Characters for a number line' (see General resources).

Equipment
An individual whiteboard and pen for each child.

Lesson

Starter

Say: *Who can remember what 'multiples' are? What is special about multiples of 2… of 10… of 5?* Count together in ones from any number, asking the children to clap at each multiple of 2. Call out random numbers, asking for the same response. Now play 'Jog and jump'. Start counting slowly from 1. When the children hear you say a multiple of 5, they should jump; for a multiple of 10, they should jog on the spot; for a multiple of both, they should do both. Ask them what they notice. (They never jog without jumping.) Can they explain this?

Main teaching activities

Whole class: Explain that today the children will be adding and subtracting numbers, and finding out whether it matters in which order we do it. Ask: *What does 'add' mean?* Encourage the children to tell you all the 'add' words they can think of. Repeat for 'subtract'.

Make a pile of single-digit number cards and another of two-digit numbers. Invite a child to pick one card from each pile. Write these numbers on the board (for example, 23 and 5). Ask the child to put the cartoon character on the class number line to mark the higher of the two numbers, then add on the other number by counting along the number line with the character (so count on five from 23). Write up the number sentence: $23 + 5 = 28$. Now ask the child to put the character on 5 and count on 23. Ask: *Is the answer the same?* Write $5 + 23 = 28$ on the board. Try another example.

Repeat with subtraction – for example, counting back 4 from 17 and writing the number sentence: 17 – 4 = 13. Now start at 4 and ask: *If we count back 17, will the answer be the same as before? What will happen?* Encourage the response that 17 cannot be taken away from the 4. If someone says the answer will be a negative number, demonstrate by counting back to –13, but don't teach the class this. Repeat several times.

Group work: Explain that the children are going to prove that it doesn't matter which way they add, but it does matter which way they subtract. Give each child a copy of the 'Add and subtract' sheet and talk through the activity with each group.

Differentiation
Less able: Give this group the version of 'Add and subtract' with numbers to 10.
More able: Give this group the version with numbers to 49.

Plenary & assessment
Ask the children whether they proved that addition can be done in any order. Invite a few children to explain. Say: *Can you think of any time when it doesn't matter in which order we subtract numbers?* If they can't answer, prompt them by writing the same number twice on the board.

Lesson 4

Starter
Ask the children to count in twos from zero to 10. Now ask them to count in twos using their fingers: 0 (no fingers), 2 (one finger) and so on to 20 (ten fingers). Repeat, but stop them (for example, at 12) and ask: *How many fingers are you holding up? How many lots of 2 is that?* Write on the board: $2 \times 6 = 12$.

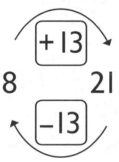

Main teaching activities
Whole class: Explain that today's lesson is about linking addition and subtraction. Write on the board: 13 + 8 = 21. Ask: *Can you think of another calculation using these numbers?* (8 + 13 = 21) Now ask the children to work out 21 – 13. Draw an arrow diagram to link the addition and the subtraction. Explain that subtraction is the inverse or opposite of addition. Write the number sentences 13 + 8 = 21 and 21 – 8 = 13. Repeat.

Group work: Give each child a copy of the 'Arrow sentences' activity sheet to complete.

Differentiation
Less able: This group uses the version of 'Arrow sentences' with totals to 10 and single-digit numbers to add and subtract.
More able: This group can use the version with totals to 40 and two-digit numbers to add and subtract.

Plenary & assessment
Ask some children whom you particularly wish to assess to write up an example of their work, using an arrow diagram and number sentences. Now write on the board: 9 + □ = 13 and 13 – □ = 9. Ask the children whether they can use an arrow diagram to find the missing numbers. Encourage them to explain their thinking. Remind them that addition is the opposite or inverse of subtraction.

middle x2

Name	Date

Add and subtract

alter
Nob

5	21	15	7
16	8	9	27
10	20	3	19
13	24	26	30

1. Choose two numbers from the grid, such as 10 and 7.

2. Make up two addition calculations, such as 10 + 7 = and 7 + 10 =.

_____   _____

3. Do you think the answers will be the same? _____

4. Work out the answers using a number line. Complete the two number sentences.

5. Make up two subtraction calculations with the same numbers, such as 10 – 7 = and 7 – 10 =.

_____   _____

6. Do you think the answers will be the same? _____

7. Work out the answers using a number line. Can you find both answers?

_____   _____

8. What can you say about addition and subtraction?

_____

_____

_____

9. Use the grid numbers to make up some more examples. Write them on the back of this sheet.

_____

top

| Name | Date |

Arrow sentences

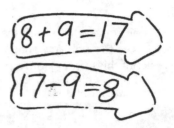

$8 + 9 = 17$

$17 - 9 = 8$

What do you need to add and take away in
these arrow sentences so that they make sense?

Write number sentences for what the arrow sentences show.
The first one has been done for you.

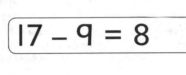

$8 + 9 = 17$

$17 - 9 = 8$

12   20

15   25

13   26

23   30

25   30

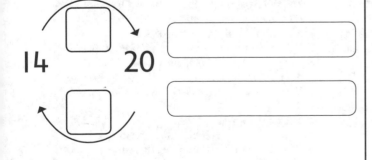

14   20

16   23

Different ways to add

This unit concentrates on three mental calculation strategies for addition. After the teaching, the learning is reinforced through approriately differentiated practical activities, that can be recorded. The last two lessons of the week put this learning into a problem solving context.

LEARNING OBJECTIVES

		Topics	Starter	Main teaching activities
Lesson	1	Mental calculation strategies (+ and −)	● **Read and write whole numbers to at least 100** in figures and words.	● **Use knowledge that addition can be done in any order to do mental calculations more efficiently.** For example: put the larger number first and count on in tens or ones.
Lesson	2	Mental calculation strategies (+ and −)	As for Lesson 1.	● **Use knowledge that addition can be done in any order to do mental calculations more efficiently.** For example: add/subtract 9 or 11: add/subtract 10 and adjust by 1.
Lesson	3	Mental calculation strategies (+ and −)	● **Know by heart multiplication facts for the 2 and 10 times-tables.**	● **Use knowledge that addition can be done in any order to do mental calculations more efficiently.** For example: identify near doubles, using doubles already known (e.g. 8 + 9, 40 + 41).
Lesson	4	Making decisions	● **Know by heart addition and subtraction facts for each number to at least 10.**	● **Choose and use appropriate operations and efficient calculation strategies** (e.g. mental, mental with jottings) **to solve problems.**

Lessons overview

Preparation
Cut out the function machines from the enlarged copies of the 'Function machine game'. Laminate the copies of CD page 'Function machine' activity for repeated use.

Learning objectives
Starter
● **Read and write whole numbers to at least 100** in figures and words.
● **Know by heart multiplication facts for the 2 and 10 times-tables.**
Main teaching activities
● **Use knowledge that addition can be done in any order to do mental calculations more efficiently.** For example: put the larger number first and count on in tens or ones; add/subtract 9 or 11: add/subtract 10 and adjust by 1; identify near doubles, using doubles already known (e.g. 8 + 9, 40 + 41).

Vocabulary
one-, two- or three-digit number, place, place value, represents, double, near double, total, addition, sum

You will need:
Photocopiable pages
A laminated copy of the 'Function machine' activity (page 22) for each child.

CD pages
Laminated 'Function machine', less able version (Autumn term, Unit 3); number cards 1–9 for each child and 0–20 for each more able child (from '0–100 Number cards'), two A3 copies of the 'Function machine' for each group, an enlarged acetate of 'Spider charts for multiplying', a set of cards from 'Near doubles cards' for each pair of children, a set of 'Near doubles game' instructions for the teacher or classroom assistant (see General resources).

Equipment
An individual whiteboard and pen for each child; a large class 100 square; an individual 100 square for each child.

Lesson

Starter

Practise reading two-digit and three-digit numbers. Ask the children to set out their number cards in order from 0 to 9. While they are getting ready, ask the class simple things like: *Show me four… seven… one more than 8; … one less than 4; … three more than 9; Double it.* Now ask the children to put a 3 in front of them, then make the 3 into 53, then make 253. Ask them to swap the 2 and the 5. Ask one of the lower-ability children to read the digits, then invite any child to read the actual number. Repeat several times.

Main teaching activities

Whole class: Explain that today the children will be adding several numbers together by starting with the largest and counting on. Recap the vocabulary of addition. Invite a child to pick two cards from a pack of number cards, hold these up and then give the higher card to a friend. The friend stands, holding up the card (for example, 7). The children note the number in their heads, then the friend sits. The original volunteer holds up the other card (for example, 4), and together everyone counts on that number from the first number (i.e. count on 4 from 7). Record this as a number sentence (7 + 4 = 11). Repeat several times.

Go on to add three numbers in the same way. Ask the children how they could check that their answer is right. Encourage them to suggest adding the numbers in a different order.

Group work: Model the following activity with two children: pick a card each from a pack of 0–10 number cards, order the three numbers from the largest to the smallest, then write the order down and total the numbers by counting on from the largest number. Let the children continue this activity in groups of three or four.

Differentiation

Less able: This group can try adding two numbers from 0–10.
More able: This group can pick three numbers from a pack of 0–20 cards.

Plenary & assessment

Invite one or two children from each group to say how they found one of their totals. Write all the totals they say on the board. Ask the children to order these from largest to smallest and then have a go at adding them all together. Ask: *Are there other strategies for adding these numbers?* Finally, say: *There are several ways to add numbers. We have been thinking about one strategy today, but over the next two days we'll be learning about others. Our aim is to know several strategies, so we can choose the best ones to use for different calculations.*

Lesson

Starter

Call out some two-digit and three-digit numbers for the children to write on their whiteboards. Now repeat the Starter from Lesson 1.

Main teaching activities

Whole class: Remind the children that 9 can be added to numbers quite easily because it is so close to 10. Use a large 100 square to demonstrate how to add 9 by adding 10 (jump down a row) and then adjusting the answer by taking away 1. Show this for single-digit numbers, then for numbers to 20. Give each child a 100 square so that they can copy what you do. Once they have understood the idea, move on to demonstrate how to add 11 by adding 10 and then one more.

Group work: Demonstrate the 'Function machine game', as explained on the CD page. Hand out the 'Function machine' activity sheet and ask the children to play the game in groups.

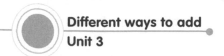

Differentiation

Less able: This group can use the version of the 'Function machine' with starting numbers provided. Provide a large 100 square to help them.
More able: Ask the children to write starting numbers from 50 to 100.

Plenary & assessment

Talk about using a similar strategy for subtracting 9, then 11. Write a few numbers on the board from which the children can subtract 9 and 11 by subtracting 10 and adjusting. They can use their 100 squares for this. Finally, write four calculations on the board, such as:

$36 + 9 = ?$ $\qquad$ $12 + 3 + 5 = ?$ $\qquad$ $47 - 11 = ?$ $\qquad$ $10 + 1 + 23 = ?$

Ask the children which of the strategies they have thought about over the last two lessons is best for answering each of these. Question the children you need to assess by asking, for example: *Why did you choose this strategy? Why is it the best one?*

Lesson

Starter

Ask the children to count slowly in twos, using one finger for each count. When they reach 10, ask them how many fingers they are holding up. Reinforce the idea that this shows that five lots of 2 make 10. Repeat for other counts up to 20. Now ask the children to look at the first spider chart on the enlarged copy of 'Spider charts for multiplying'. Ask them to count in twos for one count, two counts and so on, going round the chart. Link this to counting on fingers. Say that when they said 'eight' you were pointing at 4 on the chart, and this shows that four lots of 2 are 8. Point randomly at numbers and ask the children what that many lots of 2 are. Repeat this with tens on the second spider chart.

Main teaching activities

Whole class: Revise addition using the 'Near doubles game' and 'Near doubles cards'. Ask the children to tell you the doubles of all numbers to 15. Write them on the board: $1 + 1 = 2$, $2 + 2 = 4$ and so on. Ask: *Using what's on the board, can you tell me what 5 + 6 is?* Encourage the response: '5 add 5 add an extra 1'. Record: $5 + 6 = 5 + 5 + 1 = 11$. Repeat with most of your doubles.
Write $20 + 19$ on the board. Ask: *How can we add these using doubles?* Help the children to see that the answer is double 20 take away 1. Make a list of multiples of 10 and their doubles, from $10 + 10 = 20$ to $90 + 90 = 180$. Ask: *How can we work out 30 + 29?* Encourage the response: 'double 30 take away 1'. Record: $30 + 29 = 30 + 30 - 1 = 59$. Repeat with most of your doubles.
Group work: Explain that the children will practise this strategy by playing a pairs or Pelmanism game. Model the game using the cards and instructions from the 'Near doubles game'. Give each group a set of 'Near doubles cards' to play the game. Most of the class can use cards to 30.

Differentiation

Less able: This group can use 'Near doubles game' cards to 10.
More able: This group can use multiples and near multiples of 10.

Plenary & assessment

Invite some children to explain how they worked out the near doubles, and to write their number sentences on the board. Revisit the addition strategies used in the last three lessons. Ask the children which strategies they would use to find totals such as: $8 + 7, 30 + 31, 25 + 9, 2 + 12 + 3$. Explain that in the next lesson, they will have to choose the best strategy for various addition problems.

Lesson overview

Preparation
Copy and laminate the 'Which strategy?' gameboard for each pair of children. Cut out the calculation cards and make sets appropriate to the differentiation suggested in Lesson 4.

Learning objectives
Starter
● **Know by heart addition and subtraction facts for each number to at least 10.**
Main teaching activities
● **Choose and use appropriate operations and efficient calculation strategies** (e.g. mental, mental with jottings) **to solve problems.**

Vocabulary
multiply, times, multiplied by, multiple of, add, addition, more, plus, sum, make, total, altogether, subtract, take away, minus, how many are left?, how many less is… than…?, subtraction, double, near double, adjust

You will need:
Photocopiable pages
'Which strategy?' for each pair (page 23).

CD pages
'Calculation cards 1' and 'Calculation cards 2' for each child (Autumn term, Unit 3); number cards 0–9 for each child from '0–100 number cards'(see General resources).

Equipment
An individual whiteboard and pens for each child; an OHP.

Lesson

Starter
Rehearse addition facts for all numbers to 10. Give each child a set of number cards 1–10. Write a number on the board, such as 5. Call out a lower number, such as 2, and ask the children to show you the number card that goes with it to make 5 (3). Repeat with different lower numbers, then change the number on the board.

Main teaching activities
Whole class: Explain that today the children will be thinking about the different strategies they can use to add numbers together. Ask: *Who can tell me the strategies we have been learning this week?* Write examples of each on the board, for example: near doubles 12 + 13, 30 + 29; largest number first 36 + 5, 3 + 18 + 6; add 10 and adjust 18 + 9, 23 + 11.
Paired work: Give each child the 'Which strategy?' sheet, 'Calculation cards 1' and 'Calculation cards 2'. Ask the children to put the stack of cards face down beside the board. Demonstrate how to pick a card, read the calculation and decide which is the strategy for working it out, then place the card in the corresponding section on the board. Let most of the class use calculation cards for totals to 50.

Differentiation
Less able: This group can use calculation cards for totals to 20.
More able: This group can try a selection of calculations.

Plenary & assessment
Choose a few children to discuss the strategies they used for some of their calculations and demonstrate their recording. Use this as an assessment opportunity.
Put a calculation on the board, such as 20 + 19, and ask the children to write down as many strategies as they can for finding the answer on their whiteboards. Write their ideas on the board, then discuss the most efficient strategies. Finish by saying: *There are lots of different ways to work out calculations. We need to be able to use the ones that we find most useful.*

| Name | Date |

Function machine

How quickly can you work out +9? +11?

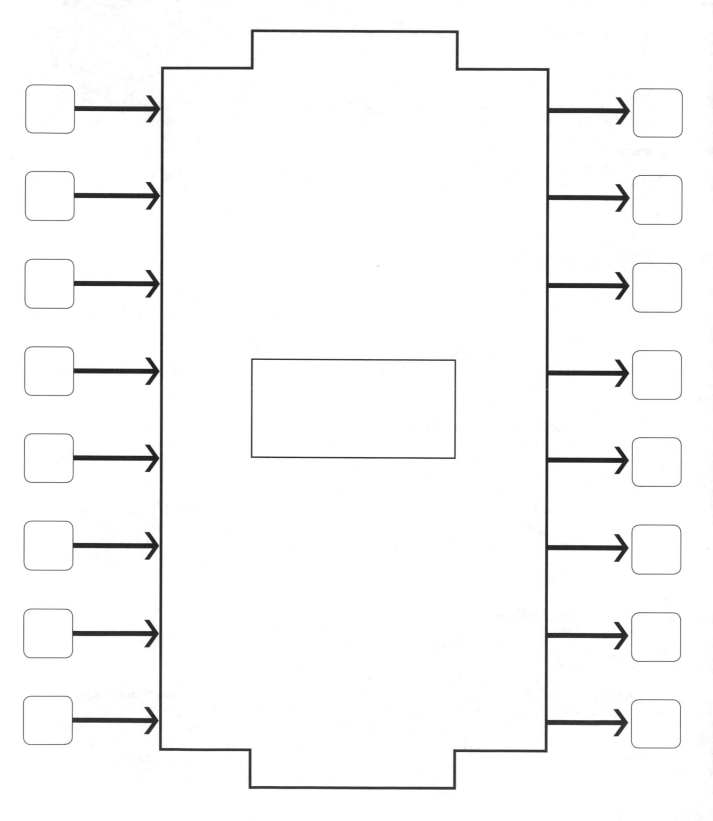

Name	Date

Which strategy?

Give each calculation card to the toy with the best strategy for that sum.

Add 9 or 11 by adding 10 and then adding or subtracting 1.	Put the largest number first and count on the others.

Partition into tens and ones.	Use near doubles.

Money problems

This chapter concentrates on money. It begins with coin recognition and ways to make certain amounts of money, linking closely to the counting activities that the children did in Unit 1. This then leads into shopping activities, introducing partitioning as a method of addition and counting on to find change.

LEARNING OBJECTIVES

	Topics	Starter	Main teaching activities
Lesson 1	Problems involving 'real life', money or measures	● **Know by heart multiplication facts for the 2 and 10 times-tables.**	● Recognise all coins and begin to use £.p notation for money.
Lesson 2	Problems involving 'real life', money or measures	● Know by heart doubles of all numbers to 10 and the corresponding halves.	● Find totals.
Lesson 3	Problems involving 'real life', money or measures. Making decisions	As for Lesson 2.	● Find totals, give change, and work out which coins to pay. ● **Choose and use appropriate operations and efficient calculation strategies** (e.g. mental, mental with jottings) **to solve problems.**
Lesson 4	Problems involving 'real life', money or measures. Making decisions	● Say the number that is 1 or 10 more or less than any given two-digit number.	As for Lesson 3.
Lesson 5	Problems involving 'real life', money or measures. Making decisions. Checking results of calculations	As for Lesson 2.	As for Lesson 3, plus: ● Repeat addition in a different order.

Lessons   overview

Preparation
Copy the 'Coin cards and labels' onto card, and colour; laminate the sheets and cut out the coins and labels. Make a copy of each coin card on acetate and cut out the coins. Prepare plastic (or real) pennies in groups of 200, 100, 50, 20, 10, 5, 2 and 1 for demonstration. Put the larger amounts into plastic bags. Copy a set of the relevant 'Shopping cards' for each child.

Learning objectives
Starter
● **Know by heart multiplication facts for the 2 and 10 times-tables.**
● Know by heart doubles of all numbers to 10 and the corresponding halves.
● Say the number that is 1 or 10 more or less than any given two-digit number.
Main teaching activities
● Recognise all coins and begin to use £.p notation for money.
● Find totals, give change, and work out which coins to pay.
● **Choose and use appropriate operations and efficient calculation strategies** (e.g. mental, mental with jottings) **to solve problems.**
● Repeat addition in a different order.

Vocabulary
money, coin, penny, pence, pound, £, price, cost, buy, bought, sell, sold, spend, spent, pay, change, costs more, costs less, how much…?, total, groups of

You will need:
Photocopiable pages
'Shopping cards 1' for each child (page 28).

CD pages
'Shopping cards 2' and '3', (Autumn term, Unit 4), number cards 0–9 for each child, acetates of 'Spider charts for multiplying' and 'Spider charts for dividing', 'Coin cards and labels'(see General resources).

Equipment
Whiteboard and pens for each child; 400 × 1p coins, Blu-Tack; 2p, 5p and 10p coins, 0–100 number line.

Lesson

Starter

Ask the children to count in twos and tens using their fingers. Make the link to 'how many lots of'. Remind them that when they count in 'lots of' they are beginning to learn the 2 and 10 times-tables. Use 'Spider charts for multiplying' to practise random 2 and 10 times-table facts. Introduce the 'Spider charts for dividing' and ask questions such as: *How many twos make this number?* (Point to 12, they say six.) *How many tens make this number?* (Point to 80, they say eight.) Encourage them to use their fingers if they need to.

Main teaching activities

Whole class: Explain that today the children will be looking at the coins in our money system. Show them some real coins and tell them that as these are very small for the whole class to see, you have prepared some larger copies. Blu-Tack each coin and its enlarged copy to the board. Hold up the coin labels and ask the children to match these to the coins. Ask: *Why do we need these different coins? What would happen if we only had pennies? What would it be like to pay for a comic that cost 50p if we only had pennies?* Using the plastic coins, show how many pennies each coin is worth. Ask the children to help you order the coins from the least to the greatest value.

Put 26 plastic pennies on the OHP. Remind the children that when you have a lot of things it is easier to count in groups than in ones. Invite someone to come to the OHP and count out ten pennies. Ask: *What could we have instead of these ten pennies?* (10p) Swap the ten pennies for the acetate 10p coin. Do the same for the next ten pennies. Now ask: *Can we make another group of ten? No, but we could change some of the remaining ones into another coin. Which one?* (5p) Replace the five pennies with the 5p acetate coin. Ask: *How many pennies are left?* (1) Add them up: 10p + 10p + 5p + 1p. Reinforce by saying: *We started off with 26 pence. From that we could get two ten pences, a five pence and a penny.* Repeat several times with amounts to 50p.

Group work: Ask ability pairs or groups to try a matching activity. They will need a selection of coins and a set of coin labels. Say: *Pick a label, take that number of pennies and then try to swap them for other coins.* Encourage the children to make each amount in three different ways.

Differentiation

Less able: This group can work with amounts to 15p.
More able: This group can find the smallest number of coins and one other mixed-coin way of making the amount on each label.

Plenary & assessment

Ask the children to show you the different ways they found to make 50p, £1 and £2.

Lesson

Starter

Say: *In Year 1 you were able to say what the doubles of the numbers up to 5 were. How would you work out double 4?* The children will probably say '4 add 4'. Call out random numbers to 5 and ask the children to show you the double of each number with their number cards. Now ask for doubles of numbers to 10, with a few doubles of numbers to 20 for more able children. Ask for some doubles of multiples of 10, before asking for halves.

Main teaching activities

Whole class: Recap Lesson 1: why all the coins are useful and how much each is worth. Order the coins from the lowest value to the highest. Invite a child to find a 2p and a 1p coin. Ask the class how much this child has altogether. Repeat with a 5p and a 2p coin. Repeat for several combinations of two and three different coins.

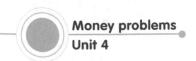
Paired work: Tell the children that they will be investigating different ways of paying for something. Show the children the shopping cards for amounts to 20p. Tell them that one child in each pair is the 'shopkeeper' and the other child is the 'shopper' who is buying the toys. The 'shopper' picks a card and finds the right coins to give to the 'shopkeeper'. The 'shopkeeper' checks that there is the correct amount of money and keeps it, while the 'shopper' keeps the toy cards. After a couple of turns they swap roles.

Give each pair a set of cards from the 'Shopping cards 1' sheet. After about 5 minutes, stop the class and add another element: they need to pick two cards (using 'Shopping cards 2') and work out the total, using any method they choose, then find the coins needed to pay that amount. Say that in the Plenary, you will discuss the methods they used. Encourage recording in this form: Total = 37p = 20p + 10p + 5p + 2p.

Differentiation

Less able: This group can use the shopping cards for amounts to 20p, only using one card each time and using 1p, 2p, 5p and 10p coins to make the amount required, so they can concentrate on the money rather than the addition.

More able: This group can pick two cards from the set with prices over £1 ('Shopping cards 3'). Ask them to use as few coins as possible.

Plenary & assessment

Hold up some shopping cards and ask for each one: *How can we make this amount using the most coins… the fewest coins?* Hold up two cards and ask some children to explain the strategies they would use to find the total.

Lesson ③

Starter

Repeat the Starter from Lesson 2. This time, introduce the idea that as well as being 5 + 5, 'double 5' is also 'two lots of 5'. This makes an initial link between addition and multiplication.

Main teaching activities

Whole class: Recap Lesson 2 by holding up some coin labels and asking for the totals and the least number of coins needed to make them. Say: *Today we will find some total prices, pay with a 20p, 50p, £1 or £2 coin, and work out the change by counting up in coins.* Work through this process slowly, using partitioning to find the total and counting out coins for the change. For example:

I am going to spend 21p and 14p. I give the shopkeeper 50p. The first thing I need to do is add the amounts I spend. Watch how I do this. (Write the calculations on the board.) *21p + 14p. I am going to partition these amounts. 21p becomes 20p and 1p. What does 14p become?* (10p and 4p.) *Now I'm going to add the tens numbers first: 20p + 10p = 30p. And then the ones numbers: 1p + 4p = 5p. Now I can recombine the tens and the ones to get 30p + 5p = 35p. My total is 35p.*

Repeat with a few examples before moving on to finding change. Go back to the first example: *To work out the change, I am going to count on from 35p to 50p using coins. What can I use to get me to 40p?* (5p) *What can I use to get from 40p to 50p?* (10p.) *So how much have I counted from 35p to 50p?* (10p and 5p, making 15p.) Demonstrate this a few times, using 20p, 50p and £1 as the coins to get change from.

Paired work: Repeat the activity from the previous lesson, but this time, when the children have found the total of two cards, they need to work out the change from 50p or £1.

Differentiation

Less able: This group can use one card (from 'Shopping cards 1') to 20p and work out the change from 20p.
More able: This group can use two cards over £1 (from 'Shopping cards 3')and work out the change from £3 or £4.

Plenary & assessment

Invite some of the children to demonstrate how they worked out their totals and the change. Ask:

- *What was the first thing you needed to do? Can you explain how you found the total?*
- *What was the next thing you did?*
- *Can you show us how you counted out the change?*

Lesson

Starter

Call out a number of pence (such as 3p). Ask the children to call out 1p more or less as quickly as they can. Repeat for several prices up to 50p, asking the children to call out the amount that is 10p more or less.

Main teaching activities

Whole class: Repeat the whole-class and paired activities from Lesson 3, but instead of counting out coins, show the children how to use a number line to find the change and then record. For example: *To find the total of 15p and 14p, we can partition the numbers and add the tens first, just as we do when we add ordinary numbers: 10p + 10p + 5p + 4p = 20p + 9p = 29p.*

To work out the change from £1, we can use a number line and count from our total of 29p up to £1, just as we do when we find small differences in ordinary numbers. Remember that £1 is 100p. 29p plus 1p gets us to 30p. Now let's count in tens to £1: 40, 50, 60, 70, 80, 90, £1. That's 70p altogether.

29p   **£1**

30p

+1p   **+70p**

So our change is 1p and 70p, which makes 71p.

To find the total of 25p and 32p, let's partition the numbers and add the tens first: 20p + 30p + 5p + 2p = 50p + 7p = 57p. Now let's use a number line and count from our total of 57p up to £1: 57p plus 3p gets us to 60p.

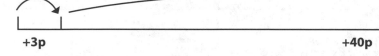

57p   60p   **£1**

+3p   **+40p**

How many tens get us to £1? Let's count… 40p.
Our change is 3p and 40p, which makes 43p.

Differentiation

As for Lesson 3.

Plenary & assessment

See Lesson 3. Your questions could include: *Can you show us how you found the difference between your total and the money you gave to the shopkeeper?*

Lesson

Repeat the Starter from Lesson 2, but use the context of money. A lot of ground was covered in the main teaching activities of Lessons 3 and 4, so continue or revisit them for consolidation purposes. The Plenary should be as in Lesson 3 or 4, but focus on checking totals. Ask the children how they can check their totals. Remind them of work they did in Unit 3 on how addition can be done in any order. Ask some children to demonstrate how they could check their answers (by adding the amounts in a different order).

Shopping cards 1

4p	3p	6p
7p	8p	6p
4p	2p	3p
14p	12p	13p
14p	12p	13p

Length and time

Children use and begin to read the vocabulary related to length and time. They estimate and measure lengths using standard units in practical activities. In practical activities they begin to estimate small units of time (seconds and minutes), review telling the time to the hour and half past, and solve time problems.

LEARNING OBJECTIVES

	Topics	Starter	Main teaching activities
Lesson 1	Measures	● **Describe and extend simple number sequences: count on or back in ones or tens, starting from any two-digit number.**	● Use and begin to read the vocabulary related to length. ● **Estimate, measure and compare lengths, using standard units** (m, cm); **suggest suitable units and equipment for such measurements.**
Lesson 2	Problems involving 'real life', money or measures	● Know by heart doubles of all numbers to 10 and the corresponding halves.	As for Lesson 1.
Lesson 3	Measures	● Say the number names in order to at least 100, from and back to zero. ● Begin to recognise two-digit multiples of 2, 5 or 10.	As for lesson 1.
Lesson 4	Measures	● **Know by heart multiplication facts for the 2 and 10 times-tables.**	● Use and begin to read the vocabulary related to time. ● Suggest suitable units to estimate or measure time. ● Use units of time and know the relationships between them (second, minute, hour, day, week).

Lessons   overview

Preparation
For Lesson 2 write up on the board the activities that the children will do during group work time. Enlarge the cards from CD page 'Measures vocabulary' to A3

Learning objectives
Starter
● **Describe and extend simple number sequences: count on or back in ones or tens, starting from any two-digit number.**
● Know by heart doubles of all numbers to 10 and the corresponding halves.
● Say the number names in order to at least 100, from and back to zero.
● Begin to recognise two-digit multiples of 2, 5 or 10.
Main teaching activities
● Use and begin to read the vocabulary related to length.
● **Estimate, measure and compare lengths, using standard units** (m, cm); **suggest suitable units and equipment for such measurements.**

Vocabulary
measure, metre, centimetre, long, short, high, low, tall, wide, narrow, deep, shallow, thick, thin

You will need:
Photocopiable pages
'Measures activities' (page 33).

CD pages
A copy for each child of the activities for length, from 'Measures activities' (Autumn term, Unit 5); number cards 0–50 from '0–100 number cards', enlarged cards from 'Measures vocabulary' (see General resources).

Equipment
A counting stick; Blu-Tack; strip of paper that is more than a metre long but less than 2 metres; metre sticks marked in 10cm intervals; canes; straws; interlocking cubes; 50cm strip of paper.

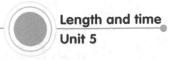

Lesson ①

Starter

Ask a child to pick a number card from 0–50 as a starting number. Ask the children to count in time in ones until you say *Stop*, at which point they count back in ones. Ask the children to pick more cards for other starting numbers. Then ask them to count in tens as you move your finger back and forth on a counting stick, jumping steps occasionally.

Main teaching activities

Whole class: Hold up the length vocabulary cards (from 'Measures vocabulary') one at a time. Invite the children to read these. The cards can be fixed to the board with Blu-Tack as a reminder of the vocabulary for length. Invite the children to put each word into a sentence to show that they understand its meaning.

Now explain that for this and the next two lessons they will be estimating and measuring length. Hold up the metre stick and ask *What in this room do you think is about 1 metre long?* Invite the children to make suggestions, then to check by holding the metre stick alongside the items suggested.

Group work: Ask the children to work in groups of about four, with a metre stick. Give each child a copy of the length activities from 'Measures activities'. Read the questions through together. Now ask the children in their groups to work through the activities on the sheet. They can make jottings onto the sheet where they need to record or make a list.

Differentiation

Throughout this unit, place the children in mixed-ability pairs or groups. Children who appear less able in terms of number skills may do well in work on shapes and measures, where the focus is more spatial. Check that the less able children are fully focused on the task and are contributing to the work being done.

Plenary & assessment

Invite children from each group to feed back on what they have done. Ask: *Did you estimate which were longer/shorter than a metre? Did you make a good guess?* Now hide the metre sticks, then show the children the strip of paper and ask for a pair to work in front of the other children to cut the paper so that they have a piece about a metre long. Ask the other children: *Do you think they have made a good estimate?* Invite another child to check how close the estimate is by using a metre stick. Discuss how making good estimates will improve with practice.

Lesson ②

Starter

Ask a child to pick two number cards up to 50. Count together from the lower up to the higher number, then back again. Ask the children to do actions (such as clapping) for each multiple of 2, 5 and 10.

Main teaching activities

Whole class: Put out in front of the children the interlocking cubes, metre sticks and canes. Explain that today you would like the children to estimate and measure items in the room and to choose appropriate units for doing this. Ask: *Look at the width of the classroom. Which unit would you choose to measure this? Metre stick? Cane? Straw? Cube? Which would be best? Why do you think that?* Encourage the children to explain why, for example, the cubes would not be suitable (so many would be needed, and there would be the issue of counting accurately how many were used). When children have decided upon a suitable unit, such as metre stick or cane, invite a child to demonstrate how they would measure the width of the classroom using the apparatus. Discuss how there is likely to be a 'bit left over' when measuring.

Group work: Ask the children to work in small groups. Explain that there are the following three activities on the board. They can make a group recording of their results on paper. Ask each group to begin with one of the activities, then to move on to another, until they have covered all three.

● Which is longer and which is shorter: across the classroom, or along the classroom? Decide which units you will use, then estimate and measure.

● How long is it round your reading book? Choose your units, then estimate and measure.

● What would you choose to measure how tall the cupboard is? Why? Now estimate and measure.

Differentiation

Less able: Check that the children make sensible choices of unit and can explain their choice.
More able: if there is time, set a challenge, such as: *How far do you think it is in metres to walk around the edge of the room?* The children can try this out!

Plenary & assessment

Discuss each activity in turn. Ask: *Which unit did you choose? Did you make a sensible choice? Why do you think that?* Encourage the children to explain in sentences, using the correct vocabulary .

Lesson 3

Starter

To reinforce multiples of 2, 5 and 10, repeat the Starter from Lesson 2 but using cards up to 100. You might limit the range of number cards from e.g. 50–100.

Main teaching activity

Whole class: Show the children the metre stick marked in 10 centimetres. Explain that there are 100 centimetres in a metre. Count along the metre stick in tens. Now ask the children to work in small groups, each group with a metre stick marked in 10 centimetres. Invite the children to agree where specific measurements are on the stick. Say, for example: *Where is 10cm? Now point to 30cm.* When the children are confident with this, invite a child to come to the front and to use the metre stick to measure the 50cm strip of paper. Invite the children to estimate how long the paper is. Ask the children to watch what happens. Check that the zero end of the stick is lined up accurately with one end of the paper. Write the measurement on the board and explain that it is 50 centimetres. Ask: *Has he/she made a good measure? How do you know that?*

Group work: Ask the children to estimate then measure the following things: the height of a chair; the width of a table; the length of a table; the height of a table. Remind them that the measurements are unlikely to be 'spot on' a decade number, and that they will need to think about whether the measurement is just over or just under the nearest 10 centimetres. The children should record their estimates and measures.

Differentiation

Less able: If the children are unsure about how to record the measurements, discuss how they write decade numbers.
More able: Encourage children to measure accurately and to read scales to the nearest division.

Plenary & assessment

Discuss with the children how well they estimated. Invite a child to demonstrate how to measure the height of the chair. Discuss where to read off the measurement on the metre stick. Ask: *Is it about… just over… a bit under…?* Repeat this for other things that the children measured.

Lesson ④ overview

Preparation
Photocopy CD page 'Measures vocabulary' for time to A3.

Learning objectives
Starter
- **Know by heart multiplication facts for the 2 and 10 times-tables.**

Main teaching activity
- Use and begin to read the vocabulary related to time.
- Suggest suitable units to estimate or measure time.
- Use units of time and know the relationships between them (second, minute, hour, day, week).

Vocabulary
day, week, fortnight, month, year, weekend, second, minute, hour, half an hour, quarter of an hour

You will need:
CD pages
'Measures vocabulary' for time (see General resources); Units of time (Autumn term, Unit 5).

Equipment
An individual whiteboard and pen for each child; geared clocks.

Lesson ④

Starter
Ask the children to write any number from 0 to 10 to the left of their whiteboard. In the middle, they write ×10. When you say *Go*, they work out the answer and write on the right. Repeat with other numbers before working with ×2 in the middle.

Main teaching activity
Whole class: Remind children about units of time using 'Measures vocabulary cards'. Show the children a geared clock. Move the hands in a clockwise direction and show o'clock times. Ask the children to say the times. Repeat this for half past times. Now say: *If we start the lesson at 10 o'clock* (show 10 o'clock) *and it finishes at 11 o'clock* (move the hands to show 11 o'clock), *we will know from the clock how long our lesson took. How long did it take?* Repeat with other such examples. On the board, write up six pairs of times, such as:
- 6 o'clock and 9 o'clock/10 o'clock and half past seven.

Group work: Ask the children to work in small groups. They use a clock face and set the time on the clock face to the first time, then to the second time, and calculate how long it is between the two times. Now ask them to put this into a sentence. For example: *I had my tea at 6 o'clock. I went to bed at 9 o'clock. This was 3 hours after tea.*

Differentiation
Less able: Decide whether to work as a group. If children find it difficult to calculate the length of time, demonstrate by moving the hands from one time to the next and asking the children to count the time. If necessary, check children's understanding of the units of time using 'Units of time'.
More able: Challenge the children to work out how long their favourite TV programme lasts.

Plenary & assessment
Invite each group to give the other groups their first two sentences and for the other children to work out the difference in times. Ask: *How did you work that out? Who has a way of doing this without using a clock?* Encourage the children to explain their methods, such as counting on in ones for hours, then half hours.

Name	Date

Measures activities

Length

Find six things in the classroom that you estimate to be longer than a metre.

Find six things in the classroom that you estimate to be shorter than a metre.

Find something that you know is exactly a metre long.

Make three piles: things that you think are longer than 1m, things that you think are shorter than 1m, and things that are exactly 1m.

Use a metre stick to measure each length.

Discuss within your group how good your estimating was.

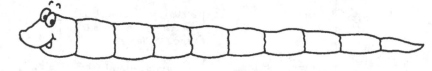

Weight

Find six things in the classroom that you estimate to be heavier than a kilogram.

Find six things in the classroom that you estimate to be lighter than a kilogram.

Find something that you know weighs exactly a kilogram.

Make three piles: things that you think are heavier than 1kg, things that you think are lighter than 1kg, and things that are exactly 1kg.

Compare each thing with a 1kg weight, using a balance scales.

Discuss within your group how good your estimating was.

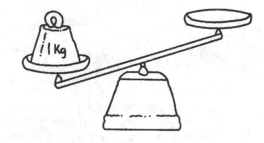

Capacity

Find four things in the classroom that you estimate will hold more than a litre.

Find four things in the classroom that you estimate will hold less than a litre.

Find something that you know will hold exactly a litre.

Make three piles: things that you think hold more than 1 litre, things that you think hold less than 1 litre, and things that hold exactly 1 litre.

Use water and a litre measuring jug to measure each capacity.

Discuss within your group how good your estimating was.

2-D and 3-D shapes

Children look at 2-D and 3-D shapes, analysing their properties and using the correct mathematical vocabulary. They will extend this by looking at the position of objects.

LEARNING OBJECTIVES

	Topics	Starter	Main teaching activities
Lesson 1	Shape and space Reasoning about numbers or shapes	● Say the number names in order to at least 100, from and back to zero. ● **Describe and extend simple number sequences: count on or back in ones or tens.**	● **Use the mathematical names for common 3-D and 2-D shapes,** including the pyramid, cylinder, pentagon, hexagon, octagon. ● **Sort shapes and describe some of their features.** ● Make and describe shapes. ● Investigate a general statement about familiar shapes by finding examples that satisfy it.
Lesson 2	Shape and space Reasoning about numbers or shapes	● **Use the mathematical names for common 3-D and 2-D shapes.** ● **Sort shapes and describe their features.**	As for Lesson 1.
Lesson 3	Shape and space	As for Lesson 2.	● **Use mathematical vocabulary to describe position, direction and movement:** e.g. describe, place, tick, draw or visualise objects in given positions.

Lessons   overview

Preparation

Prepare a collection of 3-D and 2-D shapes as listed in 'Vocabulary'. Provide two of each 2-D shape, one regular and one irregular. If necessary, photocopy 'Templates for irregular shapes' and 'Templates for regular shapes' onto card and cut them out. Make A3 card copies of '2-D shape vocabulary' and '3-D shape vocabulary' and cut out the cards.

Learning objectives
Starter
- Say the number names in order to at least 100, from and back to zero.
- **Describe and extend simple number sequences: count on or back in ones or tens.**
- **Use the mathematical names for common 3-D and 2-D shapes.**
- **Sort shapes and describe their features.**
Main teaching activities
- **Use the mathematical names for common 3-D and 2-D shapes**.
- **Sort shapes and describe some of their features**.
- Make and describe shapes.
- Investigate a general statement about familiar shapes by finding examples that satisfy it.

Vocabulary

shape, pattern, flat, curved, straight, round, solid, corner, point, face, side, edge, surface, cube, cuboid, pyramid, sphere, cone, cylinder, circle, circular, triangle, triangular, square, rectangle, rectangular, star, pentagon, hexagon, octagon

You will need:

Photocopiable pages
'3-D shapes' and '2-D shapes' (page 37–38) for each child.

CD pages
Number cards 0–50 from CD page '0–100 number cards', 'Templates for regular shapes', 'Templates for irregular shapes 1' and '2', '2-D shape vocabulary' and '3-D shape vocabulary' cards (see General resources).

Equipment
Whiteboards and pens; 3-D and 2-D shapes; a feely bag; a cardboard tube; a pentagonal prism; A4 paper; Plasticine.

Lesson

Starter

Divide the children into two groups. Ask a child to pick a number card 0–50 as a starting number. With your right hand, point towards each group at random intervals for them to count on in ones. From time to time, change to your left hand for counting backwards. Repeat for counting in tens.

Main teaching activities

This is a whole-class lesson. Show the children a cube, cuboid, pyramid, sphere, cone and cylinder. Discuss their properties: number of edges, corners and faces; the 2-D shapes of the faces. Recap on these terms as they occur. Now show the 3-D shape vocabulary cards, asking children to match the words with the shapes and properties.

Follow the instructions and discussion prompts on the '3-D shapes' activity sheet, and demonstrate as you go along, guiding the children through the instructions. It is important for continuity to follow the instructions in order: the discussion of each 3-D shape, and the 2-D shapes of its faces, should follow on naturally from the previous one.

Plenary & assessment

Put a 3-D-shape in the feely bag. Invite a child to feel the shape and describe it. Encourage the child to use all the properties that were discussed in the lesson, including the shapes of curved faces where appropriate. The class have to work out what the shape is. Repeat with different children and different shapes.

Lesson

Starter

Quickly revisit the Starter from Lesson 1. Try combining the two counts: move your hand from side to side for counting in ones and up and down for counting in tens. Do this a few times with different starting numbers.

Main teaching activities

This is a whole-class lesson. Explain that today the children will be looking at 2-D shapes. In order to make the link with 3-D shapes, show the children the 3-D shapes from Lesson 1 and discuss the 2-D shapes of their faces. Show the pictures of the 2-D shapes on 'Templates for regular shapes' and 'Templates for irregular shapes'.

Talk about the shapes. You don't need to use the terms 'regular' and 'irregular', but it is important for the children to understand that only certain shapes have the properties of equal side length and symmetry (remind the children of symmetry work in Year 1: folding shapes in half to give identical parts). Call out the names of some 2-D shapes and ask the children to draw them on their whiteboards. Then hand out the '2-D shapes' sheet for the children to complete. Demonstrate and explain what they are doing as they work.

Plenary & assessment

Attach to the board the 2-D shape name cards from the '2-D shape vocabulary' sheet. Ask the children to bring their shape and their drawing to the carpet. Call out some shape names and properties, and ask the children to stand up if their shape has the name or property that you say. Ask the children to Blu-Tack their shape on the board beside the correct name. If any children are unable to do this, ask them why. Stick their shapes on a different part of the board and ask them to try to find out their shape's name at home this evening.

Lesson ③ overview

Preparation
Make an A3 copy of the 'Position vocabulary' sheet on card and cut out the cards.

Learning objectives
Starter
- **Use the mathematical names for common 3-D and 2-D shapes.**
- **Sort shapes and describe their features.**

Main teaching activity
- **Use mathematical vocabulary to describe position, direction and movement:** describe, place, tick, draw or visualise objects in given positions.

Vocabulary
position, over, under, underneath, above, below, top, bottom, side, on, in, outside, inside, around, in front, behind, front, back, before, after, beside, next to, opposite, apart, between, middle, edge, centre, corner

You will need:
CD pages
Enlarged 'Position vocabulary cards' (see General resources).

Equipment
2-D and 3-D shapes from Lessons 1 and 2; Compare Bears or similar counting toys.

Lesson ③

Starter
Give each child a 2-D shape from Lesson 2; use a mixture of regular and irregular shapes. Call out some names and properties and ask the children to stand up if their shape has the property or name that you say (for example: triangle; pentagon with equal sides; six sides; symmetrical).

Main teaching activities
Whole class: Explain that today the children are going to think about the positions of objects. Give each child a shape, using a mixture of 2-D and 3-D shapes. Hold up each position vocabulary card in turn, and ask the children with a particular shape to put it in a place that is appropriate to that word (for example, ask whoever has a cube to put it somewhere that shows what is meant by *underneath*). Ask those children to explain what they did.

Paired work: Give each pair three or four position vocabulary cards and a counting toy. They need to make up a story about their toy that involves the words on the cards, then practise acting it out. Explain that some of them will act out their stories to the class later.

Plenary & assessment
Choose those children whom you wish to assess to act out their stories first. If you have time, invite others to share their stories.

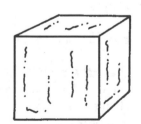

3-D shapes

You will need:
- a small lump of Plasticine
- a sheet of paper
- a pencil.

- Make the Plasticine into a sphere. Say the word 'sphere'.

- What are you doing to make your Plasticine into a sphere? What things in 'real life' are spheres?

- What are the properties of your sphere? What is special about it? Does it roll? Is it smooth? Is it round?

- Hold your sphere at arm's length. Look at it and draw the shape that you can see.

- Now turn your sphere into a cube. What are you doing to change the sphere? Will you squash in the sides? Will you take the 'roundness' away?

- What do we see in everyday life that is shaped like a cube?

- How many edges/corners/faces does your cube have? What is the shape of each face?

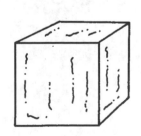

- Look at a cube from a distance and draw the 2-D shape you can see.

2-D shapes

- You will need:
- a sheet of coloured A4 paper
- a sheet of white paper
- a pencil.

• Fold the coloured paper once to make it into an irregular shape.

• Describe your shape.

• Describe the properties of your shape to your neighbour.

• Repeat this, making a second fold and then a third and fourth.

• Draw around your shape on a sheet of white paper. Write down how many sides it has, how many corners and how many lines of symmetry (if any).

• Label your shape and keep it for the Plenary.

Number sequences and investigations

This unit looks at describing and extending number sequences by counting on and back in ones, twos and tens. It looks at multiples of two and links that with odd and even numbers. There are two lessons that involve predicting and solving number problems.

LEARNING OBJECTIVES

	Topics	Starter	Main teaching activities
Lesson 1	Counting, properties of numbers and sequences	● Know by heart doubles of all numbers to 10 and the corresponding halves.	● **Describe and extend simple number sequences: count on or back in ones or tens, starting from any two-digit number.**
Lesson 2	Counting, properties of numbers and sequences	● Identify near doubles, using doubles already known (e.g. 8 + 9, 40 + 41).	● **Describe and extend simple number sequences:** count on or back in twos. ● Begin to recognise two-digit multiples of 2.
Lesson 3	Counting, properties of numbers and sequences Reasoning about numbers or shapes	● Know by heart doubles of all numbers to 10 and the corresponding halves. ● Identify near doubles, using doubles already known (e.g. 8 + 9, 40 + 41).	● **Describe and extend simple number sequences: recognise odd and even numbers** to at least 30. ● Investigate a general statement about familiar numbers by finding examples.
Lesson 4	Reasoning about numbers or shapes	● **Describe and extend simple number sequences.** ● **Begin to recognise two-digit multiples of 2, 5 and 10.**	● Solve mathematical problems or puzzles. ● Suggest extensions by asking 'What if…?' or 'What could I try next?'
Lesson 5	Reasoning about numbers or shapes	● Begin to recognise two-digit multiples of 2, 5 and 10.	As for Lesson 4. ● Use and begin to read the vocabulary of comparing and ordering numbers, including ordinal numbers.

Lessons   overview

Preparation
Photocopy all the gameboards onto card and laminate.

Learning objectives
Starter
● Know by heart doubles of all numbers to 10 and the corresponding halves.
● Identify near doubles, using doubles already known (e.g. 8 + 9, 40 + 41).
Main teaching activities
● **Describe and extend simple number sequences:**
– count on or back in ones or tens, starting from any two-digit number
– count on or back in twos
– recognise odd and even numbers to at least 30.
● Begin to recognise two-digit multiples of 2.
● Investigate a general statement about familiar numbers by finding examples.

Vocabulary
zero, one hundred, two hundred…one thousand, count on, count back, count in ones/twos/tens, multiple of, sequence, continue, predict, pattern, rule, odd, even

You will need:
CD pages
A copy of 'Diamond number line for ones' and 'Diamond number line for twos' for each pair of children; 'Odds and evens game' instructions; 0–9 number cards for each child, and a class set of '0–100 number cards', at least four A3 copies of the 'Diamond number line', a copy of 'Sun and stars' for each pair of children; an enlarged copy of 'Sun and stars' (see General resources).

Equipment
Whiteboard pens; counters.

Lesson ①

Starter

Ask the children to set their number cards 0–9 out in front of them. Call out random numbers from 1 to 10 and ask the children to show you their doubles, using number cards. Then call out even numbers to 20 and ask the children to show you their halves. Finally, mix the questions.

Main teaching activities

Whole class: Explain that today, the children will be learning about number sequences that go up and down in ones or tens. Pick a two-digit number card and ask the children to start counting forwards and then backwards from it. Repeat this a few times, counting alternately in ones and in tens. Next, invite a child to pick a card and write the number on the board. Ask the children to discuss with a partner what they think the next eight numbers will be on either side, counting on and back in ones. Ask the children what they notice. Elicit the response that the units number is one more each time. Invite some children to write these numbers on the board. Repeat for counting in tens; what do the children notice? (The units number remains the same.)

Paired work: Ask the children to play the game in pairs. Use an A3 copy of 'Diamond number line' to model the instructions on 'Diamond number line for ones'. For example: *I've picked 2 and 4, so I'm going to make 24 and write it in the first diamond. If my partner picks 8 and 2, what two numbers can we make? Can one of them be written in a diamond?* (Ask a child to write 28 in the correct place.) *If 7 and 5 are picked now, what numbers can we make? Will either of them fit on the line? No, so it's the other player's turn. What about 2 and 5? Great, 25 can be added to the line.…* Children must start with a number below 90.

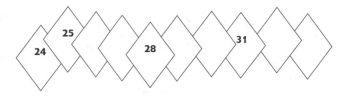

Differentiation

Less able: Give these pairs a starting number below 20 and a pile of number cards with ten extra 1s and 2s.

More able: Ask these pairs to write their starting number in the 'middle' diamond on the line, so they need to count forwards and backwards.

Plenary & assessment

Play the game again as a class, using another A3 copy of 'Diamond number line' but counting in tens. Pick single-digit number cards to make a two-digit number and write it in the middle diamond. Invite the children to pick single-digit cards and replace the tens number each time to make a new number. Ask the class to tell you what the numbers are, and invite children to write them in the correct places. Each time, ask the children what has happened to the tens number and to the units number. Reiterate the fact that the units number stays the same: only the tens number is changing.

Lesson ②

Starter

Set up as in Lesson 1. Call out pairs of numbers to 10 that are near doubles. Ask the children to find the answer by doubling one number and adjusting, then show you the answer with their cards. Ask them to explain their method and suggest alternative methods. Which way do they think is best? Extend to numbers such as 10 + 11, 20 + 21, 30 + 32.

Main teaching activities

Whole class: Have a pack of number cards 0–50 face down in front of you. Invite a child to pick one card and write the number on the board. Write up the next five numbers counting in twos, and ask the children to tell you what the sequence is. Focus on the fact that the numbers go up in twos, and explain that today the children will be counting in twos and looking for patterns in the sequences. Invite another child to pick a card and ask others to make a sequence as you did.

Draw a number line with ten divisions. Ask another child to pick a card from the pack and write it in the middle of the line. Invite other children to complete the line. Talk about whether the numbers get bigger or smaller in each direction. Repeat this a few times. If the children mention that the numbers are all either odd or even, congratulate them, but don't teach 'odd' and 'even' at this point.

Paired work: Use an A3 copy of 'Diamond number line' to model the instructions on 'Diamond number line for twos'. Let the children play the game in pairs.

Differentiation

Less able: Give these pairs a starting number below 10 and a set of single-digit number cards with ten extra 1s and 2s.
More able: Ask these pairs to write their starting number in the 'middle' diamond on the line, so they need to count forwards and backwards.

Plenary & assessment

Invite a few pairs to draw one of their completed number lines on the board and share what they noticed about this pattern. If children have already mentioned odd and even numbers, ask them to repeat this. Write a few random numbers going down from left to right onto an A3 copy of 'Diamond number line', and ask the children what the missing numbers are. For example: When the line is completed, write down the units number pattern (for example: 8, 6, 4, 2, 0, 8, 6…) and link it to even or odd numbers. Tell the children that tomorrow they will be learning more about odd and even number patterns.

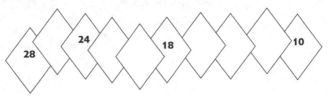

Lesson ③

Starter

Ask a mixture of doubles, halves and near doubles questions, as in Lessons 1 and 2, to reinforce these concepts.

Main teaching activities

Whole class: Explain that this lesson is about investigating odd and even numbers. Ask the children: *Can you tell me some odd and even numbers?* Write their responses on the board in two lists: odd and even. Ask: *What makes an odd number odd?* Look for: *An odd number ends with 1, 3, 5, 7 or 9*. Repeat for even numbers. Talk about street numbering: odd and even numbers are usually on opposite sides. Ask children who live in odd-numbered houses or flats to stand up, then those in even-numbered housing. Show some two-digit number cards; ask the children whether these numbers are odd or even, and invite some children to add them to your lists.
Paired work: Demonstrate the 'Odds and evens game' on an enlarged copy of the 'Sun and stars' gameboard, then give each pair a copy of the gameboard to play the game. After 10 minutes, draw the children together and ask them to tell you some of the numbers they made. Add these to the original lists.

Make two statements, one for each half of the class to investigate in pairs to see whether or not it is true:
- An even number of counters can be put into two equal piles.
- There is one left over when an odd number of counters is put into two equal piles.

Plenary & assessment

Discuss the two statements. *Are they both true?* (Yes.) *How can they be proven?* Ask the children to talk in small groups about whether they know how to recognise odd and even numbers and what they can now tell the class about them. Conclude with a whole-class discussion.

Lessons overview

Preparation

Photocopy 'Dicey digit problems' and cut into strips. Copy each set of 'Calculator cards' onto card, laminate and cut out. OHP calculators can vary, so practise first! Check that you can carry out the programming instructions on the calculator cards, and amend them if not.

Learning objectives

Starter
- **Describe and extend simple number sequences.**
- Begin to recognise two-digit multiples of 2, 5 and 10.

Main teaching activity
- **Solve mathematical problems or puzzles.**
- Suggest extensions by asking 'What if…?' or 'What could I try next?'

Vocabulary

predict, sequence, multiple of, answer, solution, addition, add, total, subtract, take away, multiply, calculate, calculation, mental calculation, jotting

You will need:

Photocopiable pages
'Dicey digit problems' strips (page 44) and a copy of 'Number investigations' (page 45) for each group. Teaching copy of 'Who came first 1' (page 51) and a copy of 'Who came first 2' (page 52) for each pair.

CD pages
'Dicey digit problems' strips and 'Number investigations' less able and more able versions (Autumn term, Unit 8), number cards 0–50, and number cards 0–9 for each group (from '0–100 number cards'), one of each set of 'Calculator cards' (see General resources).

Equipment
An OHP and OHP calculator; a whiteboard and pen for each pair; dice; dominoes.

Lesson

Starter

Use an OHP calculator to work through the three sets of calculator cards. The children need to identify the pattern each time and continue it orally until you say *Stop*. For example, key in: + 2 = = = (counts in steps of 2); 2 + 5 = = = (counts in steps of 5 from 7); or 110 – 10 = = = (counts back in steps of 10 from 100).

Main teaching activities

Whole class: Explain that you are going to give the class some problems and puzzles to solve, and will be asking them to make predictions. Do an example together: *We need to make 11 by adding three numbers. How many different ways can we do this? First predict the answer – that is, say what you think it will be.* Take some predictions and write them on the board. *Now we need to find the answer. Talk to your maths partner and write some ways of making 11 with three numbers on your whiteboards. You have two minutes. Collect the ways.* Use questioning, and ask the class to comment on each other's answers. For example: *What is the highest number that can be used? How do you know? Do you agree with that? What other thoughts do you have? Can you use three of the same number? Would it make a difference if you could only use each number once? What if you could use four numbers?*
Group work: After exploring this problem thoroughly, ask the children to work in small groups to solve some of the problem strips from 'Dicey digit problems'.

Differentiation

Less able: This group can use the version of 'Dicey digit problems' with simplified problems.
More able: This group can use the version with more complex problems.

Plenary & assessment

Take problems from each ability level and ask the children who solved them to explain what they did. Encourage them to talk about: how they made their predictions; whether they agreed on these; how they started their investigation; whether they had a 'system' or just made random guesses; how they knew they had found all the possible solutions; and how close their predictions were.

Lesson

Starter

In the Starter, hold up some number cards to 50. As you hold up each one, the children should perform an action if it is a multiple of 2, 5 or 10. For example, they could clap for multiples of 2, jump once for multiples of 5 and stick their tongues out for multiples of 10! If a number is a multiple of 2 and 5 (for example), they can carry out both actions.

Main teaching activities

Whole class: Develop the Main teaching activities from Lesson 4, asking the children to use the 'Number investigations' sheet. These problems are more extended than in Lesson 4, encouraging the children to think of more possibilities for solutions. Use the differentiated versions of the sheet. Develop the Plenary as in Lesson 4.

Group work: Show the children some ordinal number cards. Ask them what these cards show and what they mean. Stick the cards on a board and invite children to match the vocabulary words to the numbers.

Differentiation

Less able: Work with theis group, ordering the cards from 1st to 10th.
More able: See if this group can order ordinal cards up to 20th.

Plenary & assessment

Rehearse ordinal numbers and vocabulary as at the start of the main lesson. Look for the ability of each child in a pair to be able to say the ordinal number and place it in the correct position.

Main teaching activities

Whole class: Give each child a number, then begin to build an ordinal number line with the children. Do this randomly: ask the children who have 5th, 7th, 12th, 18th and 23rd (for example) to stand up, then ask which numbers go between them and ask those children to join the line. Place a few in the wrong order and ask the children to correct the line. Model the story 'Who came first? 1', using toy animals to help you.

Name	Date

Dicey digit problems

Photocopy and cut out these problem strips.

How many different ways could you score 8 by throwing three dice?

Make a prediction first, then work it out.

How many more ways could you score 8 if you had four dice?

How many different ways can you add three odd numbers to make 11?

Make a prediction first, then work it out.

What if you could only add two odd numbers to make 11? _____

What numbers can you make with the digit cards 4, 5 and 6?

You can use either two or three cards.

You can add, subtract or put the digits side by side.

Do you think you will be able to make more than 10 new

numbers? Have a go.

_____

Take ten dominoes and sort them into two groups: dominoes with an odd total of spots and dominoes with an even total.

Which group has the higher total of spots? Make a prediction first,

then work it out.

_____

Using 2, 3 and 4, and the signs + or – and =, what different answers can you make? You can use either two or three of the cards.

_____

Find an answer you could make if you used the + and the – sign in the same

calculation, e.g. 4 + 3 – 2 = 5?

_____

Name

Date

Number investigations

Photocopy and cut out these problem boxes.

0	1
2	3

Sam throws three darts at this board.

Each dart lands in a square.

They could all land in the same square.

What is the highest score he could get?

Find all the different scores he can get. _____

5	6
7	8

Pick a pair of numbers from the box.

Add them together.

Write the numbers and the answer. _____

Pick a different pair of numbers and do the same thing.

_____

Keep doing this. How many different answers can you get?

5	1	4
2	3	6

You will need a dice and some counters.

Throw the dice and put a counter on the number thrown.

Do this four times.

Add up the numbers where the two counters are.

What is your total?

Can you find other ways to make that total using the numbers 1 to 6?

Write down all the possible ways. _____

_____

Addition and subtraction problems

This unit begins with a lesson on comparing and ordering numbers, including ordinal numbers to 100. It then moves to extending the children's understanding of addition and subtraction, with some work on the mental calculation strategies of counting on and using patterns of similar calculations. Using and applying these skills is encouraged through the problem solving activities, which have an emphasis on money.

LEARNING OBJECTIVES

	Topics	Starter	Main teaching activities
Lesson 1	Place value and ordering	● **Order whole numbers to at least 100** and position them on a 100 square.	● Use and begin to read the vocabulary of comparing and ordering numbers, including ordinal numbers to 100.
Lesson 2	Understanding addition and subtraction Mental calculation strategies (+/−) Problems involving 'real life' Making decisions	● **Know by heart all addition facts for each number to at least 10.**	● Extend understanding of the operations of addition and subtraction. Use and begin to read the related vocabulary. ● Use patterns of similar calculations. ● Recognise all coins. ● Find totals. ● **Choose and use appropriate operations and efficient calculation strategies** (e.g. mental, mental with jottings) **to solve problems.**
Lesson 3	Mental calculation strategies (+/−) Making decisions	● **Know by heart multiplication facts for the 2 and 10 times-tables.**	● Find a small difference by counting up from the smaller to the larger number (e.g. 42 − 39). ● **Choose and use appropriate operations and efficient calculation strategies** (e.g. mental, mental with jottings) **to solve problems.**
Lesson 4	Problems involving 'real life', money and measures Making decisions	As for Lesson 4.	● Begin to use £.p notation for money. ● Find totals, give change and work out which coins to pay. ● **Choose and use appropriate operations and efficient calculation strategies** (e.g. mental, mental with jottings) **to solve problems.**

Lesson overview

Preparation
Make an OHT of the 'Empty 100 square'; make and laminate a copy for each pair of children. Copy 'Ordinal numbers and vocabulary' onto A3 card and cut out the cards; do the same for 'Who came first? 1'.

Learning objectives
Starter
- **Order whole numbers to at least 100** and position them on a 100 square.

Main teaching activities
- Use and begin to read the vocabulary of comparing and ordering numbers, including ordinal numbers to 100.

Vocabulary
order, compare, first, second, third… tenth… twentieth, twenty-first, twenty-second…, last, last but one, before, after, next

You will need:
Photocopiable pages
An A3 copy of 'Who came first? 1' (page 51), a copy of 'Who came first? 2' (page 52) for each child.

CD pages
'Who came first? 2', less able and more able versions (Autumn term, Unit 9), '0–100 number cards', an 'Empty 100 square' for each pair, an OHT of the 'Empty 100 square', 'Ordinal numbers and vocabulary' cards (see General resources).

Equipment
An OHP; dry-wipe markers and cloths; toy animals; scissors.

Lesson

Starter
Give each pair a laminated 'Empty 100 square'. Display the 'Empty 100 square' acetate on the OHP. Use number cards to select random numbers to 100. Model a few numbers first. Ask the children to work in pairs, plotting random numbers that you give them on their 100 squares and writing each number in the correct place. After a few, check and write them on the acetate. Repeat.

Paired work: Tell the children that they will be working in pairs to make up ordinal number stories. Give each pair a copy of 'Who came first? 2' and scissors.

Differentiation
Less able: Provide the differentiated version of 'Who came first? 2' with ordinal numbers to 10th only.
More able: Provide only the pictures. Ask this group to write their own labels. Use the differentiated version of 'Who came first? 2'.

Plenary & assessment
Rehearse ordinal numbers and vocabulary as at the start of the main lesson. Look for the ability of each child in a pair to be able to say the ordinal number and place it in the correct position.

Lessons   overview

Preparation

Make a laminated copy of 'Coin cards and labels' for each child. Provide a mixture of plastic coins in a small container and at least 12 shopping cards for each group of three children. Set up a shop counter with toys or similar items, labelled with some of the prices from 'Price labels (pence)'.

Learning objectives

Starter
- **Know by heart all addition facts for each number to at least 10.**
- **Know by heart multiplication facts for the 2 and 10 times-tables.**

Main teaching activities
- Extend understanding of the operations of addition and subtraction. Use and begin to read the related vocabulary.
- Use patterns of similar calculations.
- Find a small difference by counting up from the smaller to the larger number (e.g. 42 – 39).
- Recognise all coins and begin to use £.p notation for money.
- Find totals, give change and work out which coins to pay.
- **Choose and use appropriate operations and efficient calculation strategies** (e.g. mental, mental with jottings) **to solve problems.**

Vocabulary

money, coin, penny, pence, pound, £, spend, pay, change, total, addition, subtraction, difference between, equal to (also see 'Addition and subtraction vocabulary' sheet)

You will need:

CD pages
Number cards 0–10 from '0–100 number cards', a copy of the 'Function machine game' for each child, 'Spider charts for multiplying', a set of 'Coin cards and labels', a set of 'Price labels (pence)', a set of 'Price labels (£.p)', a copy of 'Addition and subtraction vocabulary' cards (see General resources) 'Shopping cards 1' and '2' (Autumn term, Unit 4).

Equipment
0–10 number line; Blu-Tack; individual whiteboards and pens; plastic coins, real coins and large card coins; small containers; ten different toys, fruits or similar; a Unifix pendulum; a counting stick.

Lesson

Starter

Hold up number cards 0–10 at random, and ask the children to write the number that goes with each to make 10. They can use their fingers to check and/or make jumps along a 0–10 number line. Repeat for other totals below 10, such as 8, 3, 5 or 9.

Main teaching activities

Whole class: This activity should be started in Lesson 2 and completed in Lesson 3. Explain that the rest of this unit is about adding and subtracting with money. Ask the children to tell you some words related to addition and subtraction. As they do so, show the appropriate 'Addition and subtraction vocabulary' cards and stick them on the board. Next, ask them which coins we use in our money system. Again, hold up a coin label, large card coin and real coin for each value. Attach these to the board.

Show the children your shop display. Go through the items, showing the price labels and asking how much each costs. Then ask, for example: *How much would it cost to buy a bunch of bananas and a pineapple?* Discuss strategies for calculating. Encourage rounding and adjusting; putting the largest number first and counting on; partitioning; making a 10; and counting along a number line – whichever is most appropriate for the problem.

Group work: Model the activity. *You will be working on your own today, but sharing cards and money with two others. You need to pick two shopping cards and work out the total you will spend, record the strategy you used, then find the smallest number of coins that you can use to pay. Last of all, you need to write down which coins you used.*

Differentiation

Less able: Give this group shopping cards up to 14p, so their totals are less than 30p.
More able: Ask this group to total three amounts.

Plenary & assessment

Invite a few children to give examples of their work and explain the strategies they used to find the totals. For each strategy, ask what other way could have been used and decide which is more efficient. For example, for 24p + 46p, you might compare, 'I put 46p in my head and counted on 20, then 4' with, 'I know 4 and 6 is 10, so I added 20p, 40p and 10p'. Check that the children can use the addition strategies they have been taught in previous units to add amounts of money.

Lesson  3

Starter

Use the 'Spider charts for multiplying' to practise multiplying by 10. Then give each child a copy of the 'Function machine game'. Ask the children to write random numbers up to 10 on the input side and write 10 in the middle. When you say *Go* they multiply each number by 10 and write the answer on the output side. Ask children who are struggling to write only two or three numbers on the left. Go through the answers. Repeat for multiplying by 2. If there is time, repeat both with new input numbers.

Main teaching activities

Whole class: Using your shop display, hold up a pair of items and ask the children to find the difference between their prices. Encourage them to count up from the smaller to the larger number. Draw a number line as a visual reminder and talk through the steps. For example, using a book (35p) and a horn (46p):

35p to 40p is 5p, and 46p is another 6p. 5p and 6p is 11p. The difference in price is 11p. Record: 5p + 6p = 11p
Group work: As for Lesson 2, but instead of adding up prices the children can work individually to find the difference between the prices on pairs of shopping cards.

Differentiation

Less able: Give this group only the shopping cards to 14p.
More able: These children can find bigger differences. Give them two piles of cards: one set of cards to 14p and the other set as normal. They should take one card from each pile.

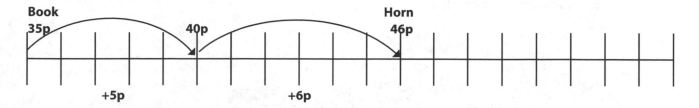

Plenary & assessment

Ask some children whom you would like to assess to explain their work and demonstrate their use of the number line. Then demonstrate how to use the same strategy for finding change from £1 and £2.

Lesson ④

Starter

Repeat from Lesson 3, but first use a counting stick to count in twos and tens. Stop at different interval marks to ask how many lots of 2 or 10 your finger is on, and how many that is altogether.

Main teaching activities

Whole class: Explain that today the children will be changing amounts of pence into pounds and pence, then working with these amounts to find totals and change. Announce that there has been an increase in the cost of all the items on your shop counter. Take off the pence labels and replace them with a selection of pounds and pence ones. As you do this, challenge the children to work out each price increase. For example: *The pineapple was 50p. Now it is £1.10. How much has it gone up?*

When you have found the price increase for each item, write some of the new prices on the board. Explain that when an amount such as £2.34 is written, the number just after the £ sign is the number of pounds and the numbers after the dot are pence. The dot separates the pounds from the pence. Point to the other new prices you have written and for each, ask how many pounds there are and how many pence. Ask: *How many pence are there in a pound… in £2 … in £4?* As a challenge, find out who can tell you how many pence there are in each price on the board.

Hold up two items with their new labels – for example, a pineapple at £1.10 and a bunch of bananas at £1.40. Ask how much they will cost altogether and invite someone to explain their strategy for addition. Then say: *If I give the shopkeeper £3, how much change will I be given?* Use a number line to find the answer by counting on.

Paired work: Give each pair of children a pile of £.p price label cards. They pick two, work out the total cost and record their strategy, then work out the change from £3.00 and record their strategy.

Differentiation

Less able: Ask this group to use one price card that is a multiple of 10p, and to work out the change from £2.

More able: This group can work out the change from £5.

Plenary & assessment

Invite some children to demonstrate their work and their strategies. Ask all the children to turn to a partner and tell them some of the things they have learned this week, and whether they have a good understanding of what they have done. Encourage them to discuss whether they used: rounding and adjusting; putting the largest number first and counting on; partitioning; making a 10; counting along a number line. After a few minutes, ask selected pairs to share their thoughts and then to do a self-assessment of how confident they feel about these strategies by putting their thumbs up, down or sideways.

Name	Date

Who came first? 1

The animals that lived in the wood at the bottom of our road decided to have a race from the wood to my house. They asked me if I would tell them who came first, who came second and so on. I said I would.

The animals in the race were Darren Duck, Ozzie Ostrich, Penny Penguin, Dora Dragon, Peter Panda, Robbie Rabbit, Neddie Bear, Tyson the Dog, Cat the Cat and Wolfgang the Wolf. They all lined up by the oak tree in the wood. Someone yelled 'GO!'. They all ran and ran as fast as they could.

As they ran through my front door, I told them where they had come in the race. This was the order: Wolfgang came first, Cat came second, Darren third, Neddie fourth, Tyson fifth, then Dora, Peter, Robbie, Ozzie and Penny.

Let's put them in order on the board. Can you find the right label to show where each animal came in the race?

Name	Date

Who came first? 2

Cut out these 20 animals. Line them up in any order.

Cut out the labels. Label the animals in the line from 1st all the way to 20th.

Then make up a story about what the animals have been doing.

You may be asked to tell the class your story during the Plenary.

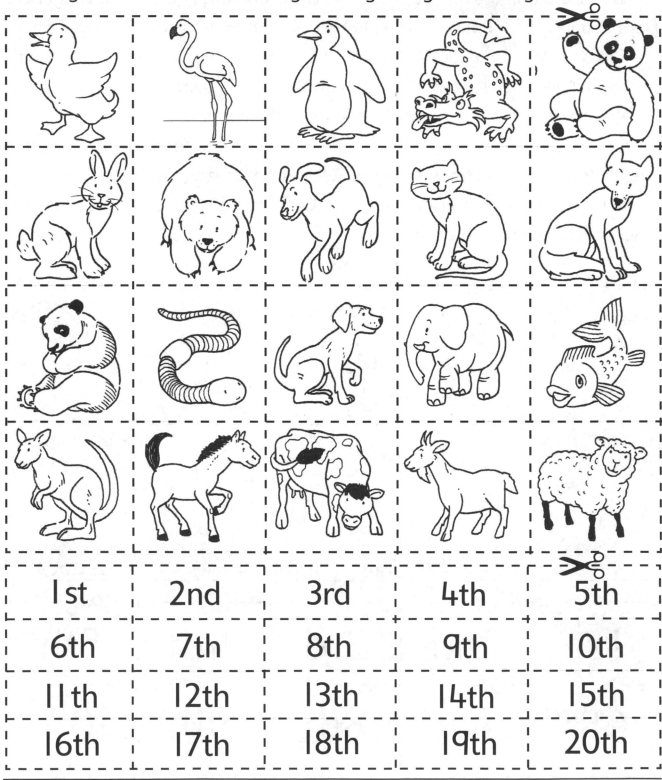

1st	2nd	3rd	4th	5th
6th	7th	8th	9th	10th
11th	12th	13th	14th	15th
16th	17th	18th	19th	20th

Multiplication and division with problem solving

The first two lessons of this unit are about understanding multiplication as repeated addition and division as repeated subtraction. They are taught using the number line, so that the children can see that they are inverse operations. The children also explore the concept of arrays and use their knowledge to solve word problems.

LEARNING OBJECTIVES

		Topics	Starter	Main teaching activities
Lesson	1	Understanding multiplication and division	● **Read and write whole numbers to at least 100** in figures and words.	● **Understand the operation of multiplication as repeated addition or as describing an array,** and begin to understand division as grouping or sharing. ● Use and read the related vocabulary. ● Use the ×, ÷ and = signs to record mental calculations in a number sentence, and recognise the use of a symbol such as □ or △ to stand for an unknown number.
Lesson	2	Understanding multiplication and division	● **Know by heart multiplication facts for the 2 and 10 times-tables.**	As for Lesson 1.
Lesson	3	Problems involving 'real life', money or measures Making decisions	● Know by heart all pairs of numbers with a total of 20 (e.g. 13 + 7, 6 + 14).	● Use mental addition and subtraction, simple multiplication and division, to solve simple word problems using one or two steps. ● Explain how the problem was solved. ● **Choose and use appropriate operations and efficient calculation strategies.**

Lessons   overview

Preparation
Photocopy 'Multiplication and division vocabulary' onto A3 card and cut out the vocabulary cards.

Learning objectives
Starter
● **Read and write whole numbers to at least 100** in figures and words.
● **Know by heart multiplication facts for the 2 and 10 times-tables.**
Main teaching activities
● **Understand the operation of multiplication as repeated addition or as describing an array,** and begin to understand division as grouping or sharing.
● Use and read the related vocabulary.
● Use the ×, ÷ and = signs to record mental calculations in a number sentence, and recognise the use of a symbol such as □ or △ to stand for an unknown number.

Vocabulary
lots of, groups of, times, multiply, multiplied by, multiple of, repeated addition, array, row, column, equal groups of, repeated subtraction, divide, divided by

You will need:
Photocopiable pages
'Things to multiply' (page 56) and 'Jumping up and down' (page 57) for each child.

CD pages
'Things to multiply', and 'Jumping up and down', less able and more able versions (Autumn term, Unit 10), '0–100 number cards', a 'Function machine game' for each child, 'Multiplication and division vocabulary' cards (see General resources).

Equipment
Individual whiteboards and pens; Multilink cubes or other counting equipment.

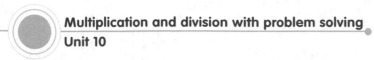

Lesson ①

Starter

Give the children some single-digit and two-digit numbers to write as numerals. Show them some single-digit and two-digit number cards to write as words. Now ask them to write a number and change it: *Write 4, make it 24, now add 10* (34), *change the 4 to a 7* (37), *add 3* (40), *take away two tens* (20), *add 100* (120), *double the tens number* (140), *add 9* (149). Repeat

Main teaching activities

Whole class: Tell the children that they are going to learn about multiplication and division. They will begin by learning to multiply and divide by 2, 10 and 5. Do they know what 'multiplication' and 'division' mean? Group the multiplication and division vocabulary cards into two groups, one for each operation.

Write 2 × 6 on the board. Choose six children to help you. Give each child two Multilink cubes. Ask: *How many Multilink does Sam have? How many does Aisha have? How many do they have altogether? Yes, six lots of 2 is 12. Two times 6 or 2 multiplied by 6 is 12.*

Write 2 + 2 + 2 + 2 + 2 + 2 = 12. Ask: *What have I written? Yes, an addition, because multiplication is like addition. Two times 6 is the same as 2 + 2 + 2 + 2 + 2 + 2. Let's count in multiples of 2 six times and see if we get the same answer.* Repeat this multiplication of 2 by other numbers below 10. Move on to multiplying by 10 as above. This links with counting in multiples of numbers, and also with division as repeated subtraction (which the children will think about later). Finish by demonstrating 'times 5'.

Group work: Ask the children to work in pairs, using counting apparatus to carry out the multiplications on 'Things to multiply'.

Differentiation

Less able: Provide the versions of 'Things to multiply', where objects are used throughout.
More able: Provide the version that moves on quickly to thinking about multiples.

Plenary & assessment

Write a multiplication on the board, such as 2 × 6. Ask what two times 6 or six lots of 2 means as a repeated addition. Then ask what six times 2 or two lots of 6 would be in repeated addition. Ask the children what they notice – that six times 2 and two times 6 have the same answer.

Lesson ②

Starter

Practise saying the 2 and 10 times-tables. Then give out 'Function machine game' sheets. Ask the children to write random numbers up to 10 on the input side and write ×10 in the middle. When you say *Go!* they write the answer on the output side. Ask children who are struggling to write two or three input numbers. Repeat with a different set of input numbers, then do the same for the 2 times-table.

Main teaching activities

Whole class: Ask the children what the opposite operation to addition is. Draw an arrow diagram on the board to jog the children's memory. Now ask: *What do you think the opposite of multiplication is? If multiplication is repeated addition, what do you think division is? Look at this example: five lots of 2 is 2 + 2 + 2 + 2 + 2 which is 10, so 10 divided by 2 must be 10 – 2 – 2 – 2 – 2 – 2.* Demonstrate this using a number line. Repeat with more examples.
Paired work: Give the children the 'Jumping up and down' activity sheet to complete in pairs.

Differentiation

Less able: Provide the version of 'Jumping up and down' that guides the child through multiplication and division by 2, using repeated addition and subtraction.

More able: This version of the sheet invites the children to draw their own number lines.

Plenary & assessment

Ask questions such as: *Why is multiplication like addition? Why is division like subtraction? What do we mean by three lots of 2? Can you draw that as an array? What about two lots of 3?*

Lesson overview

Preparation

Make and laminate A3 copies of 'Flip-flap for 20' and 'How to solve a problem'. Make acetates of 'Practice problems' and 'More practice problems'. Fold the copies of 'Flip-flap for 20' along all the lines and flatten out the sheet.

Learning objectives

Starter
- **Know by heart all pairs of numbers with a total of 20.**

Main teaching activities
- Use mental addition and subtraction, simple multiplication and division, to solve simple word problems using one or two steps.
- Explain how the problem was solved.
- **Choose and use appropriate operations and efficient calculation strategies.**

Vocabulary

lots of, groups of, times, multiply, multiplied by, multiple of, repeated, addition, array, row, column, equal groups of, repeated subtraction, divide, divided by

You will need:

CD pages
An acetate of 'Practice problems', 'Problems, problems, problems 1', 'Problems, problems, problems 2' and 'Problems, problems, problems 3', one for each child, a copy of 'Flip-flap for 20' for each child, an A3 copy of 'Flip-flap for 20' and 'How to solve a problem' (see General resources).

Equipment

Individual whiteboards and pens; Multilink cubes or other counting equipment; an OHP; dice or 0-9 number cards.

Lesson

Starter

Give the children each a copy of 'Flip-flap for 20' and ask them to count the ladybirds. Fold back the top two rows and the bottom row of your A3 'Flip-flap for 20'. Hold it so you can see ten ladybirds and the children can see ten. Ask: *If you can see ten ladybirds, how many can I see? If I fold it so you can see five ladybirds* (fold back all but the far right edge), *how many can I see?* Repeat for several numbers.

Main teaching activities

Whole class: Explain that the next lesson will be about solving real-life problems using the ideas from Lessons 1–2. Quickly recap on the meanings and methods of multiplication and division. Show the 'Practice problems' acetate problems one at a time on the OHP. For each one, ask: *What things do we need to do in order to answer this problem?* Stick the 'How to solve a problem' poster, discuss them and stick the poster on the wall. Work through each problem on the acetate, asking questions as you go.

Paired work: Ask the children to work with a partner on the 'Problems, problems, problems 1' sheet jotting on it to show their workings, perhaps using dice or number cards to generate more numbers.

Differentiation

Less able: Use the version 'Problems, problems, problems 2' with less demanding numbers.

More able: Use the version, 'Problems, problems, problems 3' with more demanding numbers.

Plenary & assessment

Invite a few children to explain how they solved one of the problems. Compare their methods. Ask questions such as: *What did you need to know before you could start to work out the answer? Which bits of the problem are important? What clue words helped?*

Name	Date

Things to multiply

You will need a tray of small things to use for counting.

For each multiplication, put the right number of things in the right number of rows.

Draw what you have done in the box.

Write the answer, then write the addition version, as shown below.

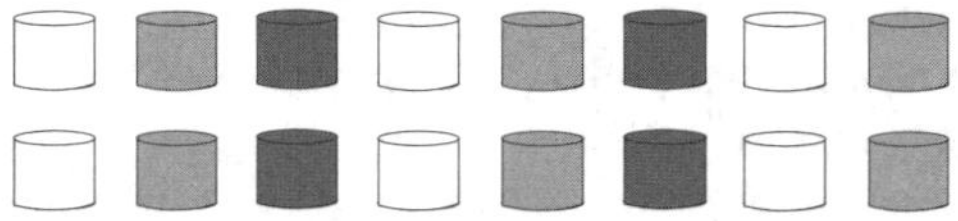

$2 \times 3 = 6$	$2 \times 8 = 16$
$2 + 2 + 2 = 6$	$2 + 2 + 2 + 2 + 2 + 2 + 2 + 2 = 16$
$2 \times 4 = \boxed{}$	$2 \times 6 = \boxed{}$
$10 \times 2 = \boxed{}$	$10 \times 4 = \boxed{}$

Now see if you can work these out by counting in twos, tens or fives.

$2 \times 7 = 2 + 2 + 2 + 2 + 2 + 2 + 2 = 14$

$2 \times 9 = $ _____

$10 \times 6 = $ _____

$10 \times 9 = $ _____

$5 \times 6 = $ _____

Name	Date

Jumping up and down

Fill the number lines to show each multiplication and its division opposite.
Count the number of arrows for the answer.

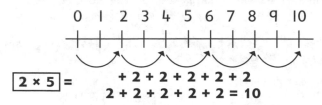

$2 \times 5 =$ + 2 + 2 + 2 + 2 + 2
2 + 2 + 2 + 2 + 2 = 10

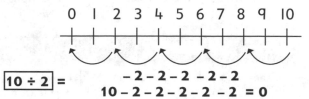

$10 \div 2 =$ – 2 – 2 – 2 – 2 – 2
10 – 2 – 2 – 2 – 2 – 2 = 0

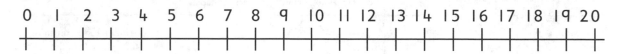

2 × 7

_____

_____

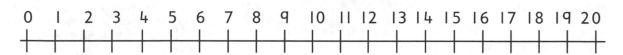

14 ÷ 2

_____

_____

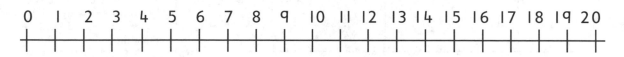

5 × 3

_____

_____

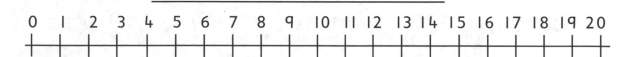

20 ÷ 5

_____

_____

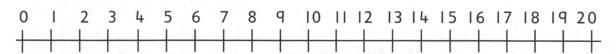

5 × 4

_____

_____

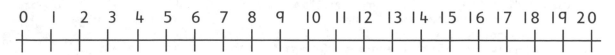

12 ÷ 2

_____

_____

Multiplication, divisions and fractions

This unit links doubling and halving to multiplying and dividing by half. Practice is provide with a game. The children are also encouraged to think about contexts in which they need to double or halve through problem solving. The last two lessons are to do with fractions and the links with multiplication and division.

LEARNING OBJECTIVES

		Topics	Starter	Main teaching activities
Lesson	1	Mental calculation strategies (×/÷)	● **Know by heart multiplication facts for the 2 and 10 times-tables.** ● Derive quickly division facts corresponding to the 2 and 10 times-tables.	● Use known number facts and place value to carry out simple multiplications and divisions.
Lesson	2	Problems involving 'real life'. Making decisions	As for Lesson 1.	● Use mental addition and subtraction, simple multiplication and division, to solve simple word problems using one or two steps. ● Explain how the problem was solved. ● **Choose and use appropriate operations and efficient calculation strategies** (e.g. mental, mental with jottings) **to solve problems.**
Lesson	3	Fractions	● Add/subtract 9 or 11: add/subtract 10 and adjust by 1.	● Begin to recognise and find one half and one quarter of shapes and small numbers of objects. ● Begin to recognise that two halves or four quarters make one whole and that two quarters and one half are equivalent.

Lessons   overview

Preparation
Cut out the 'Spider charts for multiplying' and 'Spider charts for dividing', enlarge and copy onto A3 paper. Copy 'Dartboard doubles gameboard' onto card and laminate; cut out the spinners and provide paper clips. Copy 'Halve or double?' onto acetate.

Learning objectives
Starter
● **Know by heart multiplication facts for the 2 and 10 times-tables.**
● Derive quickly division facts corresponding to the 2 and 10 times-tables.
Main teaching activity
● Use known number facts and place value to carry out simple multiplications and divisions.
● Use mental addition and subtraction, simple multiplication and division, to solve simple word problems using one or two steps.
● Explain how the problem was solved.
● **Choose and use appropriate operations and efficient calculation strategies (e.g. mental, mental with jottings) to solve problems.**

Vocabulary
double, halve, share, share equally, multiply, divide, partition, recombine

You will need:
Photocopiable pages
An acetate of 'Halve or double?' (page 61).

CD pages
'Halve or double again, 1', '2' and '3', less able and more able versions(Autumn term, Unit 11); '0–100 number cards', 'Spider charts for multiplying' and 'Spider charts for dividing' for each child, an A3 copy of 'How to solve a problem', a copy of 'Dartboard doubles spinner''Dartboard doubles game', and 'Dartboard doubles gameboard' for each group (see General resources).

Equipment
Individual whiteboards and pens; Multilink cubes or other counting equipment; counters; an OHP; scissors; paperclips.

Lesson

Starter

Count in twos from zero to ten and back. Ask the children to close their eyes as they count and imagine jumping up and down a number line. Show them the spider chart for multiplying by 2. Point randomly to numbers around the outside. The children should call out the answer when the number is multiplied. Now show the spider chart for dividing by 2: *What would you multiply 2 by to get the numbers around the outside? If I point to 18, what would you call out? That's right, 9.* Draw their attention to the fact that finding out what you would multiply 2 by to get 18 is one way of working out 18 divided by 2. Repeat.

Main teaching activities

Whole class: Tell the children that they will be working on mental calculation strategies in the next two lessons, including doubling and halving, partitioning numbers and multiplying and dividing by 10. Ask them what 'doubling' and 'halving' mean. Explain that they are the same as 'multiplying by 2' and 'dividing by 2'.

Call out a few numbers up to ten for the children to double, writing the answers on their whiteboards. Call out even numbers to 20 for halving. Move on to multiples of 10 to 100.

Group work: Tell the children that they will be working in groups of two to four to practise doubling and halving. Model the 'Dartboard doubles' game and provide the resources.

Differentiation

Less able: These children should use numbers to 10 or 20 and counting apparatus.

More able: Write extra numbers on the blank cards provided, such as 24, 22, 32 and 40. Don't use numbers with a unit digit of 5 or above.

Plenary & assessment

Can the children double and halve all the numbers they worked with? Did they manage to halve 30, 50, 70 and 90, and if so, how? Explain that there is an easy way: numbers that have an odd number of ten can be partitioned into 10 and the rest of the tens. They all know half of 10 (5), and the other number is even and therefore easy to halve.

Lesson

Starter

Give each pair of children A4 copies of the spider charts. In each pair, one child should ask multiplication and division questions (as you have done in Lesson 1) and the other child should answer them. After a couple of goes, they should swap roles. Ask several children to share their questions. End with a few key questions, such as: *If I write 2 × 6 = 12 on the board, what else do we know? How can we use our multiplication knowledge to help us divide?*

Main teaching activities

Whole class: Tell the children that in this lesson they will be solving word problems using the strategies from Lesson 1. Recap these strategies, then use the 'How to solve a problem' poster to recap the problem-solving process. Project the 'Halve or double?' acetate and talk through the problems together.

Group work: Tell the children that they may work individually or with a partner to complete the 'Halve or double again 1' activity sheet. Model how to make up problems like the example provided, using the information on this sheet.

Differentiation

Less able: Provide the version, 'Halve or double again 2' with smaller numbers.
More able: Provide the version, 'Halve or double again 3' with much larger numbers.

Plenary & assessment

Invite children from each group to ask one of their questions for the rest of the class to try to answer. Ask what strategies they used, and watch and assess the children's responses.

Lesson overview

Preparation

Cut a selection of food into halves and quarters. Copy the shapes on the 'Shapes to fold' sheet onto A3 paper for each pair of children. The recording sheet can be A3 or A4. If any children need help cutting out their shapes, do it for them before the lesson.

Learning objectives

Starter
- Add/subtract 9 or 11: add/subtract 10 and adjust by 1.

Main teaching activity
- Begin to recognise and find one half and one quarter of shapes and small numbers of objects.
- Begin to recognise that two halves or four quarters make one whole and that two quarters and one half are equivalent.

Vocabulary

part, equal parts, fraction, one whole, one half, two halves, one quarter, two… three… four quarters

You will need:

CD pages
A copy of 'Shapes to fold' and 'Shapes to fold recording sheet' for each pair (see General resources).

Equipment
A class 100 square; a 100 square for each child; an apple, a chocolate bar or other food that can be divided into quarters; Multilink cubes; counters; Plasticine; an OHP; scissors.

Lesson

Starter

Demonstrate adding and subtracting 9 and 11 on a class 100 square by adding/subtracting 10 and adjusting. Ask the children to put their finger on a number on their 100 squares, then add or subtract 9 or 11, telling you what number they get to and how they got there. Repeat several times.

Main teaching activities

Whole class: Explain that the children will be learning about fractions. Ask: *Who has heard the word 'fraction'? Can anyone tell me what it means?* Use your food examples to show 'one half' and 'one quarter'. Demonstrate that the fractions are equal, that two halves fit back together to make a whole, and that four quarters do the same.

Give everyone a piece of Plasticine. Ask them to roll it into a worm shape and then break it into halves, then quarters. Make the point that half of a half is the same as a quarter. Say: *Compare your worm with your neighbour's. Is your half the same as theirs? Does that mean it isn't a half? Why can all the half worms be different sizes? It's because half sizes are different if the whole lengths are different.*
Paired work: Model the 'Shapes to fold' activity by cutting out and folding the shapes. As you do this, ask: *What shape is this? How many parts will I have if I fold it in half? How many ways can I fold this shape in half? Who can fold this shape in half for me? Can anyone show us another way to fold it in half?*

Give an activity sheet of shapes to each pair of children. Ask them to fold these in as many ways as they can to make equal halves. Give the children the recording sheet to fill in.

Plenary & assessment

Compare the ways the children found to fold their shapes in half. Invite a few children, particularly any whom you wish to assess, to demonstrate any new ways.

Name	Date

Halve or double?

I looked in my money box and saw lots of coins.
I had fourteen 1p pieces.
I had the same amount of money in 2p pieces.

How many 2p pieces did I have? ☐

Sue had 40 marbles. Peter had half that number.

How many marbles did Peter have? ☐

Lizzie had 16 birthday cards.
Her friend Tom had double that amount.

How many birthday cards did Tom have? ☐

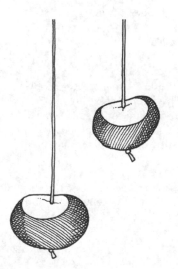

Laurie had 50 centimetres of string.
Laura had half that amount.

How long was Laura's piece of string? ☐ cm

Children use a ruler to measure and draw lines in metres and centimetres. They learn the order of the months of the year. They begin to read the time to the hour, half hour or quarter hour on an analague and 12-hour digital clock.

LEARNING OBJECTIVES

	Topics	Starter	Main teaching activity
Lesson 1	Measures	● **Know by heart multiplication facts for the 2 and 10 times-tables.** ● Derive quickly division facts corresponding to the 2 and 10 times-tables.	● **Read a simple scale to the nearest labelled division, including using a ruler to draw and measure lines to the nearest centimetre.**
Lesson 2	Measures	As for Lesson 1.	As for Lesson 1.
Lesson 3	Measures	As for Lesson 1.	As for Lesson 1.
Lesson 4	Measures	● Know by heart doubles of all numbers to 10 and the corresponding halves. ● Identify near doubles using doubles already known (e.g. 8 + 9, 40 + 41).	● Order the months of the year. ● Read the time to the hour, half hour or quarter hour.
Lesson 5	Measures	● Read the time to the hour, half hour or quarter hour on an analogue clock and a 12-hour digital clock.	As for Lesson 3.

Lessons   overview

Preparation
If necessary, make A3 copies of the 'Spider charts for multiplying' and 'Spider charts for dividing'; enlarge and cut out the 'Small spider charts' cards. Copy 'Measuring equipment' onto acetate, and cut a pointer out of card. For each table group of eight children, prepare four lines drawn on four separate pieces of paper, in thick felt pen, measuring: a) 10cm, b) between 24cm and 25cm, c) 0.5m and d) just under 1m.

Learning objectives
Starter
● **Know by heart multiplication facts for the 2 and 10 times-tables.**
● Derive quickly division facts corresponding to the 2 and 10 times-tables.
Main teaching activity
● **Read a simple scale to the nearest labelled division, including using a ruler to draw and measure lines to the nearest centimetre.**

Vocabulary
metre, centimetre, almost, between, nearly

You will need:
Photocopiable pages
A copy of 'What's my measurement?' (page 67) for each child.

CD pages
A set of '0–100 number cards', A3 copies of 'Spider charts for multiplying' and 'Spider charts for dividing', 'Small spider charts' for each child, an acetate of 'Measuring equipment', (see General resources).

Equipment
Whiteboards and pens; rulers and metre sticks marked in decades of centimetres, and in centimetres; measuring tapes (tape measure and surveyor's tape).

Lesson ①

Starter
Practise 2 and 10 times-tables facts, using the spider charts for multiplication and division as in Unit 11 Lessons 1–2.

Main teaching activities
Whole class: Explain to the children that in this and the next two lessons they will be learning how to use a ruler to measure. Ask: *What standard units do we use to measure length?* The children will almost certainly say metre, but may not remember centimetre. Write both words on the board. Ask: *How many centimetres are there in a metre? Yes, there are 100.*

Now discuss the tools that can be used for measuring in metres and centimetres. Hold up the metre stick marked in 10cm and ask, pointing to the 50cm mark, *What measurement does this show?* Repeat this for other marks. Now show the children a metre stick marked in 1cm. Put the two metre sticks together so that the children can see that the second one also shows the decades but that it also shows 1cm increments. Explain that the second one will help them to be more accurate in their measuring.

Hold up the tape measure and ask: *When would we use this?* Children may talk about being measured for new clothes, or measuring something that bends. Show them the surveyor's tape and ask *When would you use this?* Children may not have seen a tape as long as this, so if room, pull out the tape and pass it around the children so that they have a sense of its length. You may want to take them into a large space in order to do this.

Now, using a metre stick marked in centimetres, show the children how to measure the height of a chair. Ask: *How tall do you think this chair is?* Write some estimates on the board, such as 45 centimetres. Write it again, this time using the shortened form 45cm. Now invite a child to place the metre stick against the chair in order to measure its height. Invite the rest of the children to look carefully, to check that the metre stick has been placed so that it is the correct way up to take a measurement, then ask: *How tall is this chair?* Write the reading onto the board alongside the estimate. Discuss the accuracy of the measurement, to the nearest centimetre. Talk about the 'bits left over' when measuring and whether to go just above or below to the next centimetre depends upon how close the reading is to the marked centimetre.

Group work: Ask the children to work in small groups of about four. Explain that you would like them to estimate and measure five things around the room which can be measured using a metre stick marked in centimetres. Ask them to record their estimate and their measure.

Differentiation
Less able: If the children find reading numbers on the metre stick difficult, decide whether to use a metre stick marked in decades. Alternatively, work with this group, and count along the stick in ones from the nearest decade number each time in order to read off the measurement.

More able: Challenge the children to estimate, measure and record measurements greater than 1 metre. They can use a tape measure for this, or a surveyor's tape for much larger measurements.

Plenary & assessment
Invite children from each group to demonstrate with a metre stick what they estimated and measured. Ask them to write their findings onto the board for everyone to check. If the more able children have used a longer tape, ask them to demonstrate how they did this for the other children to see. Ask questions such as: *How long do you think this is? What is the measurement? Is this closer to … or …? So what shall we record?*

Lesson ②

Starter

Repeat the Starter activity from Lesson 1 once. Now let the children work in pairs to test each other, using the 'Small spider charts' as prompts.

Main teaching activities

Whole class: Project the OHT of 'Measuring equipment'. Place a pointer on it at various points for the children to read the measurement. Point to exact centimetre marks as well as marks in between. Expect answers such as: 'just more than', 'in between' and 'a bit less than' for the latter. Discuss how the ruler must be lined up with the beginning (or 0cm) of the ruler in line with one end of the line.
Paired work: Give each mixed-ability pair a 'What's my measurement?' sheet. Say: *Read the scales marked on the rulers and metre sticks and write the measurements.* Model one or more examples, emphasising the recording.

Plenary & assessment

Recap these two lessons. Ask questions such as: *Who will show me how to measure the width of this book using a ruler? Where do you place the ruler?* Ask the children to assess how they did, using the 'thumbs up' method.

Lesson ③

Repeat the Starter for lessons 1 and 2. When working in pairs, ask the children to answer correctly as many questions as they can in, say two minutes. This will encourage quick recall of multiplication facts. Using the OHT of 'Measuring equipment' and some lines that you have drawn on another acetate, revise with the children how to estimate, then measure using a ruler. Ask the children to work individually, each with some paper. On the board write some measurements, in centimetres. They use their rulers to draw the lines for the measurements on the board. Use the 'Measuring equipment' OHT during the plenary to review, again drawing lines of a given length. Ask: *Where does the line begin when we draw it?*

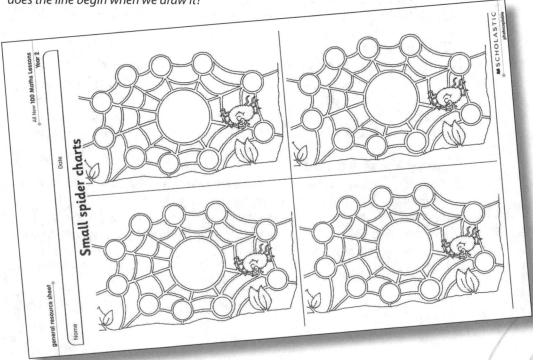

Lessons   overview

Preparation

Enlarge, copy and cut out the time vocabulary cards from 'Measures vocabulary' and the 'Months of the year cards'. Photocopy and cut out about eight sets of the cards from 'Analogue and digital time cards' and 'Clocks'. Put them into sets of about 24 matching cards. Have one complete set for class demonstration and display. Copy the 'Up the mountain gameboard' onto A3 paper.

Learning objectives

Starter
- Know by heart doubles of all numbers to 10 and the corresponding halves.
- Identify near doubles using doubles already known (e.g. 8 + 9, 40 + 41).
- Read the time to the hour, half hour or quarter hour on an analogue clock and a 12-hour digital clock.

Main teaching activities
- Order the months of the year.
- Read the time to the hour, half hour or quarter hour.

Vocabulary

time, month, year, weekend, second, minute, hour, half an hour, quarter of an hour, o'clock, half past, quarter past, quarter to, digital, analogue, clock, watch, hands, January, February…

You will need:

Photocopiable pages
Two copies of 'What's the time?' for each child (page 68).

CD pages
A set of '0–100 number cards', 'Months of the year cards', an 'Up the mountain gameboard' (A3), time vocabulary cards from 'Measures vocabulary', 'Analogue and digital time cards', 'Clocks' (see General resources).

Equipment
Individual whiteboards; Blu-Tack; a calendar; a washing line and pegs; a geared clock; a small cardboard clock for each child; an OHP; two different-coloured counters.

Lesson

Starter

Call out or show numbers to 10 and ask the children to write the doubles on their whiteboards. Call out even numbers to 20 and ask the children to write down the halves quickly. Among those numbers, call out others that were used in Unit 11 for doubling multiples of 10 or doubling numbers that can be partitioned. Write on the board (or hold up as cards) two consecutive numbers, and ask the children to add them using the near doubles strategy (for example, 6 + 7 = double 6 + 1).

Main teaching activities

Whole class: Explain that the next two lessons are about time. Ask the children to tell you any time words they know. As they say each word, Blu-Tack the vocabulary card onto the board. Ask the children what each word means. Ask them to tell you the days of the week, then the months of the year. Give out the month cards randomly to 12 children; ask the rest of the class to order them from January to December. Peg the cards on a washing line as a reminder. Ask the children what the months are divided into (weeks), what the weeks are divided into (days), and so on to hours and minutes.

Discuss analogue and digital clocks: what they look like, where they are found. Tell the children that they will be using analogue clocks, but also thinking about digital time. Use a geared clock for demonstration, and give each child a small card clock face. Write 'o'clock' on the board. Ask a child to write a number up to 12 in front of it. Ask the rest of the class to show that time on their clocks. Ask them to show you three hours later, four hours earlier and so on. Keep doing this until all or most of the class can do it correctly. This is an assessment opportunity. Each time they show you a time, ask the children what it is and how many minutes past the o'clock it is (none). Show them how digital time is given in minutes past an hour, so we don't say 'o'clock': we write the hour and two dots, then two zeros (so 3 o'clock becomes 3:00.)

Do the same for half past. Show the children your geared clock; ask them to tell you what happens to the hour hand as the minute hand moves to the 6. Ask them to show various half past times; expect them to move the hour hand to the correct place. Ask how many minutes past o'clock half past is. If necessary, ask them how many minutes there are in an hour; then establish that half an hour is half as many minutes. Ask what the digital time for half past three is. Write: 3:30. Repeat until most of the class have understood.

Compare half and quarter hours with halves and quarters of a pizza, drawing pictures on the board. Ask the children to show quarter past and quarter to times on their clocks. For each time, show them on your geared clock where the hour hand will be and ask them to show this. Ask them how many minutes past the hour a quarter past is, then a quarter to. Link this to their work in Unit 11 on finding a quarter by halving and halving again. Write examples on the board: quarter past five = 5:15, quarter to six = 5:45 and so on.

Group work: Give mixed-ability groups of up to four a selection of 12 matching analogue and digital time cards for o'clock, half past, quarter past and quarter to times. Ask the children to work together to match each analogue time to its digital equivalent.

Plenary & assessment

Together, group the matched labels in hour sets (for example, from 1 o'clock = 1:00 to quarter to two = 1:45). Start a display by drawing these times on clocks. Ask the children to use their card clocks to show various given times. For each time, ask questions such as: *How many minutes past o'clock is that? Where would the hour hand be? How would you write this time digitally?*

Lesson

Starter

Display an A3 copy of the 'Up the mountain' gameboard. Give each child a card clock. Divide the class into two teams. Attach with Blu-Tack a different-coloured counter for each team to the bottom of the mountain. Call out simple clock times for the children to show. The first child to hold up the correct time gets his or her team a move up the mountain. The first team to reach the top wins. As well as asking for times such as 4 o'clock or half past seven, try: *Half past three, now one hour after that time, half an hour earlier.* Make sure that the children place both the minute and the hour hands correctly.

Main teaching activities

Recap Lesson 4, concentrating upon quarter past, quarter to, and how to record these times. Ask the children to work in the same groups to develop their matching work in Lesson 4 by adding the clock faces from 'Clocks' and recording their work individually on two copies of 'What's the time?'.

Plenary & assessment

Show the clock face cards from 'Clocks' and invite some children to add them to the display started in Lesson 4. Using the geared clock, show some times and ask the children to write these, in digital time, onto their white boards. When you say *Show me,* they hold up their boards for you to check their times. Ask questions such as: *It is now 9:45. What time will it be in 15 minutes? What time will it be in another 15 minutes after 10:00?*

Name   Date

What's my measurement?

Read the measurement on each of these scales and write it in the box below.

Sometimes the measurement will be exact. Sometimes it will be between numbers.

If it is between numbers, you can say it is 'nearly...' or 'just over...' or 'between...'. It doesn't matter which order you do these in.

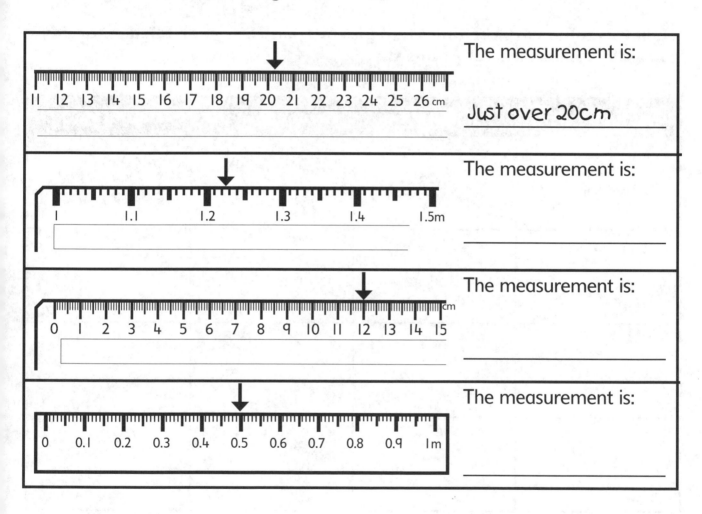

The measurement is:

Just over 20cm

The measurement is:

_____

The measurement is:

_____

The measurement is:

_____

Name		Date	

What's the time?

When you have finished matching your clocks and times, you should have 12 sets of analogue and digital times and clock pictures, like this:

quarter past 5
5:15

05:15

Fill in this table with the times and pictures. One has been filled in for you. You will need two copies of this sheet.

Analogue time	Digital time	Analogue clock	Digital clock
quarter past 5	5:15		05:15

■SCHOLASTIC

photocopiable

In the first two lessons the children solve problems and puzzles to do with shapes. In the last two lessons they learn about how to organise and use data using tables, pictograms and bar charts.

LEARNING OBJECTIVES

	Topics	Starter	Main teaching activities
Lesson 1	Reasoning about numbers or shapes	● Order months of the year. ● Read the time to the hour, half hour or quarter hour on an analogue clock and a 12-hour digital clock.	● Solve mathematical problems or puzzles, recognise simple patterns and relationships, generalise and predict. ● Suggest extensions by asking 'What if…?' or 'What could I try next?'
Lesson 2	As for Lesson 1.	As for Lesson 1.	As for Lesson 1.
Lesson 3	Organising and using data	● Add/subtract 9 or 11: add/subtract 10 and adjust by 1.	● Solve a given problem by sorting, classifying and organising information in simple ways. ● Discuss and explain results.
Lesson 4	Organising and using data	● **Know by heart multiplication facts for the 2 and 10 times-tables.** ● Derive quickly division facts corresponding to the 2 and 10 times-tables.	As for Lesson 3.

Lessons   overview

Preparation
If necessary, make an A3 copy of the 'Up the mountain' gameboard. Copy the shapes from 'Templates for irregular shapes' and 'Templates for regular shapes' onto acetate and also onto card. Each pair of children will need six shapes: three regular and three irregular. Copy one of the strips on 'Symmetry investigation' onto acetate and cut out the shapes. Make a collection of symmetrical 2-D shapes and pictures. Copy 'Puzzle practice 1' and '2' onto acetate

Learning objectives
Starter
● Order months of the year.
● Read the time to the hour, half hour or quarter hour on an analogue clock and a 12-hour digital clock.
Main teaching activities
● Solve mathematical problems or puzzles, recognise simple patterns and relationships, generalise and predict.
● Suggest extensions by asking 'What if…?' or 'What could I try next?'

Vocabulary
jotting, answer, right, correct, wrong, what could we try next?, how did you work it out?, number sentence, sign, operation, symbol

You will need:
Photocopiable pages
An acetate of 'Puzzle practice 1' and '2' (pages 73 and 74) for each pair.

CD pages
'Up the mountain' gameboard (A3), 'Templates for irregular shapes' and 'Templates for regular shapes' on card and acetate, 'Months of the year cards', 'Symmetry investigation' cut up for each two pairs of children, plus acetate (see General resources).

Equipment
Symmetrical 2-D shapes and pictures; card clocks; two counters; an OHP and OHP pen; plain paper; squared paper; scissors.

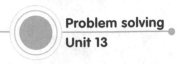
Lesson ①

Starter

Say the months of the year together. Give 12 children a month card each at random, and ask the rest of the class to put them in the right order.

Main teaching activities

Whole class: Explain that in the next two lessons the children will be solving problems and puzzles to do with shapes. Ask them what the word 'symmetrical' means. Expect them to say that one half is the same as the other. Show your examples of symmetrical items.

Figure 1

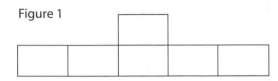

Put a regular card shape (from 'Templates for regular shapes') on the OHP. Draw round it. Demonstrate how you can flip it over so that one of its sides is still joined to the original shape to make a new shape that is symmetrical: the two halves are the same. Explain that the middle line is called the line of symmetry, because it shows where the two halves are (the fold mark from Year 1 work). Repeat this a few times using different shapes, both regular and irregular. Invite individuals to help you.

Group work: Give the children sets of shape templates ('Templates for irregular shapes' and 'Templates for regular shapes'), pens and plain paper. Ask them to work in pairs to create patterns by drawing around some of their shapes. Allow about ten minutes for this, then bring the class back together and look at some of the shapes they made. Put an acetate strip from 'Symmetry investigation' on the OHP and say: *Take the shapes you have that look like these, and use them to make a symmetrical shape. (See Figure 1.) You must use the large piece in all your shapes, but then you can add as many of the small pieces as you want. Then you can investigate other symmetrical shapes that you can make. Try to find as many different ones as you can. Draw them on squared paper, then draw the line of symmetry on each one.*

Differentiation

Organise the children in mixed-ability pairs. Children who appear 'less able' in work with numbers may be more successful in work of this kind.

Plenary & assessment

Put the acetate shapes on the OHP and invite children, particularly those whom you wish to assess, to show the class some of the shapes they made. Ask them to indicate the line of symmetry (or mirror line). Encourage their thinking by asking questions such as: *How did you start? What did you try next? How do you know your shape is symmetrical?*

Lesson ②

Starter

Give each child a card clock. Play an 'Up the mountain' game with two teams (as in Unit 12, Lesson 5): call out times for the children to show. The first child to hold up a clock with the correct time wins a point. As well as asking for times such as 4 o'clock, half past seven and quarter to six, also try: *Find half past three, now find one hour after that time, half an hour earlier…*

Main teaching activities

Whole class: Show the children the OHT of the puzzle on 'Puzzle practice 1'. Explain that each shape stands for a number. Focus on the shape names and properties. Now ask: *Which are the columns? Which are the rows? Can anyone think of a good starting point? Can we work out any numbers from this* *row? What about this column? Could we use jottings to help us? What can we try now? Can you tell me a number sentence that shows us what you have said?*

Paired work: Organise children into mixed-ability pairs. They can then work on 'Puzzle practice 2'. Any children finishing these quickly could make up puzzles of their own.

Plenary & assessment

Display the OHTs of the puzzles that the children have solved. Discuss the solutions, asking questions similar to those above. Assess whether the children can find the starting point and work systematically through the puzzle to reach a conclusion.

Lessons   overview

Preparation

Photocopy the data vocabulary onto A3 card; cut out and laminate the cards. Photocopy both sheets of 'Ways to organise data', 'Pictograms' and 'Sports block graph' onto acetate.

Learning objectives

Starter
- Add/subtract 9 or 11: add/subtract 10 and adjust by 1.
- **Know by heart multiplication facts for the 2 and 10 times-tables.**
- Derive quickly division facts corresponding to the 2 and 10 times-tables.

Main teaching activities
- Solve a given problem by sorting, classifying and organising information in simple ways.
- Discuss and explain results.

Vocabulary

count, tally, sort, vote, graph, block graph, pictogram, represent, group, set, list, label, title, most popular, least popular, most common, least common

You will need:

Photocopiable pages
A copy of 'Popular sports' (page 75) for each child.

CD pages
'Organising data vocabulary cards', acetates of 'Ways to organise data', 'Pictograms' and 'Sports block graph' (see General resources).

Equipment
A class 100 square; a 100 square for each child; an OHP; large sheets of plain paper; individual whiteboards.

Lesson

Starter

Rehearse the strategy of adding 9 and 11 to numbers by adding 10 and adjusting by 1, using a class number square. Ask the children to find specific numbers on their individual number squares and add or subtract 9 or 11. Give them a series of instructions, such as: *Find 12, add 9, add 11, add 9, add 20, add 11. Where are you?* Repeat with other starting numbers.

Main teaching activities

Whole class: Explain that the next two lessons are about how to organise and use data. What do the children think that means? If they can't tell you, show them the organising data vocabulary cards with Year 1 vocabulary and see whether these assist their thinking. Explain: *Organising data is about showing information in pictures and diagrams, so that we can see the information clearly. We can show data in lists and tables.*

Project the two OHTs of 'Ways to organise data'. For each, ask: *How is the information being shown? What things can you tell me from this list/table? What is the most common/least common…?, How many people/children were asked/involved?* Ask as many children as possible to tell you an item of information from the data. It might be very simple, such as 'The longest word is…'; or more complex, such as 'Six more… had… than…'

Group work: Give each mixed-ability group of four children some large sheets of paper. Ask each group to make up a list and then sort it into a table. They need to think of a topic. You could write a few ideas on the board to help them, such as favourite foods, books, sports or pets, or use the children's names or birthdays as in 'Ways to organise data'. Look for a table such as the one shown below as the outcome.

Favourite food

	Sausages	Pasta	Chips	Apples	Fish	Chicken
Sam	✓	✓	✓			✓
Cheryl		✓		✓	✓	✓
Faye	✓		✓			✓
Paul	✓		✓			✓

Plenary & assessment
Ask each group to share their work and explain how they decided on their topics and criteria. Ask the class questions to check whether they are able to extract information from a table.

Lesson ④

Starter
Recite the 2 and 10 times-tables together. Now count in multiples of 2 and 10 using fingers; stop the children at various intervals to ask which finger they are on and how many lots of 2 or 10 that is. Ask questions such as 2×7, 10×6, $12 \div 2$ and $40 \div 10$. The children work in pairs to support each other and write the answers on their whiteboards.

Main teaching activities
Whole class: Project the OHT of the first sheet of 'Sports block graph' and 'Pictograms'. Ask the children to tell you what is the same and what is different between them. Bring out the fact that instead of faces, there are little boxes to represent the children; these boxes are stacked up to make a block. Ask the children to tell you as much as they can about the graph. Ask children who may not find this easy first, so they can contribute before the most obvious facts have been said! Encourage the class to state all possible facts. Ask the children to discuss why this graph is a useful way of telling people about favourite sports. Elicit the response that it is clear, simple and easy to interpret.
Group work: Give mixed-ability groups of up to four children, copies of both sheets (graph and cards) from 'Sports block graph' and individual copies of the question sheet 'Popular sports' to complete.

Plenary & assessment
Invite a group to ask the questions that they made up. Ask the other children to answer them, and to describe in detail how they worked them out. Ask the children to turn to a partner and tell them about the ways of showing information that they have learned this week, and whether they have a good understanding of each one. .

Name

Date

Puzzle practice 1

Work out the value of each shape and the total of each row and column.

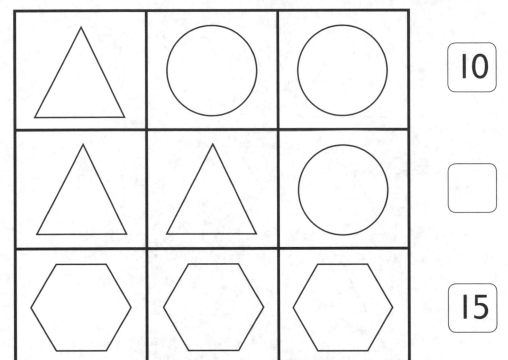

10

15

11

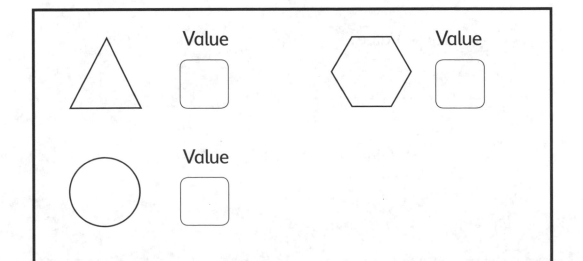

Value

Value

Value

Name	Date

Puzzle practice 2

Work out the value of each shape and the total of each row and column.

△	◯	◯	**17**
△	⬡	◯	☐
△	⬡	⬡	**13**

15	☐	☐

△ Value ☐	⬡ Value ☐
◯ Value ☐	

Name _____   Date _____

Popular sports

Look at the sports block graph.

Talk with your group. Tell each other some facts from the graph.

Cut out the pictures and numbers that come with the graph.

Look at the graph to work out how many votes each sport has.

Match each sport picture to the number of votes, like this:

13

Answer these questions:

1. Which is the most popular sport? _____

2. Which is the least popular sport? _____

3. How many children voted altogether? ☐

4. How many more children voted for tennis than for riding? ☐

5. What was the total vote for skiing and swimming? ☐

6. Which is more popular, football or rugby? How do you know? _____

_____

Make up some questions of your own. Write them here:

1._____

_____

2._____

_____

3._____

_____

Termly planning grid

EVERY DAY: **Practise and develop oral and mental skills** (e.g. counting, mental strategies, rapid recall of +, – and × facts)
• **Read and write whole numbers to at least 100 in figures and words;** say the number names in order to at least 100, from and back to zero. • **Know what each digit in a two-digit number represents, including zero as a place holder.** • **Describe and extend simple number sequences: count on or back in ones or tens, starting from any two-digit number.** • Know by heart doubles of all numbers to 10 and the corresponding halves; identify near doubles from doubles already known. • Count in hundreds from and back to zero; count on in steps of 5 to at least 30. • **Know by heart all addition and subtraction facts for each number to at least 10.** • Know by heart all pairs of numbers with a total of 20 (e.g. 13 + 7, 6 + 14); add/subtract 9 or 11: add/subtract 10 and adjust by 1. • **Know by heart multiplication facts for the 2 and 10 times-tables;** derive quickly division facts corresponding to the 2 and 10 times-tables. • **Recognise odd and even numbers** to at least 30. • Read the time to the hour, half hour and quarter hour on an analogue clock. • **Use the mathematical names for common 3-D and 2-D shapes;** sort shapes and describe some of their features. • Begin to recognise line symmetry.

Units	Days	Topics	Objectives
1	3	Counting, properties of numbers and number sequences	• **Describe and extend simple number sequences:** count on in steps of 3, 4 or 5 to at least 30, from and back to zero, then from and back to any given small number. • Begin to recognise two-digit multiples of 2, 5 or 10. • Count reliably up to 100 objects by grouping them.
2–4	15	Place value and ordering	• **Read and write whole numbers to at least 100 in figures and words.** • Compare two given two-digit numbers, say which is more or less, and give a number that lies between them.
		Estimating, rounding	• Use and begin to read the vocabulary of estimation and approximation; give a sensible estimate of at least 50 objects. • Round numbers less than 100 to the nearest 10.
		Understanding + and –	• Understand that more than two numbers can be added.
		Mental calculation strategies (+ and –)	• **Use knowledge that addition can be done in any order to do mental calculations more efficiently:** – add three small numbers by putting the largest first and/or finding a pair totalling 10; – partition into '5 and a bit' when adding 6, 7, 8 or 9, then recombine (e.g. 16 + 8 = 15 + 1 + 5 + 3 = 20 + 4 = 24); – partition additions into tens and units, then recombine.
		Problems involving 'real life', money or measures	• Use mental addition and subtraction, simple multiplication and division to solve simple word problems involving numbers in 'real life', money or measures, using one or two steps. • Explain how the problem was solved. • Recognise all coins and begin to use £.p notation for money (e.g., know that £4.65 indicates £4 and 65p). • Find totals, give change and work out which coins to pay.
		Making decisions	• **Choose and use appropriate operations and efficient calculation strategies** (e.g. mental, mental with jottings) **to solve problems.**
5–6	8	Measures	• Use and begin to read the vocabulary related to length, mass and capacity. • **Estimate, measure and compare masses, using standard units; suggest suitable units and equipment for such measurements.** • **Read a simple scale to the nearest labelled division, including using a ruler to draw and measure lines to the nearest centimere,** recording estimates and measurements as '3 and a bit metres long' or 'about 8 centimetres' or 'nearly 3 kilograms heavy'. • Use and begin to read the vocabulary related to time. • Use units of time and know the relationships between them (second, minute, hour, day, week). • Suggest suitable units to estimate or measure time.
		Shape and space	• Make and describe shapes, pictures and patterns. • Begin to recognise line symmetry. • **Use mathematical vocabulary to describe position, direction and movement:** for example, describe, place, tick, draw or visualise objects in given positions. • Recognise whole, half and quarter turns, to the left or right, clockwise, anticlockwise.
		Reasoning about numbers or shapes	• Solve mathematical problems or puzzles, recognise simple patterns and relationships, generalise and predict. Suggest extensions by asking 'What if…?' or 'What could I try next?' • **Explain how a problem was solved** orally and in writing.
7		Assess and review	

• **Read and write whole numbers to at least 100 in figures and words.** • **Describe and extend simple number sequences:** count on in steps of 3, 4 or 5 to at least 30, from and back to zero, then from and back to any given small number; say the number that is 1 or 10 more or less than any given two-digit number. • Order whole numbers to at least 100. • Derive quickly doubles of all numbers to at least 15 and the corresponding halves. • **Know by heart multiplication facts for the 2 and 10 times-tables;**
derive quickly division facts for the 2 and 10 times-tables. • **Know by heart all addition and subtraction facts for each number to at least 10.** • **Recognise odd and even numbers** to at least 30. • Know by heart all pairs of numbers with a total of 20 (e.g. 13 + 7, 6 + 14); know by heart all pairs of multiples of 10 with a total of 100 (e.g. 30 + 70). • **State the subtraction corresponding to a given addition, and vice versa.** • Read the time to the hour, half hour and quarter hour on an analogue clock and a 12-hour digital clock.

Units	Days	Topics	Objectives
8	5	Counting, properties of numbers and number sequences Reasoning about numbers or shapes	• **Describe and extend simple number sequences:** count on in steps of 3, 4 or 5 to at least 30, from and back to zero, then from and back to any given small number. • Investigate a general statement about familiar numbers by finding examples.
9	5	Place value and ordering Understanding addition and subtraction Mental calculation strategies (+ and –) Problems involving 'real life', money and measures Making decisions Reasoning about numbers or shapes	• Use and begin to read the vocabulary of comparing and ordering numbers, including ordinal numbers to 100. • Extend understanding of the operations of addition and subtraction. Use and begin to read the related vocabulary. • Partition into '5 and a bit' when adding 6, 7, 8 or 9, then recombine. • Partition additions into tens and units, then recombine. • Bridge through 10, then 20, and adjust. • **State the subtraction corresponding to a given addition, and vice versa.** • Find totals, give change and work out which coins to pay. • **Choose and use appropriate operations and efficient calculation strategies** (e.g. mental, mental with jottings) **to solve problems.** • Use mental addition and subtraction, simple multiplication and division to solve simple word problems involving numbers in 'real life', money or measures, using one or two steps. • **Explain how a problem was solved** orally and, where appropriate, in writing.
10	5	Understanding multiplication and division Mental calculation strategies (× and ÷) Problems involving 'real life', money or measures Making decisions	• **Understand the operation of multiplication as repeated addition or as describing an array,** and begin to understand division as grouping (repeated subtraction) or sharing. • Use and begin to read the related vocabulary. • Use ×, ÷ and = signs to record mental calculations in a number sentence, and recognise the use of a symbol such as □ or △ to stand for an unknown number. • Use known number facts and place value to carry out mentally simple multiplications and divisions. • Use mental addition and subtraction, simple multiplication and division, to solve simple word problems involving numbers in 'real life', money or measures, using one or two steps. • **Explain how a problem was solved** orally and, where appropriate, in writing. • **Choose and use appropriate operations and efficient calculation strategies** (e.g. mental, mental with jottings) **to solve problems.**
11		Fractions Measures	• Begin to recognise and find one half and one quarter of shapes and small numbers of objects. • Begin to recognise that two halves or four quarters make one whole and that two quarters and one half are equivalent. • Read the time .
12		Organising and using data	• Solve a given problem by sorting, classifying and organising information in simple ways, such as in a list or simple table; in a pictogram; in a block graph. • Discuss and explain results.
13	Assess and review		

This unit concentrates on counting in threes, fours and fives, in multiples of 2, 5 and 10 and estimating and counting amounts to 100 in groups of 10, 5 and 2. Where feasible it links this to the four operations and inversions. Activities to reinforce the teaching are mainly through games.

LEARNING OBJECTIVES

	Topics	Starter	Main teaching activities
Lesson 1	Counting, properties of numbers and number sequences	● **Read and write whole numbers to at least 100 in figures and words.** ● **Describe and extend simple number sequences: count on or back in ones or tens, starting from any two-digit number.**	● **Describe and extend simple number sequences**: count on in steps of 3, 4 or 5 to at least 30, from and back to zero, then from and back to any given small number.
Lesson 2	Counting, properties of numbers and number sequences	● **Recognise odd and even numbers** to at least 30.	● Begin to recognise two-digit multiples of 2, 5 or 10.
Lesson 3	Counting, properties of numbers and number sequences	● Read the time to the hour, half hour and quarter hour on an analogue clock. ● Count on in steps of 5 to at least 30.	● Count reliably up to 100 objects by grouping them. ● Give a sensible estimate of at least 50 objects.

Lessons   overview

Preparation
Make an acetate of 'Number lines'. Copy and laminate the 'Lost in space gameboard'. Copy 'Dots 1', '2' and '3' onto acetate sheets or A3 paper.

Learning objectives
Starter
● **Read and write whole numbers to at least 100 in figures and words.**
● **Describe and extend simple number sequences: count on or back in ones or tens, starting from any two-digit number.**
● **Recognise odd and even numbers** to at least 30.
● Read the time to the hour, half hour and quarter hour on an analogue clock.
● Count on in steps of 5 to at least 30.
Main teaching activities
● **Describe and extend simple number sequences**: count on in steps of 3, 4 or 5 to at least 30, from and back to zero, then from and back to any given small number.
● Begin to recognise two-digit multiples of 2, 5 or 10.
● Count reliably up to 100 objects by grouping them.
● Give a sensible estimate of at least 50 objects.

Vocabulary
two hundred… one thousand, count on, count back, count in ones/tens, odd, even, multiple of, sequence, continue, predict, count, tally, every other, how many times?

You will need:
Photocopiable pages
'How many pennies' (page 81) for each child.

CD pages
0–50 number cards from '0–100 number cards' and 'Up the mountain' gameboard, (see General resources, Autumn term), an acetate and one copy per child of 'Number lines' (0–20), '(0–30)' and '(20–50)' a copy of 'Lost in space gameboard', 'Lost in space recording sheet' for each pair, acetates or A3 copies of 'Dots 1', '2' and '3' for each child (see General resources).

Equipment
An OHP; a pendulum (cubes on string); Blu-Tack; a card clock for each child; about 50 counters; about £10 worth of pennies; some 10p, 2p and 5p coins.

Lesson

Starter

Divide the class into two teams. As you swing a pendulum, call out a range of two-digit numbers from which the teams count alternately, on and back in ones, as the pendulum swings to the left and the right. Repeat for counting in tens from numbers such as 51 and 67.

Main teaching activities

Whole class: This lesson is about counting in steps. Put the 0–30 number line on the OHP or draw it on the board. Circle the zero and ask: *If we count in threes from zero, what is the first number we come to?* Draw a loop around the numbers to 3. *What is the next number?* Each time, draw a loop from the previous number to the next multiple of 3. At 30, go back in jumps of three. Help the children to make the inverse connection by drawing arrow diagrams as in Autumn term, Unit 2. Ask questions such as: *How many jumps from 0 to 6? If I make three jumps from 0, where will I land? What about seven jumps? If we start on the number 1, will seven jumps of three still get me to 21? Why not?* Repeat, starting at different numbers.

Paired work: Demonstrate the number line activity described on 'Number lines'. Let the children work with copies of the 0–30 number line.

Differentiation

Less able: Provide the 0–20 number line.
More able: Provide the 20–50 number line.

Plenary & assessment

Invite a few pairs to draw one of their number lines on the board and demonstrate what they did. Ask the children to look for patterns. Look for awareness that when we count in fours, the numbers are always even (if the starting number is even) or odd (if it is odd); but when we count in fives, the units digit alternates between two digits, one odd and one even.

Lesson

Starter

Divide the class into two teams. Display the 'Up the mountain' gameboard and attach a counter for each team. The teams take turns to pick a number card to 50 and say whether it is odd or even. If it is odd, move the team's counter one step up. The first team to reach the top wins.

Main teaching activities

Whole class: Recite the multiples of 2, 5 and 10 together. Draw three circles on the board and as the children say the numbers, write the multiples of 2 from 0 to 20 in one circle, of 5 from 0 to 50 in the second, and of 10 from 0 to 100 in the third. Ask the children to tell you about these numbers; focus on the units digits. Discuss those numbers that appear in more than one circle.

Paired work: Demonstrate the 'Lost in space' game using the 'Lost in space gameboard' and the 'Lost in space recording sheet', then let the children play it.

Differentiation

Less able: Provide cards for numbers to 20.
More able: Provide cards for a selection of numbers to 100.

Plenary & assessment

Ask the children for examples of numbers that allowed them to move three spaces, six spaces and no spaces. Draw loops for multiples of '2 only', '5 only' and '2 and 5'. Ask which numbers will go in the loops. *Is 10 a multiple of 2? Let's count in twos to check. Can we write 10 in our '2 only' loop? Why not? What about 20 or 30? Why not?* (A multiple of 10 is also a multiple of 5 and 2.)

Lesson ③

Starter

Ask: *How many minutes are there in an hour? Half an hour? A quarter of an hour?* Ask the children to use their clocks to show you 15 minutes past seven and tell you another way of saying this (quarter past seven). Write the digital time 7:15 on the board. Repeat for other times, such as 45 minutes past two, 30 minutes past one and no minutes past eight.

Main teaching activities

Whole class: This lesson is about estimating and counting. Discuss what 'estimating' means. Put 47 counters on the OHP. Let the children see them briefly, then switch off the OHP. Ask for estimates of the number. Then show the counters again and ask the children to count: *Is there a quicker way than counting in ones?* Ask individuals to demonstrate counting in tens to 40, then fives on to 45, then twos on to 47. Point to the groups and say: *Four tens is 40, add 5 to make 45 and 2 to make 47.* Repeat with another number up to 50.

Show 50 pennies and ask the children to estimate the number, then count. Encourage counting in tens. Demonstrate exchanging each set of ten pennies for a 10p coin, then counting in tens. Repeat with 36p: three tens and six ones. *Can you think of another way to count the six?* If necessary, suggest exchanging five pennies for a 5p coin, or using 2p coins.

Group work: The children should work in groups of four or five. Demonstrate the 'How many pennies?' activity sheet. Give each group up to 50 pennies, ten 10p coins and a few 5p and 2p coins.

Differentiation

Less able: Give this group up to 30 pennies with 10p coins to exchange. Work with these children to help them learn this skill.

More able: Give this group up to 100 pennies with 10p, 5p and 2p coins. Encourage them to use all the coins.

Plenary & assessment

Show the children an OHT or A3 copy of 'Dots 1' (77 dots). Ask them to suggest the best way of counting the dots. Invite children to draw loops around groups of 10. Repeat with 'Dots 2' (72 dots) and 'Dots 3' (90 dots).

| Name | Date |

How many pennies?

Put out some pennies.

Estimate how many there are. Write your
estimate in the chart below.

Now count the pennies. Make groups of 10.
Write how many groups of 10 there are and how many are left over.
Find the total.

The first line in the chart is an example.

Estimate	Groups of 10	Left over	Total
30	2	5	25

Place value, estimating and rounding

In this unit the children will be reading and writing whole numbers to at least 100 in figures and words. They will then compare two-digit numbers and give one that lies between the two. There is then a focus on estimating amounts to 50 and rounding numbers less than 100 to the nearest 10.

LEARNING OBJECTIVES

		Topics	Starter	Main teaching activity
Lesson	1	Place value and ordering	● **Know by heart multiplication facts for the 2 and 10 times-tables.**	● **Read and write whole numbers to at least 100** in figures and words. ● Compare two given two-digit numbers, say which is more or less, and give a number that lies between them.
Lesson	2	Place value and ordering	● **Know what each digit in a two-digit number represents, including zero as a place holder.**	As for Lesson 1.
Lesson	3	Estimating, rounding	As for Lesson 2.	● Use and begin to read the vocabulary of estimation and approximation; give a sensible estimate of at least 50 objects.
Lesson	4	Estimation and rounding	As for Lesson 1.	● Use and begin to read the vocabulary of estimation and approximation; give a sensible estimate of at least 50 objects. ● Round numbers less than 100 to the nearest 10.
		Understanding addition and subtraction		● Understand that more than two numbers can be added.

Lessons   overview

Preparation
Copy the '"Follow me" cards' onto card and laminate, then cut out a set of cards. Copy 'Number words' onto A3 paper and cut out the words.

Learning objectives
Starter
● **Know by heart multiplication facts for the 2 and 10 times-tables.**
● **Know what each digit in a two-digit number represents, including zero as a place holder**.
Main teaching activities
● **Read and write whole numbers to at least 100** in figures and words.
● Compare two given two-digit numbers, say which is more or less, and give a number that lies between them.

Vocabulary
two hundred… one thousand, units, ones, tens, hundreds, digit, round, nearest, round to the nearest 10, more, larger, bigger, greater, fewer, smaller, less, most, least

You will need:
Photocopiable pages
'Which number goes where?' (page 87) for each child.

CD pages
'0–100 number cards', (see General resources, Autumn term), '0–100 number line' for each child, '0–50 number line' for each less able child, '"Follow me" cards', an A3 copy of 'Number words', 'Which number goes where?', less able and more able versions (Spring term, Unit 2)(see General resources).

Equipment
Individual whiteboards; pens and cloths.

Lesson ①

Starter

Use the 'Follow me' game to practise multiplication and division facts for 2 and 10. The children work on their own or, if lacking confidence, with a partner. Give out all the cards (at least one for each individual or pair). Choose someone to read out a question. The child who has the answer calls it out and reads their question, and so on. Record the time it takes to go round the class. Shuffle the cards and repeat. Do the children get faster with practice?

Main teaching activities

Whole class: This lesson is about writing, ordering and comparing numbers. Each child will need a set of single-digit number cards. Give the children instructions, such as: *Put a 7 on the table in front of you. Make it read 74. What did you do? Swap the digits round. What have you got now? Is that bigger or smaller than 74? Now add a card to make 147. What did you do? How much bigger is 147 than 47? Make the highest three-digit number you can using those cards. How did you do that? Why? Make it five more… 100 less …ten more….* This is a very good method for helping children grasp place value and number manipulation. Most children get this fairly easily after some practice. If any have difficulty, help them or allow them to work with a 'buddy'. Repeat the activity with the children writing and rubbing out digits on their whiteboards.

Hold up two two-digit number cards: *Which number is lower… higher?* Draw a number line and write these numbers at the ends. Invite some children to suggest a number that comes between the two, and to place these numbers on the line. Show the children the 'Number words' and ask them to find the correct words for some of these numbers. Repeat this several times, making some pairs of numbers from the same digits. For example:

34   37   40   42 43   thirty four

Group work: Distribute the 'Which number goes where?' activity sheet and demonstrate the example shown.

Differentiation

Less able: Provide the version of the 'Which number goes where?' sheet that involves making a 'teens' number. Help this group to read and understand the instructions.
More able: Provide the version that involves making 'in between' numbers from a limited choice of digits.

Plenary & assessment

Draw a number line with ten divisions on the board. Write a two-digit number at each end. Ask a child to suggest an 'in between' number and mark it in place. Continue until there are ten numbers on the line. Repeat with another pair of numbers, but use a line without divisions. Ask the children to work out where to place the numbers. Encourage them to look for the halfway mark first.

Lesson ②

Starter

As in the main teaching activity from Lesson 1, ask the children to make and manipulate numbers on their whiteboards by following your instructions. For example, they might write the number 1; make it read 21; then 12, 312, the lowest/highest three-digit number possible with these digits, five more, ten less, ten more…. Repeat with other single-digit starting numbers.

Main teaching activities

Whole class: Reinforce Lesson 1. Hold up two two-digit number cards. With the children's help, write these numbers at the ends of a number line without divisions, and place as accurately as possible some numbers that come between the two. Ask the children to find the correct number word cards for the numbers as you point to them. Repeat several times.

Group work: Let the children work in pairs with two-digit number cards. Each pair has a pile of number cards in front of them, face down on the table. They pick five cards and look at them. They then order them from smallest to largest on the 0–100 number line. For example, if they pick the cards 23, 17, 46, 89, 63:

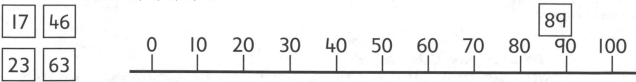

They then put the cards back, shuffle the pile and pick five more cards.

Differentiation

Less able: Ask this group to order sets of numbers to 50 from least to greatest.
More able: Ask this group to draw and complete blank number lines.

Plenary & assessment

Invite some more able children to explain how they positioned their numbers on their lines. Ask some other children to place numbers picked from cards as accurately as they can on a line you have drawn on the board. Invite the rest of the class to comment on their accuracy.

Lessons ③ ④ overview

Preparation
Copy 'Vocabulary for estimating' onto A3 paper and cut out the words. Copy 'Round it!' onto acetate. Put different numbers of beads or centicubes (up to 50) into the string bags.

Learning objectives
Starter
● **Know what each digit in a two-digit number represents, including zero as a place holder.**
● Know by heart multiplication facts fro the 2 and 10 times-tables.
Main teaching activity
● Use and begin to read the vocabulary of estimation and approximation; give a sensible estimate of at least 50 objects.
● Round numbers less than 100 to the nearest 10.
● Understand that more than two numbers can be added.

Vocabulary
guess how many, estimate, nearly, roughly, close to, about the same as, just over, just under, exact, exactly, too many, too few, enough, not enough, round to the nearest ten

You will need:
Photocopiable pages
'How close can you get?' (page 88) for each child.

CD pages
'0–100 number cards', 'Spider charts for multiplying' and 'Spider charts for dividing' (see General resources, Autumn term), an OHT of each of the 'Dots' sheets, 'Vocabulary for estimating' cards, 'Round it!' and 'Round it! gameboard' (see General Resources).

Equipment
An OHP; individual whiteboards; at least 16 small string bags; beads or centicubes; a bead string; Blu-Tack.

Lesson ③

Starter

Repeat from Lesson 2, but use different instructions (such as: *Write the number 32, take away two, double it, add three*) to explore two-digit numbers.

Main teaching activities

Whole class: This lesson is about estimating and approximating amounts up to 50. Ask: *Who can say what 'estimating' is? Can anyone tell me some estimating words?* Display the appropriate word cards, and show and discuss any words the children leave out. Put up one of the 'Dots' OHTs and ask: *Who can estimate the number of dots?* Discuss using their fingers to make a sensible estimate: *Are there more dots than you have fingers? Yes – so you know there are more than ten. Put your hands next to a friend's. Are there more dots or more fingers now?* Build up groups of ten fingers until the number is close: *Do you think we have exactly the same amount, just over or just under?* Finally count, using the grouping in tens method from Unit 1. Repeat using the dots on another OHT.

Group work: The children work in mixed-ability groups of four. Give each group three string bags. For each bag, they take turns to feel the cubes and estimate how many are in the bag, recording on the 'How close can you get?' activity sheet. Set a short time limit so they cannot count the cubes. Once everyone in the group has made a guess, they should count the cubes to find out who was closest. Finally, they can discuss and try to answer the problems at the bottom of the sheet.

Plenary & assessment

Discuss whether the children found it easy or hard to make a sensible estimate. Write 48 on the board and say: *Mrs Cook estimated there would be 48 children at the party, so she baked 48 cakes that morning. Her friends also baked cakes for the number of children they expected.* Write their estimates on the board: 53, 60, 24 and 49. Tell the children that there were 50 children at the party. Hold up these word cards from 'Vocabulary for estimating': just under, just over, too many, too few and nearest. Ask the children which word best describes each estimate. Stick the word they agree on beside each estimate.

Lesson ④

Starter

Count in twos and tens together, using fingers so that, when you stop part of the way through, the children can tell you what the multiplication fact is. For example, if you stop on 12 (the sixth finger) the multiplication fact is 2 times 6. Move on to using spider charts to reinforce these times-tables and the corresponding division facts.

Main teaching activities

Whole class: This lesson is about rounding numbers to the nearest 10. Ask: *Does anyone know what we mean by rounding?* Take suggestions and then explain. Use a bead string or draw a numbered number line 0–20 on the board. Highlight 0, 10 and 20. Mark 13 with an arrow. Explain that rounding a number to the nearest 10 means deciding which 10 number it is closest to. Ask: *Is 13 closer to 10 or 20?* Repeat with other numbers to 20. Explain that with numbers ending in 5, the rule is to round up to the higher value, so 5 is rounded to 10 and 15 to 20. Now draw a number line with 11 marks but no numbers, and write 26 on the seventh mark (where it would be if the whole line were numbered 20–30). Ask: *Which two tens numbers shall I put on this number line? Which one is 26 closest to?* Repeat with a variety of numbers up to 100.

Group work: Tell the children that they are going to practise rounding numbers to the nearest 10. Demonstrate the 'Round it!' game using an OHT of the instructions. Let the children play in pairs or small groups. They should play twice, the second time recording in the way shown in the instructions.

Plenary & assessment

Call out some random numbers for the children to round to the nearest 10. Ask them to write the answers on whiteboards and show you. Next, ask the children (working in 'buddy' pairs) to think of occasions when rounding might be helpful. Take feedback, and try to elicit the idea that rounding makes mental calculation easier. Give the example of adding/subtracting 9 or 11 by rounding to the nearest 10 and adjusting. Ask the children questions such as: 15 + 9, 13 + 11, 17 – 9, 14 + 19, 18 + 21. Explain that tomorrow they will look at another situation where rounding is useful.

Name   Date

Which number goes where?

**Choose two or more of these digits.
Make two two-digit numbers from them.**

| 7 | 5 | 2 | 4 |

Write your numbers at the ends of a number line – for example, 75 and 54.

Now think of an 'in between' number and write that on the line – for example, 61.

Write your 'in between' number in words too – for example, sixty-one.

61

54 ──────────────── 75

sixty-one

Try some more numbers, using the digits above.

1.
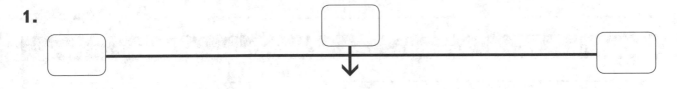

2.
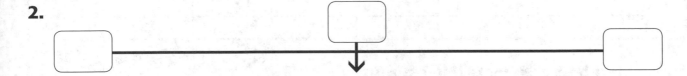

3.
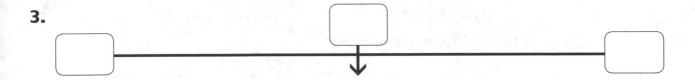

4.
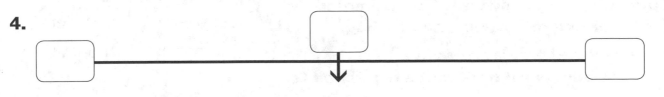

5.
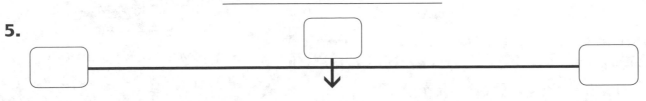

Make up some more of your own, using any digits.

Name		Date

How close can you get?

Estimate the number of things in the bag. Write your estimate in the table.

Count how many there are. Was your estimate close?

Do this for all the bags you have.

Name	Estimate	Count them	Were you close?

Name	Estimate	Count them	Were you close?

Name	Estimate	Count them	Were you close?

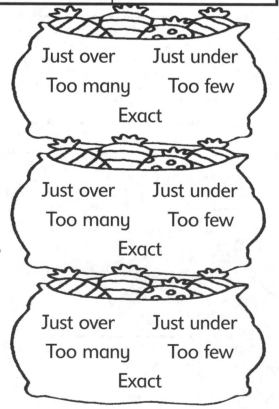

Sam had a bag of sweets. He estimated that there were 24 sweets in the bag.

He counted them. There were 45.
Tick the best word to describe his estimate.

Just over   Just under
Too many   Too few
Exact

Tina had a bag of sweets. She estimated that there were 30 sweets in the bag.

She counted them. There were 28.
Tick the best word to describe her estimate.

Just over   Just under
Too many   Too few
Exact

Sharma had a bag of sweets. He estimated that there were 28 sweets in the bag.

He counted them. There were 28.
Tick the best word to describe his estimate.

Just over   Just under
Too many   Too few
Exact

■SCHOLASTIC
photocopiable

Mental calculation strategies for addition and subtraction

This unit teaches the children about four more mental calculation strategies for addition and subtraction, for example partitioning into 5 and a bit and finding numbers that total 10. These methods are reinforced in a variety of ways, including games, which involve the children doing independent recording.

LEARNING OBJECTIVES

	Topics	Starter	Main teaching activity
Lesson 1	Mental calculation strategies (+ and –) Understanding addition and subtraction	● **Know by heart all addition and subtraction facts for each number to at least 10.**	● **Use knowledge that addition can be done in any order to do mental calculations more efficiently**: add three small numbers by putting the largest first and/or finding a pair totalling 10. ● Understand that more than two numbers can be added.
Lesson 2	Mental calculation strategies (+ and –) Understanding addition and subtraction	● **Describe and extend simple number sequences: count on or back in ones or tens, starting from any two-digit number.** ● **Recognise odd and even numbers** to at least 30.	● **Use knowledge that addition can be done in any order to do mental calculations more efficiently**: add three small numbers by putting the largest first and/or finding a pair totalling 10; partition additions into tens and units, then recombine. ● Understand that more than two numbers can be added.
Lesson 3	Mental calculation strategies (+ and –)	● **Know by heart multiplication facts for the 2 and 10 times-tables.**	● **Use knowledge that addition can be done in any order to do mental calculations more efficiently**: partition into '5 and a bit' when adding 6, 7, 8 or 9, then recombine (e.g. 16 + 8 = 15 + 1 + 5 + 3 = 20 + 4 = 24).
Lesson 4	Making decisions Mental calculation strategies (+ and –)	● Know by heart doubles of all numbers to 10 and the corresponding halves.	● **Choose and use appropriate operations and efficient calculation strategies** (e.g. mental, mental with jottings) **to solve problems**. ● Partition additions into tens and units, then recombine.

Lessons   overview

Preparation

Copy the 'Addition vocabulary cards' onto A3 paper and cut out the words. Copy 'Lost in space gameboard' and 'Find the way! gameboard' onto card and laminate, and make an acetate copy of each. Fill in the template versions of 'Making 10', '5 and a bit' and 'Partitioning tens and units' for less able and more able children.

Learning objectives

Starter
- **Know by heart all addition and subtraction facts for each number to at least 10.**
- **Describe and extend simple number sequences: count on or back in ones or tens starting from any two-digit number.**
- **Recognise odd and even numbers to at least 30**.
- **Know by heart multiplication facts for the 2 and 10 times-tables.**
- Know by heart doubles of all numbers to 10 and the corresponding halves.

Main teaching activities
- **Use knowledge that addition can be done in any order to do mental calculations more efficiently:** add three small numbers by putting the largest first and/or finding a pair totalling 10; partition additions into tens and units, then recombine; partition into '5 and a bit' when adding 6, 7, 8 or 9, then recombine (e.g. 16 + 8 = 15 + 1 + 5 + 3 = 20 + 4 = 24).
- Understand that more than two numbers can be added.
- **Choose and use appropriate operations and efficient calculation strategies** (e.g. mental, mental with jottings) **to solve problems.**

Vocabulary

add, addition, more, plus, make, sum, total, altogether, score, tens boundary

You will need:
Photocopiable pages
'Making 10' (page 93), '5 and a bit' (page 94) for each child.

CD pages
'0–100 number cards', 'Spider charts for multiplying', 'Spider charts for dividing', and 'Addition and subtraction vocabulary cards' (see General resources, Autumn term), 'Lost in space gameboard' and 'Find the way! gameboard' – one for each group of three or four and an acetate of each; a copy of the template versions of 'Making 10', and '5 and a bit', (Spring term, Unit 3) (see General resources).

Equipment
Individual whiteboards and pens; an OHP; Blu-Tack; number lines; 100 squares; counting equipment.

Lesson

Starter

and

Write a number up to 10 on the board. Time the children for two or three minutes, depending on the number, to see how many addition (adn) subtraction facts they come up with for that number, e.g. for 3: 0 + 3 = 3; 3 + 0 = 3; 3 − 3 = 0; 1 + 2 = 3; 2 + 1 = 3; 3 − 1 = 0; 3 − 2 = 1. Share facts then repeat for another number.

Main teaching activities

Whole class: Tell the class that they are going to practise some mental addition strategies and learn some new ones. Revise the vocabulary for addition, holding up word cards as the children suggest them. Attach the cards to the board with Blu-Tack. Remind the children that they already know how to add up more than two numbers by putting the largest number in their heads and counting on. Quickly revisit this strategy. Write 3, 6 and 9 on the board. Ask the children to put 9 in their heads and then count on 6 and then 3. Repeat with 7, 8 and 2, then with 60, 30 and 70.

Now introduce looking for numbers whose unit digits total 10. Write three numbers on the board, two of which total 10, such as 8, 4 and 2. Invite children to come to the board and circle the numbers that add up to 10. Now do the same with the numbers as sums: 4 + 8 + 6; 9 + 4 + 1; 3 + 7 + 9; 2 + 5 + 5. Point out that 10 is the highest number now, so they are also using the other strategy when they count on from the 10.

Gradually move on to adding two single-digit numbers and one two-digit number, such as 16 + 8 + 2. Encourage the children to hold the larger number in their heads and then count on, but now it is the 10 that will be counted: 16 + 10. Repeat several times.

Group work: The children can use the 'Making 10' activity sheet to practise what they have learned by generating their own additions from a given selection of numbers.

Differentiation

A template version of the activity sheet is provided for you to fill in with single-digit numbers for less able children and half single-digit and half two-digit numbers for more able children.

Plenary & assessment

Write on the board: 16 + 9 + 4. Ask: *How can we use both strategies to find the answer?* Aim towards adding the 6 and the 4 to make 10, which with the other 10 makes 20, then adding on the 9. Write a few more such problems on the board for the children to answer.

Lesson

Starter

Give the children different two-digit starting numbers and ask them to count on and back in ones and tens. When they count in ones, ask them to clap when they say an even number and stamp when they say an odd one. Ask them what would happen if they did this when counting in tens.

Main teaching activities

Whole class: Develop the Plenary from Lesson 1. Ask: *Who can remember what we did?* If necessary, write on the board as a clue: 17 + 3 + 8. Invite someone to circle the two numbers that make 10, then ask the children to add that 10 to the remaining 10 and then add on the 8. Let the children use their whiteboards for any jottings necessary, and for their answers. Repeat with examples such as: 14 + 6 + 5; 7 + 1 + 19. Now try some with two two-digit numbers and a single-digit number, such as: 25 + 10 + 5; 15 + 23 + 7; 24 + 12 + 6.

Paired work: Demonstrate the 'Find the way!' game, which the children can play to practise these strategies. Use an OHT of the 'Find the way! gameboard' to explain that the aim is to get through the maze by adding lines of three digits together, two of which must total 10. The children should try to use all the numbers. Ask them to record their additions and draw lines connecting the numbers that they use. Say, for example (see below): *I start on 5, and look for two numbers to add to it so the addition includes a 10. I can use 8 and 2, so I draw a line from 5 to 8 to 2, and record the sum 5 + 8 + 2 = 15. Now I am on 2, and I look for two more numbers so that the addition includes a 10. I can use the next 2 and 8 (= 12). Next I can use 9 and 1 to add to the last number, 2 (= 12). Where can I go next?*

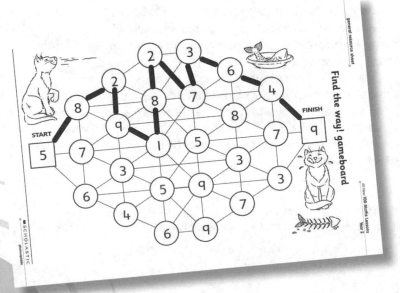

Differentiation

Children of all abilities can play this game. Provide number lines, 100 squares and counting apparatus where needed.

Plenary & assessment

Show the OHT of the 'Find the way! gameboard' and invite children to demonstrate how they got through the maze. Draw the route as they tell it to you. Write a 1 in front of some of the numbers to make teens numbers. Ask the children what difference this makes. Look for the answer that you can still find units digits to make 10 and then add on any extra tens. Suggest and demonstrate that jottings will help the children to keep track of their additions.

Mental calculation strategies for addition and subtraction
Unit 3

Lesson ③

Starter

Practise 2 and 10 multiplication and division facts using the spider charts. Invite some children to come to the front to do the pointing. Time the children to see how quickly they can go round all the facts.

Main teaching activities

Whole class: Explain that this lesson is about partitioning into '5 and a bit' when adding 6, 7, 8 or 9. Say that 5 is a good number: *We can count in fives easily, and we know that 5 and 5 is 10.* Partition the numbers from 6 to 9 into '5 and a bit', asking the children to help you: 6 = 5 + 1, and so on. Now write on the board: 6 + 8. Partition it into 5 + 1 + 5 + 3; add the fives (5 + 5 = 10) and then the other numbers (1 + 3 = 4), then recombine (10 + 4 = 14). Repeat with other examples, such as: 7 + 8; 16 + 8.
Individual work: Tell the children that they will be practising this strategy. Demonstrate how to use the '5 and a bit' activity sheet, then let the children complete it individually.

Differentiation

A template version of the activity sheet is provided for you to fill in with single-digit numbers for less able children and half single-digit and half two-digit numbers for more able children.

Plenary & assessment

Invite some children from each group to demonstrate on the board which numbers they chose, and to demonstrate and explain how they worked out the calculation.

Lesson ④

Starter

Call out numbers to 10, and some to 20, for the children to double and halve, showing you their answers with digit cards.

Main teaching activities

Whole class: Recap the addition strategy of partitioning into tens and ones and recombining. Go through a few examples. Discuss what happens when the units' digits total 10 or more, as in 34 + 27. This makes 30 + 20 + 4 + 7 = 50 + 11. Point out that 11 is 10 + 1, so you can add 50 and 10 and then add the 1 to make 61. Repeat this a few times with different starting numbers below 50.
Group work: Tell the children that they will practise this strategy by playing a game independently, but in groups of four, using the 'Lost in space gameboard'. Model the game, using an OHT. Some children may benefit from playing with a partner. Each group will need a set of 0–50 number cards and paper for recording. They take turns to pick two number cards to add by partitioning into tens and units, then move the number of spaces that the units digit of the answer shows. For example: *If I pick 27 and 38, I can partition them into 20 + 7 + 30 + 8 = 50 + 15 = 65. My unit number is 5, so I move on five spaces. The first space traveller to reach the home planet wins.* It may be helpful to pair less able children with more able children, or with an adult.

Plenary & assessment

Divide the class into three teams and play the game on an OHT of the 'Lost in space gameboard'. Choose individuals to assess by asking them to demonstrate their additions on the board for their team.

Name _____ Date _____

Making 10

| 4 | 5 | 7 | 3 | 6 | 15 |

Use these numbers to make up some addition calculations.

Your calculations must all be different, not the same one in a different order.

Each of your calculations must include two numbers that total 10.

For example:

Numbers chosen: 4 + 6 + 15

Numbers that total 10: 4 + 6 = 10

New calculation: 15 + 10 = 25

Now you try:

1
Numbers chosen: _____

Numbers that total 10: _____

New calculation: _____

2
Numbers chosen: _____

Numbers that total 10: _____

New calculation: _____

3
Numbers chosen: _____

Numbers that total 10: _____

4
Numbers chosen: _____

Numbers that total 10: _____

New calculation: _____

5
Numbers chosen: _____

Numbers that total 10: _____

New calculation: _____

6
Numbers chosen: _____

Numbers that total 10: _____

New calculation: _____

7
Numbers chosen: _____

Numbers that total 10: _____

New calculation: _____

8
Numbers chosen: _____

Numbers that total 10: _____

New calculation: _____

Name _____ Date _____

5 and a bit

| 6 | 7 | 8 | **Choose two of these numbers. One must be either 17 or 18.**
| 9 | 17 | 18 | Add them together by partitioning into '5 and a bit'.

For example:

Numbers chosen: 17 + 6   Partition: 15 + 2 + 5 + 1   Addition: 20 + 3   Total: 23

Now you try:

1

Numbers chosen: _____   Partition: _____

Addition: _____   Total: _____

2

Numbers chosen: _____   Partition: _____

Addition: _____   Total: _____

3

Numbers chosen: _____   Partition: _____

Addition: _____   Total: _____

4

Numbers chosen: _____   Partition: _____

Addition: _____   Total: _____

5

Numbers chosen: _____   Partition: _____

Addition: _____   Total: _____

6

Numbers chosen: _____   Partition: _____

Addition: _____   Total: _____

Now make up some more additions on the back of this sheet, using other two-digit numbers to add 6, 7, 8 or 9 to.

SCHOLASTIC
photocopiable

Problem solving

This unit concentrates on using the mental strategies learned in Unit 3 to solve 'real life' problems that involve money and measures. It carefully goes through the stages of problem solving. The children will work on visualising, drawing and acting out problems.

LEARNING OBJECTIVES

	Topics	Starter	Main teaching activities
Lesson 1	Problems involving 'real life', money or measures	● Read the time to the hour, half hour and quarter hour on an analogue clock.	● Use mental addition and subtraction, simple multiplication and division to solve simple word problems involving numbers in 'real life', money or measures, using one or two steps. ● Explain how the problem was solved.
Lesson 2	Problems involving 'real life', money or measures	● Know by heart all pairs of numbers with a total of 20 (e.g. 13 + 7, 6 + 14).	As for Lesson 1.
Lesson 3	Problems involving 'real life', money or measures	● Add/subtract 9 or 11: add/subtract 10 and adjust by 1.	As for Lesson 1, plus: ● Recognise all coins and begin to use £.p notation for money. ● Find totals, give change and work out which coins to pay.
Lesson 4	Making decisions	● **Know by heart multiplication facts for the 2 and 10 times-tables.** ● Derive quickly division facts corresponding to the 2 and 10 times-tables.	● **Choose and use appropriate operations and efficient calculation strategies** (e.g. mental, mental with jottings) **to solve problems**.

Lessons   overview

Preparation
Copy 'How to solve a problem' onto A3 paper. Copy 'Small spider charts' onto A4 card and laminate (as a whole sheet) for each pair. Make acetates of 'Problems' and 'Making up problems'. Copy 'Money problems' onto card and cut into strips.

Learning objectives
Starter
● Read the time to the hour, half hour and quarter hour on an analogue clock.
● Know by heart all pairs of numbers with a total of 20 (e.g. 13 + 7, 6 + 14).
● Add/subtract 9 or 11: add/subtract 10 and adjust by 1.
● **Know by heart multiplication facts for the 2 and 10 times-tables.**
● Derive quickly division facts corresponding to the 2 and 10 times-tables.
Main teaching activities
● Use mental addition and subtraction, simple multiplication and division to solve simple word problems involving numbers in 'real life', money or measures, using one or two steps.
● Explain how the problem was solved.
● Recognise all coins and begin to use £.p notation for money.
● Find totals, give change and work out which coins to pay.
● **Choose and use appropriate operations and efficient calculation strategies** (e.g. mental, mental with jottings) **to solve problems.**

Vocabulary
money, coin, penny, pence, pound, £, price, cost, buy, bought, spend, spent, pay, change, dear, costs more, cheap, costs less, cheaper, how much…?, how many…?, total

You will need:
Photocopiable pages
'Problems at the zoo' (page 99) for each child.

CD pages
'Spider charts for multiplying' 'Spider charts for dividing' per child, an A3 copy of 'How to solve a problem', and 'Small spider charts' (see General resources, Autumn term) per pair, acetates of 'Problems' and 'Making up problems', a copy of 'Visualising problems 1' per child, 'Money problems' on card; 'Problems at the zoo' less able and more able versions (see Spring term, Unit 4) (see General resources).

Equipment
Card clocks; pendulum; class 100 square; individual 100 squares, whiteboards and pens; large sheets of paper, colouring pens; coins,

Lesson ①

Starter

Give each child a card clock. Ask the children to show you various o'clock, half past, quarter to and quarter past times. Move on to questions such as: *My clock says 3 o'clock, but it is one hour slow. Show me what time it really is. My clock says 7 o'clock, but it is two hours fast… My clock says 1 o'clock, but it is half an hour slow… My clock says half past 8, but it is 15 minutes fast… .*

Main teaching activities

Whole class: Explain that the children will use the mental strategies from the previous unit to solve 'real life' problems. Project the 'Problems' OHT and display the 'How to solve a problem' poster. Use the poster to talk through the steps needed to solve the first problem. When you reach Step 4, ask the children to think of a strategy to work out the answer. Remind them of the strategies they used in Unit 3: largest number first, looking for pairs that make 10, partitioning into '5 and a bit', partitioning into tens and units; ask them to decide which one is the best. Allow them to discuss with a partner and then feed back to the class. Repeat the process with the other two problems on the OHT.

Group work: Ask the children to work in ability pairs to solve the problems on the 'Problems at the zoo' activity sheet and explain the strategies they used. Talk through the first problem.

Differentiation

Less able: Provide the version of 'Problems at the zoo' with easier numbers. Let this group use counting apparatus such as counters, beads or toy animals if necessary.
More able: Provide the version with more challenging numbers. Encourage the children to think of two strategies for each problem, decide which is better and explain why.

Plenary & assessment

Write up some basic information, such as: 3kg, 50p, potatoes, how much? Ask the children to talk to a partner and make up a problem involving this information. For example: 'I bought 3kg of potatoes. Each kilogram cost 50p. How much did I spend?' Invite some pairs to share their problems for the class to solve. Write the answers on the board. Miswrite a pounds and pence answer like this: £350. Ask the children whether this is correct and talk about why.

Lesson ②

Starter

Count in twos and tens together, using fingers so that, when you stop part of the way through, the children can tell you what the multiplication fact is. For example, if you stop on 12 (the sixth finger) the multiplication fact is 2 times 6. Move on to using spider charts to reinforce these times-tables and division facts.

Main teaching activities

Whole class: Explain that the children will work with a partner to make up their own problems, as in the Plenary of Lesson 1. Encourage them to think clearly about the information provided and the operations needed, and to check their answers. Use the 'Making up problems' OHT to talk through possible one-step and two-step problems. For example: '2m, 1m, sunflower' could be used to ask *I had three sunflowes: one was 1m tall, one wsa 2m tall and the third was as tall as both of the others together. How tall was the third sunflower?* As you model these problems, encourage the children to think visually and record with drawings instead of words.

Paired work: Pose problems for the children that involve one-step and two-step problems. Encourage them to make jottings or draw their problems as far as possible, so they don't waste time

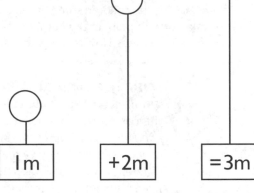

writing too many words. For example: *You have 14 monkeys and 26 bananas. What might your problem be? You have 5 ice creams, 50p and £5. What might your problem be?*

Differentiation

Less able: Use simpler numbers and times. You or another adult could scribe for this group.
More able: Provide more demanding numbers and times. Ask this group to solve each other's problems and explain how they did them.

Plenary & assessment

Invite some pairs to share their problems for the class to solve. Each time, ask: *How did you solve the problem? How many steps did you need to take? Was there any information you didn't use?*

Lesson

Starter

Recap on adding or subtracting 9 and 11 by adding or subtracting 10 and adjusting. Demonstrate on the class 100 square, then provide individual 100 squares. Ask the children to put their finger on 4. Give a series of instructions, such as: *Add on 9, add on another 9, take away 11. What number are you?* Repeat several times.

Now ask them to turn their 100 squares over and close their eyes. *Can they see the square in their heads? Put your finger on the 3 on the 100 square in your head. Go down to the next row – what number are you on now? Move your finger back one – where are you now? Go down two rows and along two – where are you? Now put your imaginary finger on 7, and add on 9 – where are you?* Repeat with a few numbers, including two-digit ones.

Main teaching activities

Whole class: Say that during the lesson the children will be seeing problems in their heads, drawing them and acting them out. Ask them to close their eyes and visualise what you say. *You are sitting in your bedroom with a money box. It is shaped like a pig; it is blue and has yellow flowers on. You take out the stopper underneath its tummy and tip the money onto your bed. You pick up one 10 pence piece, another 10 pence piece, then another and another. How many 10 pence pieces are you holding? How much is that altogether?* Act this out, asking children to collect the correct coins. Repeat in the same way with different scenarios. You can find more examples on the 'Visualising problems 1' sheet.

Group work: The children should work in mixed-ability groups to act out maths problems, so that the rest of the class can identify each problem and work out the answer. They will need a selection of coins and may use pens and paper to draw pictures, but they must try not to use words (written or spoken). Use a problem from the 'Money problems' sheet to demonstrate, then give each group a strip from that sheet. Allow time for the groups to plan their 'scenario'. They should use the correct coins, finding the totals and the change (where appropriate).

Differentiation

The children should work together in mixed-ability groups, supporting each other.

Plenary

Model a second example from the activity sheet.

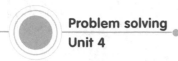

Lesson

Starter

Give each child the spider charts for multiplying and dividing by 2 and 10. Count together in multiples, using fingers. Stop at various points, such as the seventh finger, and ask: *How many lots of 2 make 14? So we can say 2 × 7 = 14.* Give the children some timed challenges to complete in pairs, using the 'Small spider charts' sheet. They take turns to point at the numbers around whichever chart you say and then give the answers. Time them for two minutes. How many times can they go round the chart?

Main teaching activities

Whole class: Explain that the type of problem called an 'investigation' can sometimes have more than one correct answer. Talk through this example: *I want to buy a bar of chocolate. It will cost me 50p. I have some coins in my pocket.* (Show five 10p pieces, two 20p pieces and four 5p pieces.) *How could I use them to pay for the chocolate?* Ask the children to work with a partner to think of as many different ways of paying as they can. They should jot down their ideas on their whiteboards to share later. After about five minutes, take feedback and find as many answers as possible: 10p × 5; 10p × 3 + 20p; 5p × 4 + 20p + 10p, and so on. Ask the children which coins they used first and why.

Group work: Write the following on the board: *Jamie has three 10p coins, three 5p coins and three 2p coins in his pocket. He uses three coins to buy some bubble gum. How much might the gum have cost? Find all the possible amounts.* The children should work in pairs on this investigation. Tell them: *There are lots of answers. How many can you find?* Children record their answers on their whiteboards.

Differentiation

Less able: If possible, ask a teaching assistant to work with this group. Give the children the actual coins to work with. Ask them to start by combining 10p and 2p coins in threes and telling you what they 'make'. Expect answers such as: 30p, 6p, 22p, 14p. Now include 5p coins.

> 10p × 3
> 5p × 3
> 2p × 3
> 10p × 2 + 2p
> 5p × 2 + 2p
> 10p × 2 + 5p
> 5p + 2p × 2
> 10p + 5p × 2
> 10p + 5p + 2p
> 10p + 2p × 2

More able: Encourage this group to be systematic, using all the 10p combinations first, then the 5p and finally the 2p combinations. Ask them to repeat the problem using four coins.

Plenary & assessment

Invite some pairs of children to talk through their work and their results. Ask the others whether they can add anything to these results. Aim for a complete list of answers, listed in a systematic way. Write them on the board as the children say them, in three columns – one for 10p starting coins, another for 5p and a third for 2p (see below). Find the total number of answers, and explain that it is easier to keep a record if we work systematically.

Name   Date

Problems at the zoo

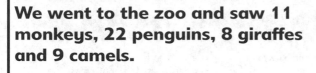

Work out the answers to these problems.

Show your working out in the boxes.

We went to the zoo and saw 11 monkeys, 22 penguins, 8 giraffes and 9 camels. How many animals did we see altogether? ☐	How I solved the problem:
At the zoo I bought a bag of nuts for the monkeys. I kept 35 and gave my friend 42. How many nuts were in the bag? ☐	How I solved the problem:
The nuts cost 40p a bag. How much would 5 bags cost? ☐	How I solved the problem:
We saw 15 adult flamingos and 9 flamingo chicks. How many flamingos did we see altogether? ☐	How I solved the problem:
It cost us £2.50 each to get into the zoo. Five of us went. What was the total cost? ☐	How I solved the problem:

Spring term
Unit 5

Mass and time

Children use and begin to read the vocabulary of mass and time. They estimate, measure and compare masses using standard equipment and read simple scales for mass. They use mental calculations to solve simple measures calculations. They estimate and measure time in practical activities.

LEARNING OBJECTIVES

	Topics	Starter	Main teaching activities
Lesson 1	Measures	● Count in hundreds from and back to zero.	● Use and begin to read the vocabulary related to length, mass and capacity. **● Estimate, measure and compare masses, using standard units (kg); suggest suitable units and equipment for such measurements.**
Lesson 2	Measures	● Know by heart doubles of all numbers to 10 and the corresponding halves. ● Identify near doubles, from doubles already known.	**● Read a simple scale to the nearest labelled division**, recording estimates and measurements as 'nearly 3 kilograms heavy'.
Lesson 3	Measures	● Count in hundreds from and back to zero. ● Know by heart doubles of all numbers to 10 and the corresponding halves. ● Identify near doubles from doubles already known.	● Use and begin to read the vocabulary related to length, mass and capacity. **● Estimate, measure and compare masses using standard units suggest suitable units and equipment for such measurements**. **● Read a simple scale to the nearest labelled division, including using a ruler to draw and measure lines to the nearest centimetre**, recording estimates and measurements as '3 and a bit metres long' or 'about 8 centimetres' or 'nearly 3 kilograms heavy'.
Lesson 4	Problems involving 'real life', money or measures	**● Read and write whole numbers to at least 100 in figures and words.** **● Know what each digit in a two-digit number represents, including zero as a place holder..**	● Use mental addition and subtraction, simple multiplication and division, to solve simple word problems involving numbers in measures, using one ot two steps. Explain how the problem was solved.

Lessons   overview

Preparation
Check that the dial scale will weigh in 100g increments to 1kg with reasonable accuracy, and adjust if necessary.

Learning objectives
Starter
- Count in hundreds from and back to zero.
- Know by heart doubles of all numbers to 10 and the corresponding halves.
- Identify near doubles, from doubles already known.

Main teaching activities
- Use and begin to read the vocabulary related to length, mass and capacity.
- **Estimate, measure and compare masses, using standard units** (kg); **suggest suitable units and equipment for such measurements**.
- **Read a simple scale to the nearest labelled division**, recording estimates and measurements as 'nearly 3 kilograms heavy'.

Vocabulary
kilogram, half-kilogram, gram, nearly, roughly, about, close to, about the same as, just over, just under

You will need:
CD pages
Enlarged weight vocabulary cards from 'Measures vocabulary' (see General resources, Autumn term).

Equipment
A counting stick; balances; dial scales; kilogram weights; 100g weights; individual whiteboards and pens; Plasticine.

Lesson

Starter
Point to jumps of 10 on a counting stick, and count with the children from zero to 100 and back in tens. Repeat, making different jumps (for example, of 30 or 20); ask the children how they knew which number went where. Do this for counting in hundreds from zero to 1000. Ask for a volunteer to use the counting stick as you have been doing for straight counting up and down in ones, tens and then hundreds. As they do this, draw three columns on the board for the ones, the tens and the hundreds numbers. Show the comparisons between 1, 10 and 100, between 2, 20 and 200 and so on, emphasising the fact that the hundreds are ten times bigger than the tens and the tens are ten times bigger than the ones. Do not let the children think that 'adding a zero' to a number makes it ten times bigger.

Main teaching activities
Whole class: Say: *During the next two lessons you will be estimating, measuring and comparing weights.* Hold up the weight cards from 'Measures vocabulary'. Invite the children to read the words and to explain how these are used in sentences. Pass the kilogram weights around the class so that everyone has the opportunity to hold one and feel its 'weight'. Ask the children to suggest some things which they think will be heavier, or lighter, than the kilogram weight. Using the bucket balance and the kilogram weight in one pan, invite a child to place one of the objects onto the other pan. Ask: *Did you make a good estimate? Which is heavier? How can you tell that by looking at the balance?* Repeat this for other suggested objects.

Now explain that the kilogram weight is too heavy to measure accurately the weight of lighter objects and that to do this we use grams. Show the children and name some 100g weights. Again, pass these around the class so that the children can 'feel' the weight. Explain that ten 100g weights weigh the same as 1kg. Ask if anyone can work out how many grams there are in 1kg. Agree that there are 1000g in a kilogram. Ask: *How many grams will a half-kilogram have?*

Now show the children a simple dial scale. Place the kilogram weight onto the scale. Invite a child to point to the position of the dial needle and read off 1kg. Repeat this with a 100g weight.

Group work: Ask the children to work in mixed-ability groups of about four. Ask them to tackle these two problems, one today and one tomorrow. It does not matter in which order they do them.

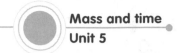

● Ask the children to find things in the classroom which they estimate are heavier, lighter and about the same weight as 100g. They check by weighing. They can record their work in a simple table. This can be repeated for other weights, such as 200g and 500g.

Object	Estimate	Measure
Pencil	Lighter than 100g	Lighter than 100g

● The children make a ball of Plasticine which they estimate weighs about 100g, then check this with a dial scale. Ask them to make Plasticine balls which weigh about 100g, 200g, 300g… to 1kg.

Plenary & assessment

As the main part of this lesson will take more time than usual, the Plenary is shorter. Ask: *How many grams are there in a kilogram? How many 100g weights weigh the same as a kilogram? How many grams are there in a half-kilogram?* Invite a child to place enough 100g weights onto a dial scale to show a half-kilogram. Now ask: *How many 100g weights do we need to show 600g… 700g… ?* Invite a child to demonstrate with the weights and the dial scale.

Lesson ②

Starter

Call out numbers to 15 for the children to double and write on their whiteboards. As they do this, ask them for their answers and write them on the board, then discuss the doubles of the related multiples of 10. For example: *6 doubled is 12, 60 doubled is 120 – double 6 and multiply by 10.*

Main teaching activities

Whole class: Review with the children what they learned yesterday. Repeat the questions from the 'Plenary & assessment'.
Group work: Continue with the work from yesterday.

Plenary & assessment

Review the first problem. Invite children from each group to give examples of items that weighed less, more or about the same as 100g. Ask: *How close were your estimates?* The children may comment that these improved with experience. Praise this response, because it is an important learning point. Review the results of the second problem. Invite children from each group to place one of their balls of plasticine onto the scales and ask other children to read off how much these weigh. Encourage the children to use the language of approximation, such as nearly, close, just over/under… in their responses.

Lessons   overview

Preparation
Enlarge and copy a selection of the pairs of near doubles cards from the 'Near doubles game'. Before each lesson, set out the equipment ready for use by groups of four. Copy 'Class R's fruit shop 2' instructions onto card, one for each group working on the problem.

Learning objectives
Starter
- Count in hundreds from and back to zero.
- Know by heart doubles of all numbers to 10 and the corresponding halves.
- Identify near doubles, from doubles already known.
- **Read and write whole numbers to at least 100 in figures and words.**
- **Know what each digit in a two-digit number represents, including zero as a place holder.**

Main teaching activities
- Use and begin to read the vocabulary related to length, mass and capacity.
- **Estimate, measure and compare masses using standard units suggest suitable units and equipment for such measurements.**
- **Read a simple scale to the nearest labelled division, including using a ruler to draw and measure lines to the nearest centimetre**, recording estimates and measurements as '3 and a bit metres long' or 'about 8 centimetres' or 'nearly 3 kilograms heavy'.
- Use mental addition and subtraction, simple multiplication and division, to solve simple word problems involving numbers in measures, using one ot two steps. Explain how the problem was solved.

Vocabulary
weight, compare, measuring scale, guess, estimate, nearly, roughly, about, close to, about the same as, just over, just under, balance, scales, lighter, heaviest, weigh, weighs, balances, today, yesterday, tomorrow, now, soon, early, late, hour, minute, second.

You will need:
Photocopiable pages
'Class R's fruit shop 1' and '2', instructions for each group (pages 105–106) for each child.

CD pages
A set of 'Near doubles cards' (see General resources, Autumn term), 'Class R's fruit shop 1', (see Spring term, Unit 5).

Equipment
Individual whiteboards and pens; calculators; Plasticine or dough; two 500g weights; two objects weighing 0.5kg; two scales (kitchen and/or balance).

Lesson

Starter
Explain that you will hold up some cards you have prepared: *If I hold up 5 and 6, you need to use a double and adjust to find the answer, so you will write down 10 + 1 or 12 – 1.* You will then ask someone what the answer is. The children should write on their whiteboards. Encourage both methods of doubling and adjusting. Use 9 and 10 as an example of a near double where it is quicker to double 10 and subtract than to double 9 and add. Do this for numbers to 20 and some near multiples of 10.

Main teaching activities
Whole class and group work: Give the children the 'Class R's fruit shop' problem card and model the problem using the teacher's notes. Then ask the children to complete the problem in groups.

Plenary & assessment
Compare the like fruits from two groups. Ask questions such as: *Which of these do you think is the heaviest/lightest? Why? Do you think this apple will be the same weight as the banana? Why/why not?* Put each fruit on the scales to find out. *How many of these fruits do you think will weigh a kilogram?* Use the scales to see how close the children's estimates were.

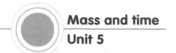
Lesson ④

Starter

Ask the children to follow your instructions, writing and changing two-digit numbers on their whiteboards. They should record all of the numbers. For example: *Write 10. Double it.* (20) *Add 5.* (25) *Add 100.* (125) *Swap the 5 and the 1. What is your number?* (521)

Main teaching activity

Whole class: Say: *There are 3kg of apples in a box. How many kilograms of apples are there in two boxes?* Invite responses and ask: *How did you work that out?* Write the number sentence $3 \times 2 = 6$ onto the board. Now say: *A bag of sugar weighs 2kg. How many bags will I need to buy so that I have 10kg of sugar?* Again, ask for responses, how the children worked out their answer, and write the number sentence $2 \times 5 = 10$ onto the board. Discuss how the children can use their mental calculation strategies to solve weight problems.

Individual work: Write some word problems onto the board for the children to solve, such as:

1. *There are two parcels to be delivered which weigh 22kg and 15kg. How much do the parcels weigh altogether?*
2. *There are five packs of carpet tiles. Each pack weighs 3kg. How much do the packs weigh in total?*
3. *A box of books weighs 25kg. Another box weighs 33kg. What is the difference in their weights?*
4. *(Two-step problem) There are 12 packets of flour in a stack on the shelves, each weighing 1kg. The shopkeeper puts another 15 packets of flour onto the stack. A customer buys five of the packs. How many kilograms of flour are left?*

Differentiation

Less able: You may like to work with these children and discuss each problem and how it could be solved.

More able: You may wish to provide more complex problems for the children to solve.

Plenary & assessment

Review the problems together. Invite children from each group to explain how they worked out their answers, and which mental strategies they used. Invite a child to write the appropriate number sentence onto the board. Ask: *How did you work this out? Who chose a different way to do this? Is there another way? Which way do you think is best? Why do you think that?*

Name   Date

Class R's fruit shop 1

Notes for the teacher or classroom assistant:

Explain to the children that this problem involves your teacher friend Miss Singh, who wants to make a shop in her classroom for her Year R children to use. She'd like your class to help by making some fruit out of Plasticine or play dough.

Give each group 1kg of Plasticine (or another malleable modelling material) and something that weighs 0.5kg (such as a 500g weight or jar of coffee).

Model exactly what you expect the children to do:

- Break the Plasticine into four pieces.
- Pick up the 0.5kg weight. Take a piece of Plasticine to make an apple and compare it with the weight (without actually weighing it). Take from or add to the Plasticine to make what you estimate to be less than 0.5kg. When you think you are about right, make the apple. Repeat this for the orange and banana. For the melon, you need to estimate more than 0.5kg.
- You must use all the Plasticine. Adjust the amounts until you are happy that all the model fruits have the correct weight.

After you have modelled this part of the activity, ask the children to have a go.

When they have done this, stop the children and model how to read 500g or 0.5kg on a set of kitchen scales. They need to use the scales to measure the weight of their model fruit. If you have a group of children who are not able to use top pan scales, they can use balance scales, putting their fruit on one side and the 500g weight on the other.

Name   Date

Class R's fruit shop 2

Instructions:

Miss Singh wants to make a shop in her Year R classroom.

She'd like you to help by making some fruit out of Plasticine or play dough.

This is what you need to do:

1. You will need 1 kg of Plasticine or play dough for your group.

2. Here is Miss Singh's list of fruit: apple, banana, orange and melon.

3. Make the apple, banana and orange each less than half a kilogram in weight. Make the melon more than half a kilogram.

4. First, estimate the weight of the Plasticine you are going to use to make each piece of fruit. You will need to use all the Plasticine.

5. When you have made your fruit, weigh each piece to see if your estimates were correct.

6. If you weren't correct, alter the fruits so they are the correct weights.

Now estimate whether each of these will weigh more or less than 1 kg:

● all the apples from all the groups_____

● all the bananas from all the groups_____

● all the melons from all the groups._____

Shape and space

The children describe shapes and patterns and then make their own using 2-D shapes. They concentrate on line symmetry and position, direction and movement. The third lesson is very practical, rehearsing known vocabulary and introducing clockwise and anticlockwise turns of varying sizes.

LEARNING OBJECTIVES

	Topics	Starter	Main teaching activities
Lesson 1	Shape and space Reasoning about numbers or shapes	● Say the number names in order to at least 100, from and back to zero. ● Describe and extend simple number sequences: count on or back in ones or tens, starting from any two-digit number.	● Make and describe shapes, pictures and patterns. ● Begin to recognise line symmetry.
Lesson 2	Reasoning about numbers or shapes	● Use the mathematical names for common 3-D and 2-D shapes. ● Sort shapes and describe some of their features. ● Begin to recognise line symmetry.	● Solve mathematical problems or puzzles, recognise simple patterns and relationships, generalise and predict.
Lesson 3	Shape and space	As for Lesson 2.	● **Use mathematical vocabulary to describe position, direction and movement**. ● Recognise whole, half and quarter turns, to the left or right, clockwise, anticlockwise.

Lessons   overview

Preparation
An acetate and one copy per child of 'Make me symmetrical' and 'Creating patterns'.

Learning objectives
Starter
● Say the number names in order to at least 100, from and back to zero.
● **Describe and extend simple number sequences: count on or back in ones or tens, starting from any two-digit number.**
● **Use the mathematical names for common 3-D and 2-D shapes.**
● **Begin to recognise line symmetry**
● **Sort shapes and describe some of their features.**
Main teaching activities
● Make and describe shapes, pictures and patterns.
● Begin to recognise line symmetry.
● Solve mathematical problems or puzzles, recognise simple patterns and relationships, generalise and predict.
● Suggest extensions by asking 'What if…?' or 'What could I try next?'
● **Explain how a problem was solved orally** and in writing.

Vocabulary
shape, pattern, flat, curved, straight, round, solid, corner, point, face, side, edge, surface, cube, buoid, pyramid, sphere, cone, cylinder, circle, circular, triangle, triangular, square, rectangle, star, pentagon, hexagon, octagon, plus: right angle

You will need:
Photocopiable pages
An acetate and one copy per child of 'Make me symmetrical' (page 110) and 'Creating patterns' (page 111).

CD pages
'0–100 number cards', acetates and enlarged copies of 'Templates for irregular shapes' and 'Templates for regular shapes', enlarged '2-D shape vocabulary' cards (see General resources, Autumn term), acetates of 'Mirror, mirror…' and 'Shape patterns', 'Creating patterns' and 'Make me symmetrical', less able and more able versions (Spring term, Unit 6) (see General resources).

Equipment
An OHP; individual whiteboards and pens; Blu-Tack; 3-D and 2-D shapes (as listed in 'Vocabulary').

Equipment
OHT; mirrors; scissors; Blu-Tack.

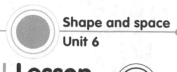
Lesson ①

Starter
Repeat the Starters from Autumn term, Unit 6, Lessons 1 and 2 in sequence. Some whole-class practice might be necessary first.

Main teaching activities
Whole class: Today the children will think about 2-D shapes and symmetry. Ask them to name and describe as many 2-D shapes as they can. Give eight children a '2-D shape vocabulary' card. Give 14 others a shape each from 'Templates for irregular shapes' and 'Templates for regular shapes'. Discuss irregular and regular shapes; compare their properties. Ask each child in turn to take their shape to the correct label. Discuss the properties of each shape: sides, angles and so on.

Now ask: *What can you tell me about symmetry?* Hold up pairs of regular and irregular shapes. *Which have the most lines of symmetry, regular or irregular shapes?* Show OHTs of a regular and an irregular hexagon. Draw one line of symmetry on the regular hexagon. *Can anyone draw another line of symmetry on this hexagon? Regular shapes have more than one line of symmetry. Can anyone draw a line of symmetry on the irregular hexagon?* Ask the vocabulary card holders to Blu-Tack their cards and shape examples to the board.

Use the 'Mirror, mirror…' OHT to demonstrate how to find lines of symmetry using a mirror. (You won't be able to see the reflection while doing this.) Ask the children to help you fill in the mirror image of the squared pattern at the bottom of the sheet.
Paired work: Ask the children to complete the 'Make me symmetrical' activity sheet, working in pairs.

Differentiation
Less able: Provide the version of the activity sheet with simpler patterns to reverse.
More able: Provide the version with more complex patterns.

Plenary & assessment
Using an OHT of the activity sheet, work through the first two patterns. Ask: *Where on the other side of our mirror line should we colour this square? Why? When we have finished colouring this side, what should we see?* (The original pattern in reverse.) *Can anyone see another line of symmetry?*

Lesson ②

Starter
Give each child a shape and a different shape vocabulary card, using a mixture of 3-D and 2-D regular and irregular shapes. Call out some names and properties. Ask the children to stand up if their shape or vocabulary card has that property or name.

Main teaching activities
Whole class: Today the children will investigate shape patterns. Display the 'Shape patterns' OHT, and ask the children to describe the first pattern. Use the questions on the OHT to discuss the first two patterns. Repeat with the other two patterns, asking similar questions.
Paired/individual work: The children may work on their own or with a partner. Use an OHT of the 'Creating patterns' activity sheet to demonstrate this shape and pattern investigation, then ask the children to work through it.

Differentiation
Less able: Provide the version of 'Creating patterns' with simpler shape templates.
More able: Provide the more open-ended version of the activity.

Plenary & assessment

Look at the shapes the children have made; ask some children to sketch their work on the board. Discuss the properties of these shapes: the number of sides, angles and lines of symmetry.

Lesson overview

Preparation

Photocopy 'Position vocabulary' onto A3 card and cut out the cards.

Learning objectives

Starter

- **Use the mathematical names for common 3-D and 2-D shapes.**
- **Sort shapes and describe some of their features**.
- Begin to recognise line symmetry.

Main teaching activities

- **Use mathematical vocabulary to describe position, direction and movement**.
- Recognise whole, half and quarter turns, to the left or right, clockwise, anticlockwise.

Vocabulary

over, under, underneath, above, below, top, bottom, side, outside, inside, around, in front, behind, front, back, beside, next to, opposite, between, middle, edge, centre, corner, direction, clockwise, anticlockwise, whole turn, half turn, quarter turn, right angle, straight line.

You will need:

CD page
'Position vocabulary' cards (see General resources).

Equipment
Individual whiteboards and pens; an OHP; a Roamer or similar floor robot; the NNS ICT program *Unit the Robot*.

Lesson

Starter

Repeat the Starter from Lesson 2. Assess the children's confidence with symmetry after Lesson 2.

Main teaching activities

Whole class: Explain that today, the children will revise their work on positions of objects, then think about moving and turning them. Ask them to give you some position vocabulary. As they do so, hold up the vocabulary cards. Ask them to use their whiteboards: *Draw a circle under a line. Draw a square over a circle. Draw a pentagon beside a triangle.*

Write these words on the board: 'clockwise', 'anticlockwise', 'whole turn', 'half turn', 'quarter turn', 'right angle', 'straight line'. Point to the words and say: *Who can tell me what a turn is? Can you show me? What is a quarter turn? What type of angle does it make? Which direction is clockwise? What about anticlockwise? Everyone stand up. Turn clockwise for a quarter of a turn. Turn anticlockwise to make a right angle turn. Turn anticlockwise to make a turn the size of a straight line.*

Group activity: Demonstrate the program *Unit the Robot* with a floor robot. Let groups of children have a turn at this program. If a PC is not available, choose an adult or a child to be the 'robot' and orally 'program' them with instructions to move around the classroom.

Differentiation

Less able: Encourage peer buddying for any child who is having difficulty.
More able: Ask the children for more complicated programming.

Plenary & assessment

Discuss how the children got on with the computer program. Invite some children to 'program' a human robot (an adult or child) to get around the classroom by moving and turning. Assess whether they know the necessary vocabulary and use it correctly.

Name   Date

Make me symmetrical

**This is an example
of a symmetrical pattern:**

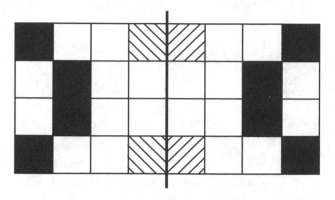

One side of each pattern has been coloured in.
Colour in the other side so each pattern is symmetrical.

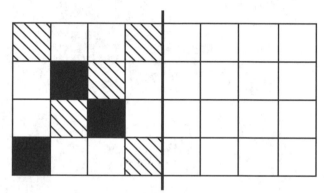
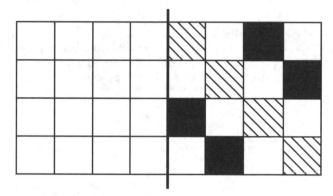

Now make up a symmetrical pattern of your own.

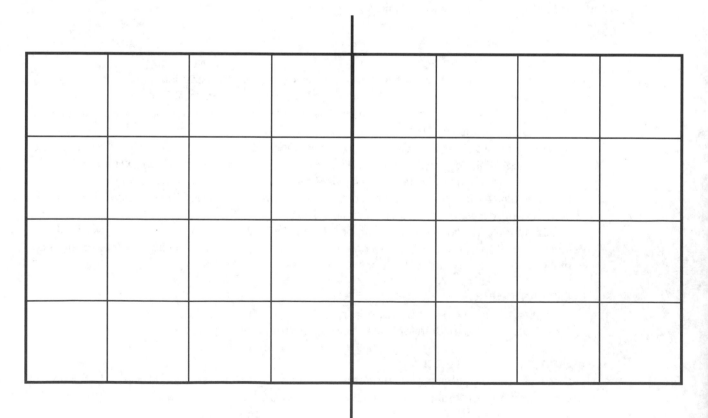

Name	Date

Creating patterns

Cut out the square, triangle and pentagon templates at the bottom of this sheet.

Use them to make new shapes like this:

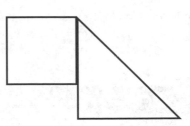

Now you try. Draw and name your new shapes in these boxes:

My new shape is a hexagon.

1. Use the square and the triangle.

My new shape is a

2. Use the pentagon and the square.

My new shape is a

3. Use the pentagon and the triangle.

My new shape is a

4. Use all three templates.

My new shape is a

Use two of your new shapes to make a pattern on another sheet of paper.

Here is an example:

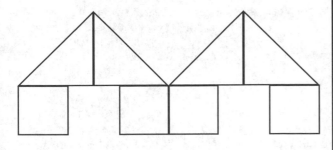

These are the shapes to cut out and use:

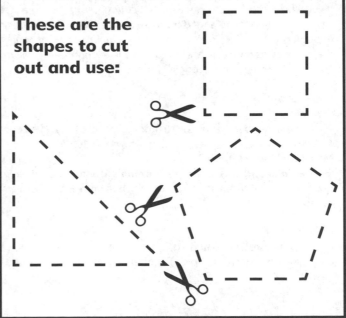

Looking for patterns in number sequences

In this unit, counting in steps of different sizes is rehearsed through games activities, and then the class moves forward to investigate patterns made by these counts. From here the class investigate 2-D shapes with three, four and five sides. The last lesson deals with proving or disproving general statements about numbers and shapes.

LEARNING OBJECTIVES

		Topics	Starter	Main teaching activities
Lesson	1	Counting, properties of numbers and number sequences	● Say the number that is 1 or 10 more or less than any given two-digit number.	● **Describe and extend simple number sequences**: count on in steps of 3, 4 or 5 to at least 30, from and back to zero, then from and back to any given small number.
Lesson	2	Counting, properties of numbers and number sequences	● **Recognise odd and even numbers** to at least 30.	As for Lesson 1.
Lesson	3	Counting, properties of numbers and number sequences	As for Lessons 1 and 2.	As for Lesson 1.
Lesson	4	Reasoning about numbers or shapes	● **Read and write whole numbers to at least 100 in figures and words.**	● Investigate a general statement about familiar numbers or shapes by finding examples that satisfy it.

Lessons

Preparation
Copy the 'Up the mountain' gameboard onto A3 paper. Copy the 'Doubles and halves "follow me" cards' onto card and cut out the cards. Make acetates of 'Diamond number line' and '100 square patterns'. Copy onto card and laminate enough copies of the 'Count it' gameboard for one between four children; copy the game cards onto card and cut out. Make enough sets for all groups to use. Make an A3 copy of the 'Count it' gameboard.

Learning objectives
Starter
● Say the number that is 1 or 10 more or less than any given two-digit number.
● Recognise odd and even numbers to at least 30.
Main teaching activities
● **Describe and extend simple number sequences:** count on in steps of 3, 4 or 5 to at least 30, from and back to zero, then from and back to any given small number.

Vocabulary
zero, one hundred, two hundred… one thousand, count on, count back, count on in ones/twos/tens, multiple of, sequence, continue, predict, pattern, rule, odd, even

You will need:
CD pages
'0–100 number cards', 'Up the mountain' gameboard, an acetate of 'Diamond number line' (see General resources, Autumn term), a copy of '100 square patterns' for teacher/LSA, 'Doubles and halves "follow me" cards', one copy of the 'Count it! Gameboard' for each group of four, plus a set of 'Count it! cards' for each group, an A3 copy of the 'Count it! Gameboard', a copy of the 'Count it! Instructions' (see General resources).

Equipment
A dice; a class 100 square; individual whiteboards and pens; individual 100 squares; a counting stick; a collection of play money to 50p; counters; counting apparatus; an OHP; three coloured OHP pens.

Lesson ①

Starter

Use a class 100 square to count on and back in tens and ones. For example, find 36 and ask: *What is 10 more?* *…10 less? …1 more? …4 less?* Now ask the children to imagine the class 100 square in their heads. Say a number, for example 23, and ask them to look at it in their minds: *Which number is below it on your 100 square?* (33) *… above it?* (13) *… two squares to the right?* (25)… *three to the left?* (20) Repeat several times with other numbers. If any children struggle with this, give them a 100 square to use.

Play a game using the 'Up the mountain' gameboard, a pile of two-digit number cards and a dice. Divide the class into two teams, who take turns to pick a card and throw the dice. If the dice lands on an even number, they add ten to the number on the card and write the answer on their whiteboards, then move two spaces up the mountain if they were correct. If they throw an odd number, they add one to the number and move one space. Encourage them to use a mental picture if possible. All the children in the team should write the answer. The first team to reach the top of the mountain wins.

Main teaching activities

Whole class: Explain that the next three lessons will focus on counting backwards and forwards from different numbers in steps of 3, 4 and 5. In this lesson, the children will practise counting in twos, fives and tens from and back to different small numbers, then move on to counting in threes.

Using a counting stick, give the children a small starting number (such as 0, 2 or 5) and move your finger up and down, asking them to count in jumps of 2, then 5, then 10. Make jumps along the stick, asking the children to predict what number you are pointing to and say how they know. Expect answers such as: 'That is 15 because it's five jumps of 2, which is 10, and 10 onto 5 is 15'. Repeat a few times with different starting numbers.

Move on to counting in threes. Begin with the starting number of zero, at the beginning of the stick. Count on and back. Now jump along the line as you did previously. Ask which number you are pointing at and how the children know. Look for answers such as: 'That is 12 because it's four jumps, and four lots of 3 is 12' or 'The next one is 9 because I know 2 onto 6 is 8 and then I added 1 more'. Repeat several times, using different small starting numbers.

Individual/paired work: Ask the children to work individually or with a partner on the following task. Use the OHP to model the activity: show the children the 'Diamond number line'. Have a pile of number cards in front of you. Pick one and write the number at the beginning of your line. Ask the children to complete the line by counting on in threes, writing on their whiteboards. Provide two-digit starting numbers up to 20.

Differentiation

Less able: Give these individuals or pairs a starting number below 10.
More able: Ask these individuals or pairs to put their starting two-digit number in the 'middle' diamond of the line, so that they need to count forwards and backwards.

Plenary & assessment

Pick a number between 20 and 30, write it on the board and ask the children to help you make a sequence of numbers counting forwards and back in threes from the number. For example, starting with 26, the sequence would be: 11 14 17 20 23 26 29 32 35 38 41. Ask the children what they notice about the numbers. Look for the answer: 'The pattern goes odd, even, odd, even'. Repeat for fives: *Does the same thing happen? Can the children draw a conclusion from this? What about sevens?* Write a count in sevens (from zero) on the board.

Project the OHT of the '100 square patterns'. Use the coloured OHT pens to follow the instructions for Lesson 1 on the sheet. By the end of the lesson, expect the children to know that when we count in odd numbers, the pattern is always odd, even, odd, even.

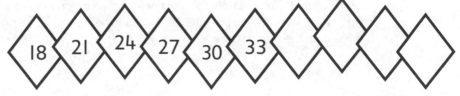

Lesson ②

Starter

Call out some numbers from 1 to 15 for the children to double, and some even numbers to 30 for the children to halve, writing on their whiteboards. Use the 40 'Doubles and halves "follow me" cards' to play a 'Follow me' game. Let the children work in pairs, with at least two cards per pair.

Main teaching activities

Repeat the whole-class and group work from Lesson 1, but this time work on counting in fours.

Plenary & assessment

Pick a number between 20 and 30. Write it on the board, and ask the children to help you make a sequence of numbers going forwards and back in fours from the number – for example, starting with 18, the number sequence would be: 2 6 10 14 18 22 26 30 34. Repeat with an odd starting number. Ask the children what they notice. Look for such answers as 'The units/ones numbers repeat: 2, 6, 0, 4, 8, 2, 6', or 'If the starting number is even, all the numbers are even. If it is odd, all the numbers are odd.' Repeat for counting in twos: *Does the same thing happen?* Can the children draw a conclusion from this? *What about sixes?* Write a count in sixes (from zero) on the board to see whether the same thing happens.

Project the OHT of the '100 square patterns'. Follow the instructions for Lesson 2 on the sheet. By the end of the lesson, expect the children to know that when we count in even numbers, the pattern is: all even numbers if the starting number is even, all odd numbers if the starting number is odd.

Lesson ③

Starter

Use the 'Doubles and halves "follow me" cards' and see whether the class can go round the questions faster than they did in Lesson 2.

Main teaching activities

Group work: Say that today, the children will be playing a game to help them practise counting in steps of different sizes. Give each group of four a copy of the 'Count it!' gameboard, a selection of the 'Count it!' cards and a pot of coins (to 50p). Model how to play the game, using the A3 gameboard and the instructions.

Differentiation

Less able: Provide the cards for counting forwards and backwards in twos and tens only. Let the children use counting apparatus and a 100 square or number line to help.
More able: Use all the cards and expect this group to count in their heads.

Plenary & assessment

Play the 'Count it!' game again as a class, using the A3 gameboard. Write the counting that you do on the board – for example, for 'Start on 4 and count on in 4s to 24', write 4, 8, 12, 16, 20, 24. Focus on any patterns (for example, all the numbers being even) and predict from looking at the pattern what digit the next number will end with (in this case, 8 so the next number is 28).

Lessons

Preparation
Copy 'Investigation cards' onto card, then cut out a set of cards for each group.

Learning objectives
Starter
- **Read and write whole numbers to at least 100** in figures and words.
- **Describe and extend simple number sequences:** count on in steps of 3, 4 or 5 to at least 30, from and back to zero, then from and back to any given small number.

Main teaching activities
- Investigate a general statement about familiar numbers or shapes by finding examples that satisfy it.

Vocabulary
zero, one hundred, two hundred…, one thousand, count on, count back, count on in ones/twos/tens, multiple of, sequence, continue, predict, pattern, rule, odd, even

You will need:
Photocopiable pages
'Investigation cards' (page 116) and 'Investigation cards answers' (page 117) for each pair.

CD pages
'Templates for irregular shapes', and 'Templates for regular shapes', (see General resources, Autumn term) 'Count it! Gameboard', differentiated 'Investigation cards' and 'Investigation cards answers', less able version (Spring term, Unit 8) (see General resources).

Equipment
Individual whiteboards and pens; cubes.

Lesson

Starter
Ask the children to follow your instructions for writing and operating on two-digit numbers up to 30, using their whiteboards. For example: *Write 15. Double it.* (30) *Add 5.* (35) *Add 100.* (135) *Swap the 5 and the 1. What is your number?* (531) Also ask them to write some two-digit numbers in words, encouraging them to look for clues in the number vocabulary (which should, ideally, be displayed all the time in your classroom).

Main teaching activities
Whole class: Explain that the children will now use what they learned in Lessons 1–3 to carry out investigations. Say: *In this lesson, I am going to give you some statements to investigate to see whether they are wrong or right. What do I mean by that? Let us do an example together.* (Draw a circle on the board.) *My statement is: 'This is a circle.' Is that right? Are you sure? How do you know? It has the properties of a circle. It is flat and 2-D. It has no sides or corners.*

Invite a few children to make a statement like this about a shape. Ask them to draw examples. Then demonstrate the process for numbers: *Here is my statement: 'Six is an even number.' I know that's right because all even numbers of things can be divided exactly into two piles, with nothing left over. Watch me divide these six cubes equally into two piles.*

Paired work: Give each pair of children a selection from half of the 'Investigation cards', including a selection of possible answers to choose from. They should copy the 'best fit' answer onto their sheet. Let them choose which card to do first, but they need to have worked on at least two by the end of the lesson.

Differentiation
Less able: Provide the version of 'Investigation cards' with one answer for each statement. Once the children have found the right answer, they should copy it onto their sheet. They may need some help with the reading.
More able: Provide the version without answers and ask the children to give their own reasons.

Plenary & assessment
Take each statement in turn and ask the children to explain their investigation. Discuss whether the children think the examples provided are enough to show that the statement is always right. If they don't, try to improve on them.

Name   Date

Investigation cards

Statement cards

Cut out the statement and answer cards and give them to pairs of children.

Ask them to choose the best answer to match each statement.

This is a cube.	**I think this because**
This is a hexagon.	**I think this because**
This is a right angle.	**I think this because**
Odd numbers won't divide equally by 2.	**I think this because**
8 + 9 = 17	**I think this because**
If a number ends in 0, it will divide exactly by 10.	**I think this because**
You can make 12 using 3 lots of 4 things.	**I think this because**
There are 3 numbers less than 10 that divide exactly by 3.	**I think this because**

Name   Date

Investigation cards answers

it is a 3-D shape.	it is a 3-D shape with 6 faces.	it is a 3-D shape with 6 square faces.
it is a 2-D shape.	it is a 2-D shape with 6 sides.	it is a 2-D shape with 6 sides and 6 corners.
there are 2 lines.	the 2 lines are joined together.	the 2 lines join to make quarter of a turn.
they end with a 1, 3, 5, 7 or 9.	they are not even numbers.	when you divide them by 2, you always have 1 left over.
one number is odd and the other is even.	the answer is less than 20.	If I put 8 things and 9 things together, I will have 17 altogether.
it is an even number.	it ends with 0.	numbers ending in 0 are multiples of 10 and so are in the 10x table.
you can't because 3 + 4 equals 7.	4 lots of 3 is: ● ● ●　○ ○ ○　⊛ ⊛ ⊛　◎ ◎ ◎	3 lots of 4 is: ● ● ● ●　○ ○ ○ ○　◎ ◎ ◎ ◎
3, 6 and 9 are less than 10.	3, 6 and 9 are in the 3x table and are less than 10.	3, 6 and 9 cubes will all divide equally between 3 groups, and are all below 10.

Spring term
Unit 9

Using addition and subtraction strategies to answer problems involving money and measures

In this unit the children compare two-digit numbers in the context of money and measures and find numbers that go between them. They will also work on some mental calculation strategies for addition and subtraction, and on employing these to solve word problems involving money and measures.

LEARNING OBJECTIVES

	Topics	Starter	Main teaching activities
Lesson **1**	Place value and ordering	● **Know by heart multiplication facts for the 2 and 10 times-tables.** ● Derive quickly division facts for the 2 and 10 times-tables.	● Compare two given two-digit numbers, say which is more or less, and give a number which lies between them.
Lesson **2**	Understanding addition and subtraction Mental calculation strategies (+ and –) Problems involving 'real life', money and measures Making decisions	● **Know by heart all addition and subtraction facts for each number to at least 10.**	● Extend understanding of the operations of addition and subtraction. ● Use and begin to read the related vocabulary. ● Partition into '5 and a bit' when adding 6, 7, 8 or 9, then recombine. ● Partition additions into tens and units, then recombine. ● Find totals, give change and work out which coins to pay. ● **Choose and use appropriate operations and efficient calculation strategies** (e.g. mental, mental with jottings) **to solve problems**.
Lesson **3**	Making decisions Mental calculation strategies (+ and –) Reasoning about numbers or shapes	● Know by heart all pairs of numbers with a total of 20 (e.g. 13 + 7, 6 + 14).	● **Choose and use appropriate operations and efficient calculation strategies** (e.g. mental, mental with jottings) **to solve problems.** ● Use mental addition and subtraction, simple multiplication and division to solve simple word problems involving numbers in 'real life', money or measures, using one or two steps. ● **Explain how a problem was solved** orally and, where appropriate, in writing.
Lesson **4**	Making decisions Mental calculation strategies (+ and –)	● Order whole numbers to at least 100.	As for Lesson 3, plus: ● Partition into '5 and a bit' when adding 6, 7, 8 or 9, then recombine. ● Partition additions into tens and units, then recombine. ● Bridge through 10, then 20, and adjust. ● **State the subtraction corresponding to a given addition, and vice versa.**

Lesson overview

Preparation
Make A3 copies of 'Spider charts for multiplying' and 'Spider charts for dividing'. Copy, laminate and cut out the 'Small spider charts' for each child. Make sticky note labels for 20cm, 40cm, 60cm, 75cm, 95cm and 55cm.

Learning objectives
Starter
- **Know by heart multiplication facts for the 2 and 10 times-tables.**
- Derive quickly division facts for the 2 and 10 times-tables.

Main teaching activities
- Compare two given two-digit numbers, say which is more or less, and give a number which lies between them.

Vocabulary
order, compare, larger, largest, bigger, biggest, greater, greatest, smaller, smallest, less, least, size, halfway between

You will need:
Photocopiable pages
'Ordering money and lengths' (page 123) for each child.

CD pages
'0–100 number cards', A3 copies of 'Spider charts for multiplying', 'Spider charts for dividing' and 'Small spider charts' for each child (see General resources, Autumn term), 'Ordering money and lengths', less able and more able versions (Spring term, Unit 9) (see General resources).

Equipment
Coins; an OHP; a metre stick; Post-It Notes.

Lesson

Starter
Use the whole-class spider charts to practise 2 and 10 times-table facts and corresponding division facts. Do this twice. Ask the children to practise with a partner using the 'Small spider charts', taking turns to play 'teacher'. Make sure they point to the numbers randomly and not in order. After a few minutes, ask for volunteer pairs to demonstrate how fast they can 'dodge' around the chart.

Main teaching activities
Whole class: Explain that today the children will compare two-digit numbers, say which one is more and find numbers that go in between them. They will be thinking about money and length. Discuss the vocabulary 'more', 'less', 'greater', 'larger', 'smaller'.

Show the children a 1p coin and a 10p coin. Ask: *Which is worth more?* Draw a blank number line with ten divisions. Ask which coins can go in between the 1p and 10p on the number line. Invite individuals to put coins in the right places. Repeat with 10p and £1 coins. Discuss the link between 2p and 20p coins, and between 5p and 50p.

Show a metre stick with 10cm markings. Invite a child to show where 20cm is, and another to show 40cm. Place the sticky notes in these places. Ask: *Which is the greater length?* Invite two other children to give a length between these two and point to it on the metre stick. Repeat with other measurements, such as 60cm and 75cm or 95cm and 55cm.

Draw a life-sized 1m line on the board with 10cm divisions. Ask two children to pick two 0–100 number cards and plot the numbers in the correct places. Ask for other numbers that will fit in between those plotted, and that also fit criteria you ask for (such as even numbers or multiples of 5).

Paired work: Ask the children to work in pairs, plotting amounts of money and lengths on number lines. Model the 'Ordering money and lengths' activity sheet.

Differentiation
Less able: Provide the version of the activity sheet with simpler quantities and number lines.
More able: Provide the version with more complex quantities.

Plenary & assessment
Draw a 0 to £1 number line on the board. Call out some amounts (such as 60p, 15p, 91p) and ask particular children to plot them on the line. Ask: *How did you decide where to put the number? What number could go in between that number and this one? Why do you think that?*

Lessons   overview

Preparation

If necessary, make laminated cards of the 'Function machine game' and an A3 copy of 'How to solve a problem' as a poster. Sort a mixture of plastic coins into a small container for each group of three children. Display the ten items as if on a shop counter and label them with prices from' Price labels (pence)' and 'Price labels (£.p)'. Make enough shopping cards for at least 12 per group. Prepare 50cm, 1m, 1.5m and 2m lengths of ribbon or string. Make cards from 'Measures and money cards' for each pair or group, by ability (see Differentiation on page 121). Make OHTs of 'Recording sheet 1', 'Recording sheet 2' and 'Measures and money cards'; cut up the latter.

Learning objectives

Starter
- **Know by heart all addition and subtraction facts for each number to at least 10.**
- Know by heart all pairs of numbers with a total of 20 (e.g. 13 + 7, 6 + 14).
- **Order whole numbers to at least 100.**

Main teaching activities
- Extend understanding of the operations of addition and subtraction.
- Use and begin to read the related vocabulary.
- Partition into '5 and a bit' when adding 6, 7, 8 or 9, then recombine.
- Partition additions into tens and units, then recombine.
- Bridge through 10, then 20, and adjust.
- **State the subtraction corresponding to a given addition, and vice versa.**
- Find totals, give change and work out which coins to pay.
- **Choose and use appropriate operations and efficient calculation strategies** (e.g. mental, mental with jottings) **to solve problems.**
- Use mental addition and subtraction, simple multiplication and division to solve simple word problems involving numbers in 'real life', money or measures, using one or two steps.
- **Explain how a problem was solved** orally and, where appropriate, in writing.

Vocabulary

money, coin, penny, pence, pound, £, spend, pay, change, total, addition, subtraction, difference, equal

You will need:
Photocopiable pages
'Measures and money problems' (page 124) for each child.

CD pages
'0–100 number cards', a copy of the 'Function machine game' and a set of 'Coin cards and labels', 'Price labels (pence)' and 'Price labels (£.p)' for each child, 'Addition and subtraction vocabulary' cards, an A3 copy of 'How to solve a problem' (see General resources, Autumn term), 'Shopping cards 1' and '2' (Autumn term, Unit 4) OHTs of 'Recording sheet 1' and 'Recording sheet 2', and a copy for each child, a set of 'Measures and money cards' for each pair or group; 'Measures and money problems', more able, and less able versions (Spring term, Unit 9) (see General resources).

Equipment
Individual whiteboards and pens; Blu-Tack; plastic and real coins; small containers; ten different toys, food items or similar; a pendulum; a counting stick; ribbon or string.

Lesson

Starter

Hold up a number from 0 to 10. Ask the children to write the number that adds to it to make 10 on their whiteboards. Ask for other pairs to make 10. Use fingers and jump along a number line to check. Repeat for totals below 10. See how many pairs of numbers the children can find to make the total in one minute.

Main teaching activities

Whole class: Explain that for the rest of this week, the children will practise mental addition and subtraction using money and length. Ask them to tell you words about addition and subtraction; as they do so, show the vocabulary cards and stick them on the board. Now ask them which coins we use; as they do so, hold up the labels and coins. Show the children the ten labelled items. Ask what each item costs. Ask questions such as: *How much does a bunch of bananas and a pineapple cost altogether?* Discuss strategies for calculating; encourage the children to use rounding and adjusting, counting on from the largest number, partitioning or counting along a number line.

Group work: Distribute the 'Recording sheet 1', one copy to each child. Model how they are going to use it. *You will be working on your own today, but sharing cards and money with two others. You need to have two piles of shopping cards: one for pence and the other for pounds and pence. Pick two cards, one from each pile, and work out the total you will spend. Record how you worked it out, then find the least number of coins that you need to pay. Write down what these coins are.* Distribute the 'Recording sheet 1', one copy to each child.

Differentiation
Less able: Give this group shopping cards only to 50p.
More able: Ask this group to pick three shopping cards (a mixture of the two types).

Plenary & assessment
Invite a few children to give examples of their work and explain their strategies. For each strategy, ask for an alternative and let the class decide which is more efficient.

Lesson

Starter
Draw a number line on the board with 20 divisions. Mark on 11, then jump up in ones to 20. Ask: *How many jumps? What goes with 11 to make 20?* Repeat a few times. Swing a pendulum and call out a number; as it swings the other way, the children call out the complement to make 20.

Main teaching activity
Whole class: Repeat the activity from Lesson 2, but use ribbon or string. *Today we are going to solve money problems that involve length. I would like to buy 2m of ribbon.* (Show this.) *Each metre costs 50p. How much will I spend? I have 10p, 20p and 50p coins in my purse. What coins could I use to pay for my ribbon? Is there another way? Think of as many ways as you can. If I have a £2 coin in my purse, how much change will I need? I want to buy 4m of ribbon. I have £1.80 in my purse. Do I have enough to buy the ribbon? How much more do I need? Which of these lengths of ribbon can be put together to make 4m? I have lengths of 50cm, 1m, 1m 50cm and 2m.* Repeat with similar scenarios and questions.
Group work: Provide the 'Measures and money cards' sheet 1, and a copy of 'Recording sheet 2' for each pair. Model how the children use these. *Work with a friend. You have two piles of cards: one to tell you what you are going to buy, the other to tell you how much money you have. You need to work out how much you will spend and then decide whether you have enough money. If you do, work out how much you will have left over; if you don't, work out how much more you need.* Work through two or three examples.

Differentiation
Less able: Provide the 'Measures and money cards' sheet 2, with money to £1. Work with this group, reading the problems and giving guidance.
More able: Provide the 'Measures and money cards' sheet 3, with larger amounts of money.

Plenary & assessment
Write a problem on the board based on the measures and money cards, such as: *Suzie needs a skipping rope. She buys 5m. Each metre costs £1.25. How much does she spend? She gives the shopkeeper seven pound coins. How much change is she given?* Ask the children what they must do to solve the problem. Ask questions such as: *What is the problem asking you to find out? Which words tell us that? How can you work out how much she spent? Is there another way?* Show the poster of 'How to solve a problem' and work through each point for this problem. Invite some children to talk through problems they solved, sharing their methods and relating them to the poster. Use questions as above to assess the children's problem-solving skills.

Lesson ④

Starter

Give each child a number card at random from 0–100. Ask five children to come to the front and stand with their numbers held up, ordered from lowest to highest. Invite other children to stand in the place appropriate to their number. Ask the class to check that they are standing in the right places and explain why. When the line is ten children long, ask the original five to sit down and another five to go to the places appropriate to their numbers. Repeat until everyone has had a go. Ask questions such as: *Who is holding the number closest to 34? Who is holding an odd number between 20 and 30?*

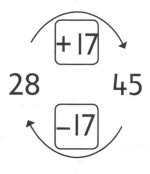

Main teaching activities

Whole class: Explain that this lesson is about solving 'real-life' problems. The children will be thinking about how to solve two-step problems and the best strategies to use. Discuss strategies for addition and subtraction, particularly: partitioning into '5 and a bit' and recombining when adding 6, 7, 8 or 9; partitioning into tens and units; adding 10 or 20 and then adjusting; using the inverse operation. Ask the children what they must do to solve a problem. Show the poster of 'How to solve a problem' and write a problem from the Plenary of Lesson 3 on the OHP. Work through it using the four strategies above. Discuss which strategy is most efficient.

Paired/individual work: Ask the children to work individually or with a partner on the 'Measures and money problems' activity sheet, finding the best strategy to answer each problem. Model an example from the sheet.

Differentiation

Less able: Provide the version of 'Measures and money problems' with simpler quantities. Work with this group: take them through the problems step by step, give guidance and discuss their strategies.

More able: Provide the version with more complex quantities.

Plenary & assessment

Invite some children to explain how they solved their problems. Question them carefully about the steps they used and why they chose particular strategies. Ask how they could check their answers. Encourage them to think about using the inverse operation. Demonstrate this using arrow diagrams (see Autumn term, Units 2 and 10).

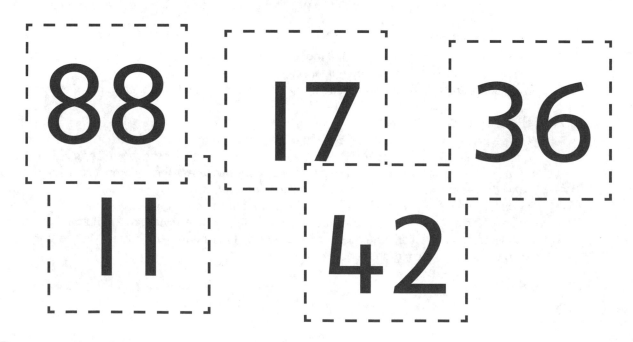

Name   Date

Ordering money and lengths

1. Mark these on the number line.

50p   30p   10p   90p   70p   25p   75p   55p

0   20p   40p   60p   80p   £1

2. Mark these on the number line.

30cm   90cm   10cm   50cm   70cm   65cm   15cm   95cm

0   20   40   60   80   1m

3. Mark these on the number line.

75p   20p   5p   80p   45p   10p   35p   60p

0   £1

4. Mark these on the number line.

15cm   30cm   60cm   55cm   95cm   25cm   5cm   65cm

0   1m

5. Try these!

£1   £5   £3   £7   £4.50   £8.50   £1.50   £6.50

0   £2   £4   £6   £8   £10

| Name | Date |

Measures and money problems

Solve these problems.

Show what you did.

For example:

Ben found some string.

He found 8cm in his cupboard.

He found 7cm under his bed.

He wanted 20cm. How much more did he need?

I did this: 5 + 3 + 5 + 2 = 10 + 5 = 15

15 to 20 is 5.

My answer is: 5cm

Now you try:

Sally found some ribbon.

She found 18cm in her cupboard.

She found 19cm in her pocket.

She wanted 50cm.

How much more did she need?

I did this:

My answer is:

Tyrone spent 75p on some rope and 90p on some string.

He gave the shop keeper £5.

How much change did he need?

I did this:

My answer is:

Hyatt found some ribbon.

She found 29cm in her bedroom.

She found 39cm in her pocket.

She used 60cm.

How much did she have left over?

I did this:

My answer is:

Kulvinder bought 5 metres of rope.

The rope cost 50p a metre.

He had £2.

How much more money did he need?

I did this:

My answer is:

Shelley needed 1m of wool.

Her mother gave her a piece 30cm long.

Her sister gave her a piece 49cm long.

How much more did she need?

I did this:

My answer is:

Multiplication and division and problem solving

In this unit the children will focus on multiplication and division. They will rehearse and practise what they did last term and then apply their learning to problem-solving situations. They will also think about the stages in which a problem is solved.

LEARNING OBJECTIVES

	Topics	Starter	Main teaching activities
Lesson 1	Understanding multiplication and division	● **Read and write whole numbers to at least 100 in figures and words.**	● **Understand the operation of multiplication as repeated addition or as describing an array**, and begin to understand division as grouping (repeated subtraction) or sharing. ● Use and begin to read the related vocabulary. ● Use ×, ÷ and = signs to record mental calculations in a number sentence, and recognise the use of a symbol such as □ or △ to stand for an unknown number.
Lesson 2	Understanding multiplication and division	● Know by heart multiplication facts for the 2 and 10 times-tables. ● Derive quickly division facts for the 2 and 10 times-tables.	As for Lesson 1.
Lesson 3	Understanding multiplication and division	● Know by heart all pairs of numbers with a total of 20 (e.g. 13 + 7, 6 + 14).	As for Lesson 1.
Lesson 4	Problems involving 'real life', money or measures Reasoning about numbers or shapes Making decisions Mental calculation strategies (× and ÷)	● Know by heart all pairs of numbers with a total of 20 (e.g. 13 + 7, 6 + 14). ● Know by heart all pairs of multiples of 10 with a total of 100 (e.g. 30 + 70).	● Use mental addition and subtraction, simple multiplication and division to solve simple word problems involving numbers in 'real life', money or measures, using one or two steps. ● **Explain how a problem was solved** orally and, where appropriate, in writing. ● **Choose and use appropriate operations and efficient calculation strategies** (e.g. mental, mental with jottings) **to solve problems.** ● Use known number facts and place value to carry out simple multiplications and divisions.

Lessons

Preparation

Photocopy 'Multiplication and division vocabulary' onto card and cut out the words. Photocopy the 'Home we go!' gameboard onto card and laminate for each group of three children. Make a pack of 0–30 number cards for each group. Make an A3 copy of 'Flip-flap for 20'.

Learning objectives

Starter
- **Read and write whole numbers to at least 100 in figures and words.**
- **Know by heart multiplication facts for the 2 and 10 times-tables.**
- Derive quickly division facts for the 2 and 10 times-tables.
- Know by heart all pairs of numbers with a total of 20 (e.g. 13 + 7, 6 + 14).

Main teaching activities
- **Understand the operation of multiplication as repeated addition or as describing an array,** and begin to understand division as grouping (repeated subtraction) or sharing.
- Use and begin to read the related vocabulary.
- Use ×, ÷ and = signs to record mental calculations in a number sentence, and recognise the use of a symbol such as □ or △ to stand for an unknown number.

Vocabulary

lots of, groups of, times, multiply, multiplied by, multiple of, repeated addition, array, row, column, equal groups of, repeated subtraction, divide, divided by

You will need:
Photocopiable pages
'Array for maths!' (page 130) and 'Group that!' (page 131) for each child.

CD pages
0–30 number cards for each group, 'Spider charts for multiplying' and 'Spider charts for dividing', 'Multiplication and division vocabulary' cards, an A3 copy of 'Flip-flap for 20' (see General resources, Autumn term), 'Home we go!' gameboard and instructions for each group; 'Array for maths!' and 'Group that!', less able and more able versions (Spring term, Unit 10) (see General resources).

Equipment
Whiteboards and pens; Multilink or cubes; counters; number lines; a pendulum.

Lesson

Starter

Ask the children to write single-digit and two-digit numbers on their whiteboards. Show them number cards and ask them to write these as words. Then say: *Write 2. Make it say 22. Now add 10.* (32) *Change the 2 to a 7. What number do you have now?* (37) *Add 3.* (40) *Take away two tens.* (20) *Add 100.* (120) *Double the tens number.* (140) *Add 9. What number do you have now?* (149) *Write the number in words.* Repeat several times.

Main teaching activities

Whole class: This week the children will be learning about multiplication and division. Revise the meaning of 'multiply' and 'divide', and ask for related vocabulary. Use the vocabulary cards to reinforce or share the words. Sort the words into two groups: multiplication and division. Say: *Today we will be concentrating on the words 'repeated addition', 'repeated subtraction', 'arrays' and 'groups'.* Write the number 6 on the board. Ask someone to draw an array of six dots. You may need to demonstrate. Ask the class how the array can be recorded as a number sentence: 2 + 2 + 2 = 6

Explain that this repeated addition can be written as 2 × 3 = 6 (three groups of two). Link this to the 2 times-table by counting 2, 4, 6 on fingers. Ask whether there is another way of making an array. Link this to the 3 times-table by counting 3, 6… using fingers. Repeat with two arrays for 10 (5 × 2 and 2 × 5). Ask the children to draw arrays of 8 on their whiteboards and write number sentences. Ask those that do this quickly to try 12. Can they find more than two arrays?

Paired work: Ask the children to work in pairs to make arrays and derive two number sentences from each array. Model the example from the 'Array for maths!' activity sheet.

Differentiation

Less able: Provide the version of 'Array for maths!' with lower numbers. If possible, ask a teaching assistant to work with these children. Let them make the arrays with counters before drawing them.
More able: Provide the version that asks for three different arrays for 24.

Plenary & assessment

Invite one pair to draw and explain one of their arrays. Use their work to introduce division in terms of grouping or repeated subtraction. (Note: an example of division by grouping is: *I have eight sweets and I put them in bags with two in each.* An example of division by sharing is: *I have eight sweets and I share them equally with my friend.*) Explain that since division is the opposite of multiplication and multiplication is repeated addition, division must be repeated subtraction. If the children's example is 3 × 4, explain that if four groups of 3 are 12, then to divide you can take away four groups of 3 from 12. Draw the groups on the board (see left). Record this as 12 ÷ 3 = 4. Use an array to show that if 2 × 5 = 10 then 10 ÷ 2 = 5.

Lesson

Starter

Practise saying the 2 and 10 times-tables, then use the class spider charts to ask for random facts. Count in multiples of 2 and 10 using fingers, saying 'Stop' at certain points and asking the children how many lots of 2 or 10 make that number. For example: *2, 4, 6, 8, 10, 12, Stop! How many fingers are you holding up? So how many twos make 12?*

Main teaching activities

Whole class: Recap on arrays and the link to division. Start with the example from the Plenary of Lesson 1, using cubes or similar objects to demonstrate. Say: *I have 12 cubes and I am going to divide them into groups of 4. Here's one group of 4. Salman, you hold them. Here's another. Sue, you hold these. And here is another, which I will hold. How many groups of 4 have I got? Yes, three. So 12 divided by 4 is 3, which we can record as 12 ÷ 4 = 3.* Repeat with other numbers and divisors, such as 12 ÷ 3 = 4, 12 ÷ 2 = 6 and 12 ÷ 6 = 2. Use the children in your demonstrations and ask questions: *What am I dividing by? How many are there in each group? How many groups have I taken away? How can I record that?* Demonstrate by recording:12 ÷ 4.
Individual work: Ask the children to practise dividing by grouping. Distribute the 'Group that!' activity sheet and check that they understand what to do.

1 group   **2 groups**   **3 groups**

Differentiation

Less able: Provide the version of 'Group that!' with numbers to 12.
More able: Provide the version where the children have to draw the arrays.

Plenary & assessment

Ask one child from each group to show the class an example of their work. Take an example such as 12 ÷ 2 and explain that we can also say this as 'How many twos make 12?' and that our times-table knowledge can help us to work out divisions. Show a few examples, such as: 8 divided by 2 is four groups (8 − 2 − 2 −2 −2). *How many twos make 8?* Answer is four (2 + 2 + 2 + 2).Draw the groupings on the board, then count up in twos using your fingers.

Lesson ③

Starter

Use the A3 copy of 'Flip-flap for 20'. Show some ladybirds and ask the children to write on their whiteboards how many more they need to make 20. Ask more able children to write this as a calculation (such as 13 + 7 = 20). Give less able children a 0–20 number line to help them. Repeat for most of the numbers to 20. Now use a pendulum: as it swings one way, you call out a number; as it swings the other way, the children call out its complement to make 20.

Main teaching activities

Whole class: Write 18 ÷ 2 on the board and ask: *How can we answer this? Let's work out 18 ÷ 2 by counting in twos together, using our fingers: 2, 4, 6… 18. How many twos is that? How many fingers?* (9) *Try 15 ÷ 3. What should we count in this time?* (threes) Ask similar questions for the children to answer on their whiteboards. Make the divisors the numbers they have counted in steps of: 2, 3, 4, 5 and 10.
Group work: Ask the children to practise this by playing a game in groups of three or four. Model the 'Home we go!' game.

Differentiation

Less able: Let these children use number lines, counters or pennies to help them group. Adult support would be helpful.
More able: Encourage these children to record their work like this: '12 ÷ 3 is 4 groups of 3' and '15 ÷ 2 is 7 groups of 2 and 1 left over'.

Plenary & assessment

Play 'Home we go!' in two teams. Make sure everyone counts. Use this as an opportunity to bring in remainders very briefly. For example, with 11 ÷ 3, count in threes: 3, 6, 9, 12. 11 is higher than 9, but lower than 12. Draw 11 dots on the board and say: *We can get three groups of 3 from 11, but then we have two left over. So we can say that 11 ÷ 3 is 3 remainder 2.* (See figure below.) This is mainly for more able children.

Lessons ④

Learning objectives
Starter
- Know by heart all pairs of numbers with a total of 20 (e.g. 13 + 7, 6 + 14).
- Know by heart all pairs of multiples of ten with a total of 100 (e.g. 30 + 70).

Main teaching activities
- Use mental addition, and subtraction, simple multiplication and division, to solve simple word problems involving numbers in 'real life', money or measures, using one or two steps.
- **Explain how a problem was solved** orally and, where appropriate, in writing.
- **Choose and use appropriate operations and efficient calculation strategies** (e.g. mental, mental with jottings) **to solve problems.**
- Use known number facts and place value to carry out simple multiplications and divisions.

Vocabulary
lots of, groups of, times, multiply, multiplied by, multiple of, repeated addition, array, row, column, equal groups of, repeated subtraction, divide, divided by

You will need:
CD pages
An A3 copy of 'How to solve a problem' (see General resources, Autumn term), 'Flip-flap for 10' for each child, plus one A3 copy, an OHT of the 'Party problems example', 'Party problems 1', '2' and '3' (General resources).

Equipment
Individual whiteboards and pens; items to count; an OHP; counting apparatus.

Lesson ④

Starter

Remind the children how to use a 'flip-flap' (see Autumn term, Unit 10, Lesson 4). Fold your A3 'Flip-flap for 10' so that when you hold it up towards the children, they can see one snail. Say: *If this snail represents ten snails, how many will two snails represent?* (20) *How about three?* Ask the children to write the answers on their whiteboards. Each time, ask: *How many more do I need for 100?* Use a pendulum (as in Lesson 3) to practise number bonds of multiples of 10 to 100.

Main teaching activities

Whole class: Explain that this lesson is about solving 'real-life' problems, using multiplication and division. Write the five stages of problem solving ('How to solve a problem') on the board. Show the 'How to solve a problem' poster and stick it on the wall as a constant reminder. Using the OHT of 'Party problems', work through the exemplar problem. Ask questions as you go along, such as: *What is the question? What do we need to know to find the answer? How many packets of biscuits can you see? How many biscuits are in each one? What are four lots of 10? What else do we need to find out? How many biscuits are there altogether? How did you work out the last part?*

Group work: Ask the children to work with a partner from their group. Give out the 'Party problems 1' activity sheet. Say that the children can jot down their workings on it.

Differentiation

Less able: Provide the version of 'Party problems 2' activity sheet with smaller numbers. Make counting apparatus available if needed.

More able: Provide 'Party problems 3' with larger numbers. Talk through a problem similar to question 2 on the sheet, such as: *Sam needs 17 little cakes. The shop sells them in packs of 10. How many packs does he need?* Discuss the fact that he will have to buy a second pack.

Plenary & assessment

Invite a few children, particularly any you want to assess, to explain how they solved one of their problems. Discuss and compare methods. Ask questions such as: *How did you know what was being asked? What information did you need? Explain hwo you worked it out. How did you know if you were right. What did you do if there were some things left over?*

Name   Date

Array for maths!

You will need a container of small counters.

Take the number of counters that is written in the box.
Make up an array. Draw under the number in the box.
Then draw the other array that goes with it.

Write the two number sentences for the two arrays like this:

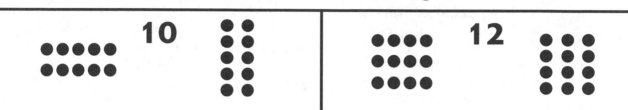

10	**12**
2 × 5 = 10 5 × 2 = 10	___ × ___ = 12 ___ × ___ = 12

15	**18**
___ × ___ = 15 ___ × ___ = 15	___ × ___ = 18 ___ × ___ = 18

12 not the same as before!	**18** not the same as before!
___ × ___ = 12 ___ × ___ = 12	___ × ___ = 18 ___ × ___ = 18

24	**24** not the same as before!
___ × ___ = 24 ___ × ___ = 24	___ × ___ = 24 ___ × ___ = 24

Now choose some more numbers up to 30.
Use them to make your own arrays on the back of this sheet.

Name	Date

Group that!

For each of these:

- Look at the number that the dots need to be divided by.
- Group the dots.
- Work out how many groups there are.
- Complete the number sentence.

Here is an example:

8 ÷ 2

4 groups of 2

8 ÷ 2 = 4

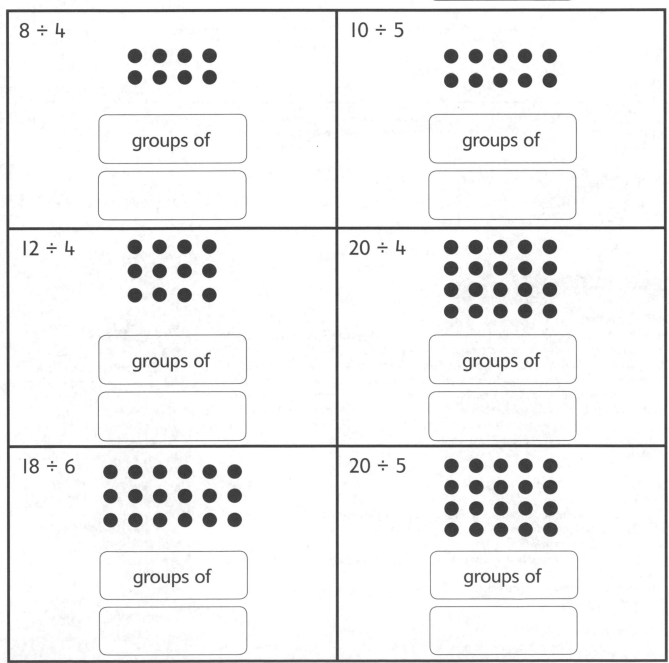

8 ÷ 4

●●●●
●●●●

groups of

10 ÷ 5

●●●●●
●●●●●

groups of

12 ÷ 4

●●●●
●●●●
●●●●

groups of

20 ÷ 4

●●●●●
●●●●●
●●●●●
●●●●●

groups of

18 ÷ 6

●●●●●●
●●●●●●
●●●●●●

groups of

20 ÷ 5

●●●●●
●●●●●
●●●●●
●●●●●

groups of

On the back of this sheet, make up some for a friend to do.

...ions and time

...on fractions, with an emphasis on halves and quarters of numbers of ... tell the time in both digital and anologue modes.

		Starter	Main teaching activities
		● **Know by heart multiplication facts for the 2 and 10 times-tables.** ● Derive quickly division facts for the 2 and 10 times-tables.	● Begin to recognise and find one half and one quarter of shapes and small numbers of objects. ● Begin to recognise that two halves or four quarters = one whole; two quarters and one half are equal.
Lesson 2	Fractions	As for Lesson 1.	As for Lesson 1.
Lesson 3	Measures	● Derive quickly doubles of all numbers to at least 15 and the corresponding halves.	● Read the time.
Lesson 4	Measures	● **State the subtraction corresponding to a given addition, and vice versa.**	As for Lesson 3.

Lessons

Preparation
Make A3 copies of 'Spider charts for multiplying' and 'Spider charts for dividing'; copy and laminate 'Small spider charts' and cut out at least two charts per child; copy and laminate the 'Spin a fraction cards', cut out the spinners. Copy 'Fraction strips' onto acetate and cut out. Make one copy of 'Pennies game', and a copy of 'Pennies recording sheet 1','2' or '3' for each child, according to ability. Copy 'Fraction number line' to A3 and laminate it; copy and laminate the 'Fraction cards'. Make some sets of the 'Spin a fraction' cards. Prepare five Multilink towers: 1) two red, one yellow and one green; 2) three red, two yellow and one green; 3) four red, two yellow and two green; 4) five red, two yellow and three green; 5) six red, three yellow and three green.

Learning objectives
Starter
● **Know by heart multiplication facts for the 2 and 10 times-tables.**
● Derive quickly division facts for the 2 and 10 times-tables.
Main teaching activities
● Begin to recognise and find one half and one quarter of shapes and small numbers of objects.
● Begin to recognise that two halves or four quarters = one whole and that two quarters and one half are equal.

Vocabulary
part, equal parts, fraction, one whole, one half, two halves, one quarter, two... three ... four quarters

You will need:
CD pages
'0–100 number cards', 'Spider charts for multiplying' and 'Spider charts for dividing', 'Small spider charts' for each child (see General resources, Autumn term), an OHT of 'Fraction strips', 'Pennies' game', 'Pennies recording sheet 1','2' or '3' 'Fraction number line and cards', 'Fraction spinner' and 'Spin a fraction' (see General resources).

Equipment
Paperclips; Multilink; counters; pennies; OHP; A4 paper.

Lesson

Starter

Count in two from zero to 20 and back. Ask the children to close their eyes as they count and imagine jumping up and down a number line. Stop them part-way along their line – say at 14 – and ask how many jumps they have made. Repeat a few times, then move on to counting in tens. Show the children the spider chart for multiplying by 2. Recap on how it is used. Now show the spider chart for dividing by 2 and ask: *What would you multiply 2 by to get the numbers around the outside? If I pointed to 18, what would you say?* (9) *Point to random numbers.* Now say: *When I point to a number, tell me what that number is divided by 2. If I pointed to 18, what would you say?* (9) *What do you notice?* Emphasise that finding what you multiply 2 by to get 18 is a way of finding 18 ÷ 2. Repeat with the 10 times-table.

Main teaching activities

Whole class: Explain that the next two lessons are about fractions. *Who can tell me things about fractions?* Write down the children's statements on the board. Look for (and if necessary, prompt) statements such as: 'a fraction is part of a whole thing'; 'half is when you divide something into two equal parts'; 'a quarter is when you divide something into four equal parts'; 'two halves or four quarters make a whole'; 'one quarter is half of a half'; 'three quarters is a half plus one quarter'.

Use the 'Fraction strips' OHT to demonstrate these relationships. Ask questions as you do this. Put four counters on the 'whole' strip. Give another four to a volunteer to put correctly on the 'halves' strip (two in each section), and to another volunteer to put on the 'quarters' strip. Repeat with eight counters, then 12, 16 and 20. Now try ten counters. What happens? Ask the children to say another number that can only be divided into halves. Ask them to say a number that can only be divided into quarters and not into halves. Can they explain why this is impossible?

Group work: Ask the children to practise finding fractions of numbers by playing 'Spin a fraction'.

Differentiation

Less able: These children can use the number spinner and find halves only.

More able: These children can use the fraction spinner and the 'Spin a fraction cards'. You could also ask them to record their work (for example: $\frac{1}{4}$ of 36 = 9).

Plenary & assessment

Show the Multilink towers and plain paper. Make statements, asking the children to tell you whether they are true or false. Each time, ask them to explain their response. First, take a sheet of paper and fold it once, but not in half. Say: *I have folded this sheet of paper in half. True or false?* Here are some other statements you can make: *I am folding this paper into four equal pieces, so I have folded it in half.* (F) 1. *One quarter of this tower is yellow.* (T) *Three quarters are a mixture of red and green.* (T) 2. *One quarter of this tower is green.* (F) *One half is yellow.* (F) 3. *One quarter of this tower is green.* (T) *Half is red.* (T) 4. *One quarter of this tower is red.* (F) *Half is made up from the yellow and green cubes.* (T) 5. *The red and yellow cubes make up three quarters of this tower.* (T) *The green makes up one half.* (F)

Lesson ②

Starter
Give the children their own small spider charts. They should work with a partner. One child does what you did in Lesson 1 (which you may need to model) and the other responds. After a couple of turns, they swap roles.

Main teaching activity
Whole class: Ask the children to tell you all they can about fractions. Compare this with what they said at the start of Lesson 1. Are they more confident? Explain that they are going to practise working out halves and quarters and looking for patterns.
Paired work: Model the 'Pennies game' using the instructions on the CD page. Let the children play Version 1 in pairs, taking pennies from a pile of up to 40.

Differentiation
Less able: These children can play Version 2, taking pennies from a pile of up to 20.
More able: These children can take pennies from a pile of up to 80.

Plenary & assessment
Discuss the game. Did any children notice which numbers could be divided into halves and quarters? Look for the answer: multiples of 4. Show the children the 'Fraction number line' and ask them to place some of the fraction cards correctly on the line. Discuss where each card should go and what clues the number line provides.

Lessons ③ ④ overview

Preparation
If necessary: copy and laminate the gameboard and copy and cut out the cards and spinners from 'Dartboard doubles' game; copy the 'Up the mountain' gameboard onto A3, and make a laminated A4 copy on card for each group of four; copy and laminate the 'Analogue and digital time cards' and 'Addition and subtraction cards'. Copy 'Get on the bus!' onto A3 or an OHT.

Learning objectives
Starter
● Derive quickly doubles of all numbers to at least 15 and the corresponding halves.
● **State the subtraction corresponding to a given addition, and vice versa.**
Main teaching activities
● Read the time.

Vocabulary
time, month, year, weekend, second, minute, hour, half an hour, quarter of an hour, digital, analogue, clock, watch, hands, January, February… fortnight, yesterday, today, tomorrow, now, soon, early, late, takes less time, takes longer, how long ago?, how long will it be to…?, o'clock, half past, quarter to, quarter past

You will need:
CD pages
An A3 copy of 'Up the mountain' gameboard and a copy for each group, plus 'Up the mountain 2', time vocabulary cards from 'Measures vocabulary', 'Dartboard doubles' game, 'Analogue and digital time cards' (see General resources, Autumn term), 'Addition and subtraction cards' (see General resources).

Equipment
Individual whiteboards and pens; an analogue card clock for each child; a real digital clock; dice; counters. The NNS ITP *Tell the Time* would be useful.

Lesson 3

Starter

Play the 'Dartboard doubles' game. Adapt the instructions for the class to play in two or three teams.

Main teaching activities

Whole class: Explain that the next two lessons are about time. Give each child a card clock. Ask the children to give you some facts about it. Look for: 'The numbers going round from 1 to 12 show us what the hour is' 'The minute hand shows us parts of an hour, such as 'o'clock' (hand on 12), 'half past' (hand on 6), 'quarter past' (hand on 3) or 'quarter to' (hand on 9)'; 'The little marks in between the numbers are minutes; there are five minutes from one number to the next.'

Ask the children to put a finger on the 12, then move to the 1. *How many minutes is that?* Carry on so the children are counting in fives. Ask them to put the hour hand on the 12. Count round in fives again; when you reach 3, ask how many minutes past the o'clock that is. Write on the board '15 minutes past 12'. Ask them how else we can say that, reminding them that the minute hand has gone a quarter of the way round. (Quarter past 12.) Show the digital clock and say: H*ow would you see this time on a digital clock or a video/DVD recorder? The hour number goes first and then the number of minutes past, so you will see 12:15.* Repeat this for 30 minutes past 12, 45 minutes past 12 and 1 o'clock. Link quarter past 12 to 12:15, and link 15 to three lots of 5, or 3 × 5.

Call out analogue and digital times for the children to show on their clocks, such as: *3:45, quarter past 6, 2:30, 15 minutes past 11.* Divide the class into two teams to play 'Up the mountain'. Call out a time, wait until everyone has shown it (the children can help each other) and then throw a dice. If an even number is thrown, the first team moves up the mountain; if an odd number is thrown, the second team moves. Expecting all the children to show the time will ensure that they all participate.

Plenary & assessment

Ask the children to show you how confident they are with times by showing a thumbs up, down or level sign. Talk about the vocabulary of time. Show the time vocabulary cards or write them on the board, asking the children to explain what they mean.

Lesson 4

Starter

Show the 'Addition and subtraction cards' and ask the children to write the corresponding addition or subtraction. For example, if you show 12 + 7 = 19 they should write 19 – 7 = 12. Ask them to explain their responses and demonstrate with jumps of 1 along a number line.

Main teaching activities

Whole class: Recap Lesson 3 and ask the children to play 'Up the mountain' again to help them practise finding analogue and digital times.
Group work: Put the children into mixed-ability groups of four to play as two pairs. Model the game using the appropriate instructions.

Plenary & assessment

Ask the children to give a thumbs-up sign if they think they can find times more quickly now than they could before. Make a note of any who cannot, so that you can target them specifically with oral and mental starter activities related to time. Set the children some problems that they can answer using their clocks, such as: *My clock says 3 o'clock, but it is one hour slow. Show me what time it really is. My clock says half past seven, but it is half an hour fast. What time is it really?*

Data handling

In this unit the children will be revisiting work on lists, pictograms and block graphs. They will be analysing and interpreting them and devising questions to ask. As a progression they will then construct their own.

LEARNING OBJECTIVES

	Topics	Starter	Main teaching activities
Lesson 1	Organising and using data	Read the time to the hour, half hour or quarter hour.	Solve a given problem by sorting, classifying and organising information in simple ways. Discuss and explain results.
Lesson 2	Organising and using data	Count on in steps of 3, 4 or 5 to at least 30, from and back to zero.	As for Lesson 1.
Lesson 3	Organising and using data	Say the number that is 1 or 10 more or less than any given two-digit number.	As for Lesson 1.
Lesson 4	Fractions	**Know by heart all addition and subtraction facts for each number to at least 10.**	As for Lesson 1.
Lesson 5	Mental calculation strategies (+ and –)	Know by heart multiplication facts for the 2 and 10 times-tables. Derive quickly division facts for the 2 and 10 times-tables.	As for Lesson 1.

Lessons overview

Preparation
Make an A3 copy of the 'Up the mountain' gameboard. Copy 'Organising data vocabulary cards' onto A3 card and cut out. Make OHTs of 'Ways to organise data', 'Pictograms' and 'Sports block graph'. Draw smiley faces on some Post-it Notes. On squared paper, draw horizontal and vertical axes and label them 'Number of children' and 'Colour of paint' respectively, with the title 'Which colour?' Prepare another A1 sheet with vertical and horizontal axes, labelled 'Number of children' and 'Favourite sport', the numbers 1–20 on the vertical axis and the title 'Favourite sports'.

Learning objectives
Starter
- Read the time to the hour, half hour or quarter hour.
- Count on in steps of 3, 4 or 5 to at least 30, from and back to zero.
- Say the number that is 1 or 10 more or less than any given two-digit number.
- **Know by heart all addition and subtraction facts for each number to at least 10.**
- **Know by heart multiplication facts for the 2 and 10 times-tables.**
- Derive quickly division facts for the 2 and 10 times-tables.
Main teaching activities
- Solve a given problem by sorting, classifying and organising information in simple ways.
- Discuss and explain results.

Vocabulary
count, tally, sort, vote, graph, block graph, pictogram, represent, group, set, list label, title, most popular, least popular, most common, least common

You will need:
Photocopiable pages
'Lists and tables' (page 140), and 'Our sports graph' (page 141) for each child.

CD pages
'0–100 number cards', 'Up the mountain' gameboard, 'Function machine game' for each child, 'Organising data vocabulary cards', acetates of 'Ways to organise data', 'Pictograms' and 'Sports block graph' (see General resources, Autumn term), 'Lists and tables', 'Which colour?', and 'Our sports graph', less able and more able versions (Spring term, Unit 12).

Equipment
Card clocks; counters; counting stick; a pendulum; class 100 square; individual whiteboards and pens; OHP; Post-it Notes; A1 squared paper; Blu-Tack.

Lesson

Starter

Blu-Tack the 'Up the mountain' gameboard to the board. Give each child a card clock. Divide the class into two teams and play 'Up the mountain', as in Unit 11, Lessons 3 and 4. As well as asking for times such as 4 o'clock, half past seven or quarter to 6, say: *Find half past 3. Now find one hour later… half an hour earlier.*

Main teaching activities

Whole class: Remind the children of last term's work on organising and using data. Ask: *Can you remember what we mean by 'data' and 'organising and using data'? What words can we use about this topic?* Write any words they say on the board, and use the vocabulary cards to prompt when necessary. Discuss the meanings of these words. Ask who remembers the ways of organising data that they used last term. List them: counting, tallying, sorting, voting and making graphs, such as block graphs and pictograms. Explain that these are ways we can represent, group or list information. This saves us having to write lots of words, and helps us to see information easily. It also helps us to find out what things are most or least popular and common.

Show the OHTs used in the Autumn term, Unit 13 ('Ways to organise data', 'Sports block graph' and 'Pictograms') to revise the ways of organising information. For each type of display (list, table, block graph and pictogram), ask questions such as: *How is the information shown here? What does it tell us? What four things can you tell me from this table? Which is the most popular… ? Which is the least common… ? How many people were asked?*

Paired work: Ask the children to work in pairs, making a list and a table and answering some questions about them. Distribute the 'Lists and tables' activity sheet. Demonstrate how to answer the questions, using the examples provided.

Differentiation

Less able: Provide the version of 'Lists and tables' with a simpler list and table.
More able: Ask children who finish early to make up a table of other things that they like and dislike, and to write some questions about it.

Plenary & assessment

Ask a few pairs to share their work on the activity sheet. They need to explain how they decided which numbers and words to put in their list and table, and how they found the answers to the questions. Now ask other children for their own lists, tables and questions. Can the class answer these questions?

Lesson

Starter

Use the pendulum to count with the children on and back in steps of five, then three and four. Encourage them to use fingers, so that when you stop counting they can tell you how many lots of 4 (for example) make 24. Remind them that when they count from zero they are counting in 'lots of' or 'multiples of' the number. Use the counting stick to count in these steps from and back to other small numbers (for example, count in fives from 2 to 77, in threes from 5 to 35 and in fours from 7 to 47).

Main teaching activity

Whole class: The whole-class work will take one lesson and the group work another lesson. Show the 'Pictograms' OHT. Ask: *What is this called? Give me as much information from it as you can.* Tell the children that they are going to solve this problem using a pictogram: *The school caretaker needs to*

paint the door of our classroom. He has some paints in his shed, but doesn't know which colour to use. He wants your advice. We want to find out which is the most popular colour. Here are the colour choices: red, yellow, blue, brown and orange. Give the children some time to talk to a friend and discuss their favourite colour. Make a tally of their choices on the board. Say: *Each smiley face represents one child. How many faces do we need for red?* Invite some children to add the Post-it Notes to your A1 skeleton pictogram. Repeat for the other four colours.

Analyse the class pictogram with the children, asking them to tell you as many facts about it as possible, ask each other questions and come to a conclusion about which paint is most popular.

Lesson

Starter

Invite children to take turns to pick a two-digit number card from your pack, and ask the others to write on their whiteboards the number that is one or ten more or less than that number. Encourage any children who are struggling to look at the class 100 square.

Main teaching activities

Group work: Discuss and review the pictogram work in Lesson 2. Explain that today the children will be answering questions from a pictogram and making up their own. Distribute and model the 'Which colour?' sheet. The children could work in mixed-ability pairs; if you prefer them to work in ability groups, use the differentiation below.

Differentiation

Less able: Provide adult help to encourage the children to talk about the graph.
More able: Ask children who finish early to make up some questions for the class to answer.

Plenary & assessment

Work through the questions on the activity sheet. Invite a few pairs to share the pictograms they made up. Invite more able children to ask the class their questions. Finally, ask the class to make up some more questions. Assess how confidently they give correct answers.

Lesson

Starter

Write a number up to 10 on the board. Ask the children to write as many addition and subtraction facts for this number as they can in one minute (or two minutes, depending on the number). For example, given 4 they could write: $1 + 3 = 4$; $2 + 2 = 4$; $4 - 2 = 2$; $4 - 1 = 3$; $4 - 3 = 1$. Discuss their answers, taking one each from several children. Ask less able children to share their answers first.

Main teaching activity

Whole class: The whole-class work will take one lesson and the group work another lesson. Explain that the children are now going to look at block graphs. Ask: *Who can remember this?* Show the OHT of 'Sports block graph'. Ask the children to tell you as much as they can about it. Encourage them to state all possible facts. Ask children who may find this difficult first, when the more obvious facts have not been said.

If your class is quite competitive, divide them into two teams and play 'Spot the info', using the 'Up the mountain' gameboard and counters. Every time a team spots a new piece of information, they can move their counter two steps closer to the top of the mountain.

Ask the children to turn to their neighbours and discuss why this is a useful way to tell people about favourite sports. (Look for: it is a picture; it is clear and simple; it is easy to interpret.)

Now say: *We are going to make our own block graph to show our favourite sports.* Collect about six examples of sports the children like. Ask them to choose their favourite one from the list. Give them each a Post-it Note and ask them to draw a stick picture of themselves playing the sport on it. While they are doing this, write the sport names and appropriate numbers (for the vertical axis) on Post-it Notes notes.

Gather the class together. Show them your labels and numbers, and invite children to stick them onto your A1 skeleton graph. Ask them to explain why they have put them in those places. Do the other children agree? Now invite everyone to come to the front and add their stick picture to the correct column, starting from the horizontal axis. Discuss what this graph shows, and ask questions (particularly of the How many more/less… type). Encourage the class to ask each other similar questions, perhaps after talking to a friend and making up a question together. Finally, ask: *Which is the most popular sport for this class?*

Lesson

Starter

Recite the 2 and 10 times-tables with the children. Now count in multiples of 2 and 10, using fingers. Stop the children at various intervals, asking which finger they have got to and how many lots of 2 or 10 that is. Give each child a laminated 'Function machine game', pen and cloth. Ask them to write any numbers from 1 to 10 on the input side and '× 2' in the middle; then, when you say *Go*, to fill in the output side as quickly as possible. Ask them to rub out the outputs and replace × 2 with × 10, then write the new outputs. Ask children who do this quickly to repeat with × 5.

Main teaching activity

Group work: Show the class block graph from yesterday. Say: *Today you are going to make your own block graph. You need to help* (name the PE teacher) *decide what things to buy for the sports cupboard.* Model what the children must do, using large squared paper: *With your partner, you need to choose five sports that we play – or you'd like to play – at school. You need to finish a skeleton graph like the one we used yesterday* (show this) *by adding labels like this* (label the axes and fill in sports and numbers up to 9, as on the 'Our sports graph' activity sheet). Use 1–9 number cards to pick the number of children that choose each sport. *Once you have picked a card, you cannot use it again. Draw blocks of the right height for each sport – so if you pick 5, colour in five squares above that sport.*

Differentiation

Less able: Provide the version of 'Our sports graph' with pre-labelled axes and five numbers to use.
More able: Provide the version with no numbers on the graph. If you think any children may be able to draw the graph on squared paper, let them have a go.

Plenary & assessment

Ask each pair to join with another pair, share their graphs and say four facts that their graph shows. Invite some pairs to share their graphs and facts with the class. Let the more able group ask the class a few of their questions.

Recap on this unit by asking questions such as: *Why are lists, tables, pictograms and block graphs useful for showing information? What is the difference between a list and a table? What does a pictogram look like? What about a block graph?*

Name	Date

Lists and tables

Make a list of more than 5 odd numbers.

Like this: Now it's your turn. Don't use mine!

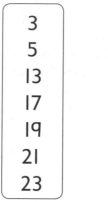

3
5
13
17
19
21
23

How many numbers are there in your list?

Which is the highest number?

Which is the lowest number?

Make a table to show the colours you both like and the colours you don't like.

Like this:

Sal likes	Rob likes	Sal doesn't like	Rob doesn't like
Red	Blue	Black	Pink
Pink	Black	Brown	Yellow
Blue	Silver	Grey	Purple
Yellow	Orange	Orange	Grey

Now you try:

_____ likes	_____ likes	_____ doesn't like	_____ doesn't like

Which colours do you both like?

Which colours do you both not like?

What are your favourite colours?

Name   Date

Our sports graph

Model this activity for the children first.

Label the side and bottom boxes. Use these words to help you:

Number of children   Sports

Choose five sports and write them in the five boxes at the bottom of the graph.
Use 1–9 number cards to pick the number of children that choose each sport.
When you have picked a card, you cannot use it again.
Colour in that number of squares above the sport.

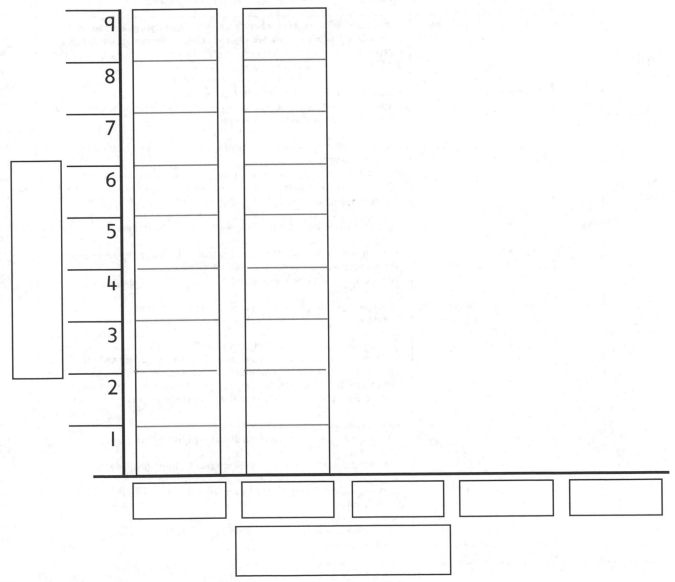

What does your graph tell you?

Write down as many points as you can on the back of this sheet.

EVERY DAY: Practise and develop oral and mental skills (e.g. counting, mental strategies, rapid recall of +, – and × facts)

- Begin to know multiplication facts for the 5 times-table.
- **State the subtraction corresponding to a given addition and vice versa.**
- Count on in steps of 3, 4 and 5 to at least 30.
- Derive quickly doubles of multiples of 5 to 50 (e.g. 20 × 2 or 35 × 2) and halves of multiples of 10 to 100 (eg half of 70).
- **Know by heart multiplication facts for the 2 and 5 times-tables.**
- Derive quickly division facts corresponding to the 2 and 10 times-tables.
- **Recognise odd and even numbers** to at least 30.
- **Know by heart all addition and subtraction facts for each number to at least 10.**
- Know by heart all pairs of numbers with a total of 20 (e.g. 13 + 7, 6 + 14) and all pairs of multiples of 10 with a total of 100.
- **Know by heart multiplication facts for the 2 and 10 times-tables.**
- Derive quickly division facts corresponding to the 2 and 10 times-tables.
- Read the time to the hour, half hour or quarter hour on an analogue clock and a 12-hour digital clock.
- Order the months of the year.
- **Use the mathematical names for common 3-D and 2-D shapes.**

Units	Days	Topics	Objectives
1	3	Counting, properties of numbers and number sequences	• **Describe and extend simple number sequences:** count on in steps of 3, 4 or 5 to at least 30, from and back to zero, then from and back to any given small number; recognise odd and even numbers to at least 30.
2–4	15	Place value and ordering	• **Read and write whole numbers to at least 100 in figures and words.** • **Know what each digit in a two-digit number represents**, including zero as a place holder, and partition two-digit numbers into a multiple of tens and ones. • Use the = sign to represent equality.
		Estimating, rounding	• Round numbers less than 100 to the nearest 10. • Use and begin to read the vocabulary of estimation and approximation; give a sensible estimate of at least 50 objects.
		Understanding addition and subtraction	• **Understand that subtraction is the inverse of addition** (subtraction reverses addition). • Use the +, – and = signs to record mental additions and subtractions in a number sentence, and recognise the use of a symbol such as □ or △ to stand for an unknown number. • Use known number facts and place value to add/subtract mentally.
		Mental calculation strategies (+ and –)	• Use mental addition and subtraction, simple multiplication and division to solve simple word problems, using one or two steps. • Explain how the problem was solved
		Problems involving 'real life', money or measures	• Recognise all coins and begin to use £.p notation for money. • Find totals, give change, and work out which coins to pay.
5–6	7	Measures, including problems	• Use and begin to read the vocabulary related to capacity. • **Estimate, measure and compare capacities, using standard units** (m, cm, kg, litre)**; suggest suitable units and equipment for such measurements.** • **Read a simple scale to the nearest labelled division, including using a ruler to draw and measure lines to the nearest centimere.**
		Shape and space	• Relate solid shapes to pictures of them. • **Use mathematical vocabulary to describe position, direction and movement**. • Know that a right angle is a measure of a quarter turn, and recognise right angles in squares and rectangles. • Give instructions for moving along a route in straight lines and round right-angled corners.
		Reasoning about numbers or shapes	• Investigate a general statement about familiar numbers or shapes by finding examples that satisfy it.
7		Assess and review	

EVERY DAY: Practise and develop oral and mental skills (e.g. counting, mental strategies, rapid recall of +, – and × facts)

- **State the subtraction corresponding to a given addition and vice versa.**
- Find one half and one quarter of small numbers.
- Add/subtract 9 or 11: add/subtract 10 or 20 and adjust by 1.
- **Read and write whole numbers to at least 100** in figures and words.
- Derive quickly doubles of multiples of 5 to 50 and halves of multiples of 10 to 100.
- Begin to know multiplication facts for the 5 times-table.
- Count on in steps of 3, 4 and 5 to at least 30.
- **Know by heart all addition and subtraction facts for each number to at least 10.**
- Know by heart all pairs of numbers with a total of 20, and multiples of 10 with a total of 100.
- Know by heart all pairs of multiples of 10 with a total of 100.
- **Know by heart multiplication facts and division facts for the 2 and 10 times-tables.**
- **Describe and extend simple number sequences.**

Units	Days	Topics	Objectives
8	3	Counting, properties of numbers and number sequences	• **Describe and extend simple number sequences**: count on in steps of 3, 4 or 5 to at least 30, from and back to zero, then from and back to any given small number.
		Reasoning about numbers or shapes	• Solve mathematical problems or puzzles, recognise simple patterns and relationships, generalise and predict. • **Explain how a problem was solved** orally and, where appropriate, in writing.
9–10	8	Place value and ordering	• **Order whole numbers to at least 100,** and position them on a number line and 100 square.
		Understanding + and – Mental calculation strategies (+ / –)	• Extend understanding of the operations of addition and subtraction. • Add/subtract 19 or 21.
		Understanding × and ÷	• **Know and use halving as the inverse of doubling.**
		Mental calculation strategies (× / ÷)	• Use known number facts and place value to carry out mentally simple multiplications and divisions.
		Rapid recall of + and – facts	• Know by heart all pairs of numbers with a total of 20.
		Problems involving 'real life', money and measures	• Use mental addition and subtraction, simple multiplication and division to solve simple word problems, using one or two steps. • Explain how the problem was solved. • Recognise all coins and begin to use £.p notation for money, • Find totals, give change, and work out which coins to pay.
		Making decisions	• **Explain how a problem was solved** orally and in writing. • **Choose and use appropriate operations and efficient calculation strategies.**
11	5	Understanding × and ÷	• Know and use halving as the inverse of doubling.
		Mental calculation strategies (× / ÷)	• Use known number facts and place value to carry out mentally simple multiplications and divisions.
		Making decisions	• Recognise all coins and begin to use £.p notation for money. • Find totals, give change, and work out which coins to pay. • Explain how a problem was solved, orally and in writing.
12–13	10	Measures	• Suggest suitable units to estimate or measure time. • Read the time to the hour, half hour or quarter hour on an analogue clock and a 12-hour digital clock, and understand the notation 7:30.
		Organising and using data	• Solve a given problem by sorting, classifying and organising information in simple ways, such as: in a list or simple table; in a pictogram; in a block graph. • Discuss and explain results.
13		Assess and review	

Number sequences

This unit focuses on counting in multiples of the numbers 2, 3, 4, 5 and 10. The children will need to think of what steps to count in from zero to get to different numbers. They also will be considering multiples of 2, 5 and 10 and odd and even numbers.

LEARNING OBJECTIVES

		Topics	Starter	Main teaching activities
Lesson	1	Counting, properties of numbers and number sequences	● Begin to know multiplication facts for the 5 times-table.	● **Describe and extend simple number sequences**: count on in steps of 3, 4 or 5 to at least 30, from and back to zero, then from and back to any given small number.
Lesson	2	Counting, properties of numbers and number sequences	● Read the time to the hour, half hour or quarter hour on an analogue clock. ● Count on in steps of 5 to at least 30.	As for Lesson 1.
Lesson	3	Counting, properties of numbers and number sequences	● Derive quickly doubles of multiples of 5 to 50 (e.g. 20 × 2 or 35 × 2).	● **Describe and extend simple number sequences: recognise odd and even number**s to at least 30.

Lessons overview

Preparation
If necessary, copy and laminate the gameboard and cards for the 'Count it!' game.

Learning objectives
Starter
● Begin to know multiplication facts for the 5 times-table.
● Read the time to the hour, half hour or quarter hour on an analogue clock.
● Count on in steps of 5 to at least 30.
● Derive quickly doubles of multiples of 5 to 50 (e.g. 20 × 2 or 35 × 2).

Main teaching activities
● **Describe and extend simple number sequences**:
 – count on in steps of 3, 4 or 5 to at least 30, from and back to zero, then from and back to any given small number
 – recognise odd and even numbers to at least 30.

Vocabulary
two hundred… one thousand, count on, count back, count in ones/tens, odd, even, multiple of, sequence, continue, predict, count, tally, how many… ?

You will need:
Photocopiable pages
'Jump to it!' (page 147), and 'Odd or even?' (page 148) for each child.

CD pages
'0–100 number cards' (see General resources, Autumn term), 'Count it!' gameboard and cards (see General resources, Spring term), OHT of 'Spider charts for ×5 and ÷5', 'Jump to it!' and 'Odd or even?' less able and more able versions (see Summer term, Unit 1) (see General resources).

Equipment
An OHP; counters; a card clock for each child; a pot of coins to 20p; Unifix or similar cubes; individual whiteboards.

Lesson

Starter

Count together in fives, using fingers. Stop at various points to ask the children how many fingers they are holding up and how many lots of 5 they have. Project 'Spider charts for ×5 and ÷5' and and use it to revise 5 times-table facts.

Main teaching activities

Whole class: This lesson and Lesson 2 are about counting on in steps of 3, 4 and 5. Ask the class to count in threes, fours and fives from zero, then from 1 and 2. Play a whole-class collaborative game of 'Count it!', as in Spring term, Unit 8, Lesson 3. After about five minutes, finish the game and count the money earned. Encourage the children to look for 10p, 5p and 2p pieces, then for groups of pennies that total any of those coins, and to add these first.

Write the number 6 on the board. Ask the children what steps they could count in from zero to reach 6. Look for the answers 3 and 2. For each answer they give, count in steps of that number from zero to check that they are right. Repeat for 12 (look for the answers 2, 3 and 4). Now ask about both 6 and 12; look for the answers 2 and 3. Ask: *Why not 4?* (6 is not in the fours pattern/not a multiple of 4.)

Paired work: Give pairs the 'Jump to it!' activity sheet. Explain the activity, which is similar to the class work. The children have to find numbers that they can count in to reach the target numbers on the sheet, drawing the jumps along the number lines.

Differentiation

Less able: Provide the version of 'Jump to it!' with lower totals.
More able: Provide the version with higher totals and a further challenge. Encourage the children to tell you that the solution to the challenge must end in 5 or 0 to be in the fives sequence, and must be even to be in the fours sequence, so it must end in 0. The answer is 60.

Plenary & assessment

Discuss the challenge, asking some more able children how they found the answer. Make the link between the number of jumps from zero and multiplication. For example, ask the children what steps they can count in to get to 12. Draw jumps of 2, 3 and 4 on 0–12 number lines. Help the children to see that six jumps of two reach 12, so two times 6 is 12 or 2 × 6 = 12. Repeat for 3 × 4 and 4 × 3.

Lesson

Starter

Give the children a card clock each. Ask: *How many minutes are there from one number to the next?* Count in lots of 5 minutes around the clock. Ask the children what they notice. Look for the answer that the hour numbers multiplied by 5 give the numbers of minutes. Point to the 3: *How many minutes would that be past an o'clock time? How could you work it out quickly? How many minutes from o'clock to the 4… the 6… the 8?* Look at the number of minutes between hour numbers, such as from 4 to 9 or 2 to 7. Ask the children to show you 15 minutes past 7, 45 minutes past 2, 30 minutes past 1, no minutes past 8 and so on. Each time, ask how they know. Encourage them to refer to 5 times-table facts.

Main teaching activities

Whole class: This lesson is about counting on in steps of 3, 4 and 5 from different numbers. Practise counting in these steps from numbers such as 1, 2 and 4. Ask what steps the children can count in to get from 2 to 12 (fives) and from 3 to 19 (fours). Demonstrate using a number line as in Lesson 1.
Group work: Write some different number ranges on the 'Jump to it!' template, e.g. 0–20, 2–20, 6–21, 8–32 and 7–31. The children count on in steps of 3, 4 and 5 to find if they land on a target number, e.g. 13, 15, 26, 32 and 31.

Differentiation

Less able: Provide the template sheet 'Jump to it!' with lower totals and number lines, e.g. 1–20 [to jump to 13], 1–20 [7], 2–20 [8], 2–20 [17] and 4–20 [20]. Adult help will be useful, especially at the start.
More able: Provide a template where some questions require two answers, and there is a further challenge, for example, number lines 1–20 [jump to 13], 2–20 [15], 5–31 [31], 8–32 [32] and 7–31 [31].

Plenary & assessment

Work through some of the questions. Discuss the challenge; draw the number line and the jumps. Ask the class what they notice about sequences like this. (Counting in threes gives numbers that are odd, even, odd, even and so on; counting in fours gives numbers that are always odd or even; counting in fives gives a pattern where the last digit is repeated every other number.) Ask: *Are these multiples of 3, 4 and 5? Why not?* (Multiples must start from zero.)

Lesson ③

Starter

Count in fives to 50. Ask for two volunteers to call out the multiples of 5 in turn to 50; ask the rest of the class to write down on their whiteboards the double of each number called out. Ask the class how they worked out each answer. Encourage recall, counting on or partitioning and recombining.

Main teaching activities

Whole class: Hold up two single-digit number cards and ask the class to say as many differences between them as possible. Focus on odd and even numbers. Ask: *Can you remember what makes a number odd or even?* Show two towers of Unifix cubes or similar, one with eight cubes and the other with nine. Ask: *What will happen if I split the even tower into two?* (Each new tower will have the same number of cubes.) *What will happen if I split the odd tower into two?* (One tower will have one more cube.) Demonstrate again with towers of 10 and 13 cubes, then 11 and 14. Ask: *What can you tell me about an even/odd number now?* (It can/cannot be divided equally into two halves.)
Group work: Give out the 'Odd or even?' gameboard and recording sheet. Model the game.

Differentiation

Less able: Provide the gameboard with lower numbers.
More able: Provide the gameboard with higher numbers and different rules.

Plenary & assessment

Ask the children for examples of odd and even numbers. Can they explain how they know whether a number is odd or even? Ask them to demonstrate with cubes.

Name	Date

Jump to it!

Can you count in 3s, 4s and 5s to these numbers?

Start from zero each time.

Draw your jumps on the number lines.

For example: 20

I can count in 4s and 5s.

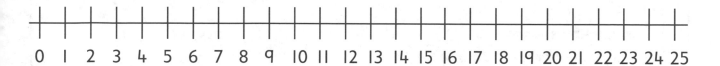

0 1 2 3 4 5 6 7 8 9 10 11 12 13 14 15 16 17 18 19 20 21 22 23 24 25

Now you try: 12

I can count in

0 1 2 3 4 5 6 7 8 9 10 11 12 13 14 15 16 17 18 19 20 21 22 23 24 25

15

I can count in

0 1 2 3 4 5 6 7 8 9 10 11 12 13 14 15 16 17 18 19 20 21 22 23 24 25

18

I can count in

0 1 2 3 4 5 6 7 8 9 10 11 12 13 14 15 16 17 18 19 20 21 22 23 24 25

25

I can count in

0 1 2 3 4 5 6 7 8 9 10 11 12 13 14 15 16 17 18 19 20 21 22 23 24 25

Odd or even?

Note for teacher or classroom assistant:

Model this game clearly, so the children don't need to read the instructions in order to play. Explain how to fill in the recording sheet.

You need:
- number cards to 30
- counters, one colour each.

Take turns to:
1. pick a number card
2. decide whether it is odd or even
3. make two cube towers from the number in your head and decide how many cubes are in each tower
4. fill in the recording sheet as your teacher explained
5. cover those numbers on the grid with your counters
6. play until all the numbers are covered.

The winner is the player with the most counters on the board at the end.

Example:

I picked 25. It is an odd number. My two towers have 12 cubes and 13 cubes. I can cover the numbers 12 and 13 on my grid, and write 25 on my recording sheet.

1	2	3	4	5	6
7	8	9	10	11	12
13	14	15	15	14	13
12	11	10	9	8	7
6	5	4	3	2	1

Rounding, missing numbers and the equals sign

This unit focuses on counting in multiples of the numbers 2, 3, 4, 5 and 10. The children will need to think of what steps to count in from zero to get to different numbers. They will also be considering multiples of 2, 5 and 10 and odd and even numbers.

LEARNING OBJECTIVES

		Topics	Starter	Main teaching activities
Lesson	**1**	Place value and ordering Estimating and rounding	● **Know by heart multiplication facts for the 2 and 10 times-tables.** ● Derive quickly division facts corresponding to the 2 and 10 times-tables.	● **Order whole numbers to at least 100,** and position them on a number line and 100 square. ● Round numbers less than 100 to the nearest 10.
Lesson	**2**	Estimating and rounding	● Derive quickly halves of multiples of 10 to 100 (e.g. half of 70).	● Round numbers less than 100 to the nearest 10. ● Use and begin to read the vocabulary of estimation and approximation.
Lesson	**3**	Place value and ordering	As for Lesson 2.	● **Know what each digit in a two-digit number represents, including zero as a place holder,** and partition two-digit numbers into a multiple of tens and ones. ● Use the = sign to represent equality.
Lesson	**4**	Understanding addition and subtraction	● Know by heart all pairs of numbers with a total of 20 (e.g. 13 + 7, 6 + 14). ● Know by heart all pairs of multiples of 10 with a total of 100.	● **Understand that subtraction is the inverse of addition** (subtraction reverses addition). ● Use the +, – and = signs to record mental additions and subtractions in a number sentence, and recognise the use of a symbol such as □ or △ to stand for an unknown number.
Lesson	**5**	Understanding addition and subtraction	● As for Lesson 1.	● Use the +, – and = signs to record mental additions and subtractions in a number sentence, and recognise the use of a symbol such as □ or △ to stand for an unknown number.

Lessons overview

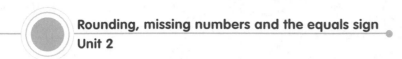

Preparation

If necessary, copy and laminate the gameboard and cards for the 'Count it!' game.

Learning objectives

Starter

- **Know by heart multiplication facts for the 2 and 10 times-tables.**
- Derive quickly division facts corresponding to the 2 and 10 times-tables.
- Derive quickly halves of multiples of 10 to 100 (e.g. half of 70).
- Know by heart all pairs of numbers with a total of 20 (e.g. 13 + 7, 6 + 14).
- Know by heart all pairs of multiples of 10 with a total of 100.

Main teaching activities

- **Order whole numbers to at least 100,** and position them on a number line and 100 square.
- Round numbers less than 100 to the nearest 10.
- Use and begin to read the vocabulary of estimation and approximation.
- **Know what each digit in a two-digit number represents, including zero as a place holder,** and partition two-digit numbers into a multiple of tens and ones.
- Use the = sign to represent equality.
- **Understand that subtraction is the inverse of addition** (subtraction reverses addition).
- Use the +, – and = signs to record mental additions and subtractions in a number sentence, and recognise the use of a symbol such as □ or △ to stand for an unknown number.

Vocabulary

two hundred… one thousand, units, ones, tens, hundreds, digit, round, more, larger, bigger, fewer, smaller, less, most, nearest, round to the nearest 10, exact, exactly, multiply, divide

You will need:

Photocopiable pages

'Lunch money' (page 154) and 'What's in the box' (page 156) for each child; 'In the balance' (page 155) and 'What am I?' (page 157) for each pair.

CD pages

'0–100 number cards', 'Arrow cards' for each less able child, 'Up the mountain' gameboard, 'Spider charts for multiplying' and 'Spider charts for dividing' (see General resources, Autumn term), 'Round it!' instructions and gameboard, 'Number words' (see General resources, Spring term), 'Time "Follow me" cards', an OHT of 'Plenary questions', and 'Lunch money', 'What's in the box?', 'In the balance' and 'What am I?', less able, more able and template versions (see Summer term, Unit 2) (see General resources).

Equipment

A class 100 square; individual whiteboards; balance scales; 1kg and two 500g weights; pendulum; an OHT.

Lesson ①

Starter

Use the spider charts for multiplication and division by 2 and 10, as before. Do this twice. Play the multiplication and division 'Follow me' game as in Spring term, Unit 2, Lesson 1, reminding the children of the rules. Record how long it takes to go round the class.

Main teaching activities

Whole class: This lesson is about ordering numbers to 100 and rounding them to the nearest 10. You will need a pile of two-digit number cards. Invite five children to pick a card each and show them to the class, who should order them from the smallest to the largest by telling the children where to stand. Repeat a few times. The last time, ask the children to find the numbers on a class 100 square. Mark these numbers. Say: *We are going to round these numbers to the nearest 10.* Remind the children how they learned to add/subtract 9 or 11 by adding/subtracting 10 and adjusting. Explain that it is useful to round to tens because these are easy numbers to work with.

Round the numbers on the class 100 square. Ask, for example: *Is 23 closer to 20 or 30?* On the 100 square, count how far 23 is from each number. Record on the board: 23 □ 20. Repeat with the other numbers. Pick more number cards and repeat several times. Hold up cards for the children to round on their whiteboards. Let children refer to the class 100 square if they need to.

Hold up a card with 5 as the 'units' digit. Ask which multiple of 10 it is closest to. Establish that it is halfway between two multiples of 10. Explain that the rule is to round numbers ending in 5 up, not down.

Group work: Explain that the children will now practise this in pairs or small groups. Demonstrate the game 'Round it!' using the instruction sheet, then distribute 'Round it! Gameboard 2'. When the children have played the game once, they should play again and record their work.

Differentiation

Less able: Give these children 'Round it! Gameboard 3', with 10 and 20 only. Ask the children to generate numbers from 10 to 19 using arrow cards.

More able: The children could try the challenge described on the instruction sheet.

Plenary & assessment

Call out random numbers for the children to round on their whiteboards. Now ask the children to talk to a partner about when they think rounding might be helpful. Take feedback; look for the idea of estimating the answer to a calculation (for example, when adding up prices in a shop).

Lesson

Starter

Use the 'Up the mountain' gameboard for a whole-class game to practise halving multiples of 10 to 100. Follow the instructions for this lesson, given on the activity sheet.

Main teaching activities

Whole class: Ask the children what they learned in Lesson 1. Call out a few numbers for them to round on their whiteboards. Include numbers that end in 5. Ask why it can be useful to round. Recap on adding or subtracting 10 and adjusting as a strategy for adding or subtracting 9 or 11. Move on to estimating the answers to problems through rounding: *Imagine I am in a shop and I have 30p. I would like to buy three chews. They cost 9p each. Do I have enough money? How can I decide quickly?* Ask the children to talk to each other and come up with suggestions. Discuss how useful this strategy is for shopping. Give another example: *I am in the shop and I have 50p. I want to buy a bag of crisps for 32p and a can of cola for 29p. Have I got enough money?* Ask the children what they think, then work through the problem on the board. Repeat with two or three more problems from 'Lunch money'.

Group work: Demonstrate how to complete the rest of 'Lunch money'. Emphasise that the children do not need to calculate the exact answers, only estimate the answers by rounding.

Differentiation

Less able: Provide the version of 'Lunch money' with smaller amounts. The children should work in pairs.

More able: Provide the version where the full calculation is used to check.

Plenary & assessment

Invite some children to explain how they made their estimations. Make sure every problem done is covered. Check each estimate by working out the answer. Allow the children to mark their work and write the answer.

Lesson ③

Starter

Repeat the Starter from Lesson 2, but offer bonus points for telling you a quarter of the number as well as half. You may need to remind the children that a quarter is half of a half, and encourage them to find a quarter by halving and halving again.

Main teaching activities

Whole class: Say that this lesson is about the special jobs of zero and the equals sign. Write the number 25 on the board. Ask the children to partition 25 into tens and units on their whiteboards. Write 20 + 5 = 25 on the board and ask them to check they have written that. Make 25 using arrow cards; invite two children to help you. Ask the child with the 5 to move away. Say: *What is left in the place of the 5? What would the number say if the zero wasn't there? The zero holds the place for the units or ones numbers. We call it a place holder.* Repeat this with 49, 18, 67 and 34. Then write 104 on the board. Ask which number the zero is the placeholder for. Repeat with 108 and 2045.

Ask the children what the = sign means. Invite a child to draw one on the board. Many children think the = sign means 'the answer'. It is very important for them to understand that it means 'what is on one side of the = sign is the same as what is on the other side'. Demonstrate this with balance scales. Put a 1kg weight in one side and ask whether the two sides are equal. Add a 500g weight to the other side and ask whether both sides are equal now. Add another 500g weight. Write a number sentence on the board to show this: 1kg = 500g + 500g.

Write on the board: 10 + 5 = 11 + □ . Ask: *What can you put in the box to make this number sentence true? How do you know?* Encourage the children to work out the left-hand side and then decide how to make the other side the same (10 + 5 = 15, 11 + 4 = 15 so the missing number must be 4). Repeat with other numbers, with the box in different places, for example:
12 – □ = 10 – 1, 20 – 6 = □ + 4, □ + 10 = 10 x 2.
Paired work: Demonstrate the example from the 'In the balance' activity sheet. Let the children complete the sheet in pairs.

Differentiation

Less able: Provide the version of 'In the balance' with simpler calculations.
More able: Provide the version with more complex calculations.

Plenary & assessment

Invite some children to go through some of the number sentences they made equal. Write an incorrect number sentence on the board, such as: 11 + 5 = 20 – 10. Ask: *Is that correct? How can I make the two sides equal? On your whiteboards, change one of the numbers so that the number sentence is correct. Show me.* Repeat with other incorrect number sentences.

Lesson ④

Starter

Use a simple pendulum (as before) to practise number pairs to make 20 (for example, if you call out 13 the children call out 7) and pairs of multiples of 10 to make 100 (for example, 20 and 80).

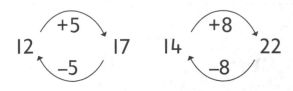

Main teaching activities

Whole class: Write these 'arrow diagrams' (see left) on the board:
Ask the children what these show. Ask them to write down two number sentences for each diagram on their whiteboards. Use the arrow diagrams to make up questions, such as: $\Box + 5 = 17$, $\Box - 5 = 12$, $14 + \Box = 22$. Ask the children to find the answers, using arrow diagrams. Repeat with several similar examples, including higher two-digit numbers.
Group work: Distribute the 'What's in the box?' activity sheet and model the example, then let the children complete the sheet.

Differentiation

Less able: Present the version of the activity sheet with lower totals.
More able: Present the version with higher totals.

Plenary & assessment

Project the OHT of 'Plenary questions'. Work through these SATs-type problems. Ask the children such questions as: *What do you need to do here? What strategy can you use to help you?*

Lesson ⑤

Starter

Repeat the Starter from Lesson 1. Record how long it takes to go round the class. Can the children beat their previous time?

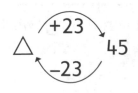

Main teaching activity

Whole class: Remind the children of the problems they solved in Lesson 4. Explain that today they will use other symbols for the missing numbers. Pick two number cards to 50 (such as 45 and 23) and make a number sentence with the $\triangle$ symbol representing the first number and the cards as the second and answer numbers. Relate this to an arrow diagram:

Ask: *What do we know that can help us?* Write these number sentences on the board:
$\triangle + 23 = 45 \qquad 45 - 23 = \triangle$

Which sentence can help us see what the triangle stands for? (The subtraction sentence.) Work through five or six examples.
Paired work: Demonstrate the 'What am I?' activity sheet. Ask pairs of children to complete it.

Differentiation

Less able: Provide the version of 'What am I?' with lower numbers.
More able: Provide the version with higher numbers.

Plenary & assessment

Ask some volunteers to share an example of their work and explain what they did.
    Look at number sentences with symbols in the middle. Write on the board: $23 + \triangle = 45$. Can the children tell you how to solve this? Ask what other sentences they can make from it. Say that because addition can be done in any order, $\triangle + 23 = 45$. Use an arrow diagram to show that $\triangle = 22$. Repeat with examples from the children's work.

| Name | Date |

Lunch money

Work in small groups of 3 or 4.

Imagine you are in a café.

Estimate whether you have enough money by rounding the prices to the nearest 10p.

> **For example:**
> I have 70p. I would like to buy a drink for 39p and a biscuit for 42p.
> Have I got enough money?
> In your head, round the amounts: 40p and 40p. Add them: 80p.   Answer: No.

I have 80p. I would like to buy chips for 51p and a drink for 43p. Have I got enough money? _____ Why?	I have £1. I would like to buy a sausage for 51p and a burger for 58p. Have I got enough money? _____ Why?
I have 90p. I would like to buy a slice of cake for 48p and a sandwich for 52p. Have I got enough money? _____ Why?	I have 80p, I would like to buy 3 fish fingers for 21p each. Have I got enough money? _____ Why?
I have £2. I would like to buy a bag of chips for 68p and a piece of fish for £1.29. Have I got enough money? _____	I have £1. I would like to buy a drink for 54p and crisps for 38p. Have I got enough money? _____

■SCHOLASTIC

photocopiable

Name   Date

In the balance

Make these balances equal.
Here's an example:

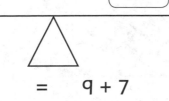

$$10 + 6 \quad = \quad 9 + \boxed{7}$$

$$16 \quad = \quad 9 + 7$$

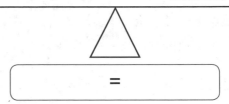

$$13 + 5 \quad = \quad 9 + \boxed{}$$

$$\boxed{\quad = \quad}$$

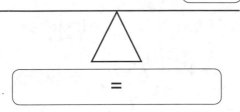

$$12 + 12 \quad = \quad 20 + \boxed{}$$

$$\boxed{\quad = \quad}$$

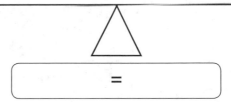

$$25 + 10 \quad = \quad 20 + \boxed{}$$

$$\boxed{\quad = \quad}$$

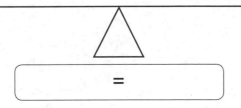

$$15 + 16 \quad = \quad 20 + \boxed{}$$

$$\boxed{\quad = \quad}$$

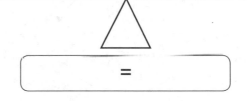

$$12 + 8 \quad = \quad 10 + \boxed{}$$

$$\boxed{\quad = \quad}$$

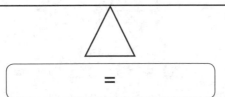

$$15 + 9 \quad = \quad 11 + \boxed{}$$

$$\boxed{\quad = \quad}$$

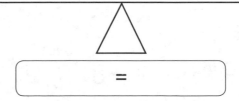

$$20 + 10 \quad = \quad 15 + \boxed{}$$

$$\boxed{\quad = \quad}$$

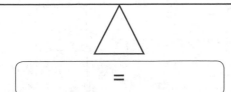

$$30 + 8 \quad = \quad 20 + \boxed{}$$

$$\boxed{\quad = \quad}$$

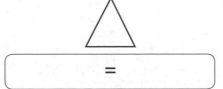

$$35 + 25 \quad = \quad 40 + \boxed{}$$

$$\boxed{\quad = \quad}$$

Name	Date

What's in the box?

Work out what number needs to go in the box.

Write down what you did to find the answer. Use the 'arrow diagram' to help you.

Here is an example:
12 + 6 = 18
I did 18 − 6 = 12 so
12 goes in the box.

$\boxed{12}$ +6 ↘ 18 −6 ↙

Now you try:

+ 9 = 15
I did: $\boxed{}$
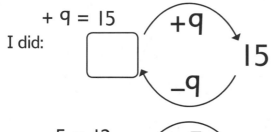

+ 17 = 28
I did: $\boxed{}$

− 5 = 12
I did: 12
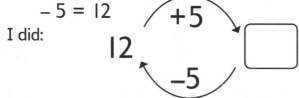

− 14 = 7
I did: 7
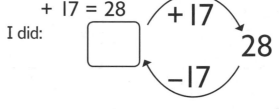

− 23 = 21
I did: 21
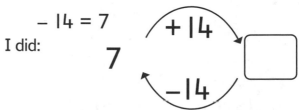

15 + ⬚ = 23
I did: 15   23

+ 13 = 27
I did: $\boxed{}$ 27

+ 15 = 31
I did: $\boxed{}$ 31

− 8 = 17
I did: 17
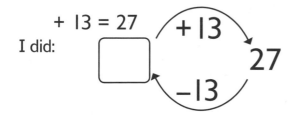

− 20 = 35
I did: 35

− 31 = 25
I did: 25
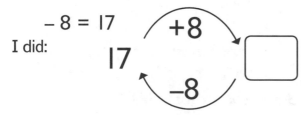

30 + ⬚ = 42
I did: 30   42

Name	Date

What am I?

Work out what number the △ stands for.

Write down what you did to find the answer. Use the 'arrow diagram' to help you.

Here is an example:

△ + 12 = 18

Number sentences:

△ + 12 = 18

18 − 12 = △

The one that helps me is:

18 − 12 = △	△ = 6

Now you try:

△ + 6 = 15

Number sentences:

△ + ___ = ___

___ − ___ = △

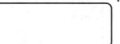

The one that helps me is:

	△ =

△ + 12 = 23

Number sentences:

△ + ___ = ___

___ − ___ = △

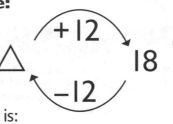

The one that helps me is:

	△ =

△ + 24 = 46

Number sentences:

△ + ___ = ___

___ − ___ = △

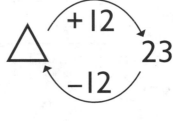

The one that helps me is:

	△ =

△ − 23 = 27

Number sentences:

△ − ___ = ___

___ + ___ = △

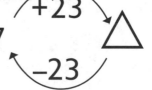

The one that helps me is:

	△ =

△ − 24 = 57

Number sentences:

△ − ___ = ___

___ + ___ = △

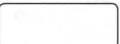

The one that helps me is:

	△ =

△ − 31 = 53

Number sentences:

△ − ___ = ___

___ + ___ = △

The one that helps me is:

	△ =

Mental calculation strategies for addition and subtraction

This unit looks at mental calculation strategies for addition and subtraction. It begins with partitioning by keeping the first numbers whole and partitioning the second, for both operations. The children then learn about using number bonds to 10 and multiples of ten to 100 as a way of helping them add. Bridging through ten, near doubles and finding the difference by counting up are also covered.

LEARNING OBJECTIVES

		Topics	Starter	Main teaching activities
Lesson	1	Mental calculation strategies (+ and –)	● **Know by heart all addition and subtraction facts for each number to at least 10.**	● Use known number facts and place value to add/subtract mentally.
Lesson	2	Mental calculation strategies (+ and –)	● **Recognise odd and even numbers** to at least 30.	As for Lesson 1.
Lesson	3	Mental calculation strategies (+ and –)	● **Know by heart multiplication facts for the 2 and 10 times-tables**.	As for Lesson 1.
Lesson	4	Mental calculation strategies (+ and –)	● **Use the mathematical names for common 3-D and 2-D shapes**. ● Describe some of their features.	As for Lesson 1.
Lesson	5	Mental calculation strategies (+ and –)	As for Lesson 4.	As for Lesson 1.

Lessons overview

Preparation

Copy 'Near doubles game' cards and 'Addition and subtraction vocabulary' cards to A3 and cut out the cards. Fill in the templates of 'Keeping it whole' appropriately for the less and more able groups. Cut out the 'Near doubles game' cards. If necessary, make and laminate a copy of the 'Lost in space and 'Recording sheet' for each group of three or fours. Make OHTs of the 'Lost in space gameboard' and 'Find the way! gameboard'. Copy both the 'Home we go!' gameboard and instructions for this unit onto A3 for each group.

Learning objectives

Starter
- **Know by heart all addition and subtraction facts for each number to at least 10.**
- **Recognise odd and even numbers** to at least 30.
- **Know by heart multiplication facts for the 2 and 10 times-tables.**
- **Use the mathematical names for common 3-D and 2-D shapes.**
- **Describe some of their features.**

Main teaching activities
- Use known number facts and place value to add/subtract mentally.

Vocabulary

add, addition, more, plus, make, sum, total, altogether, score, tens boundary, difference, subtract, subtraction, take away

You will need:

Photocopiable pages
'Keeping it whole' (page 163) and 'Number bonds' (page 164) for each child.

CD pages
'0-100 number cards', 'Spider charts for multiplying' and 'Spider charts for dividing, 'Near doubles cards' for each group, 'Addition and subtraction vocabulary' cards, (see General resources, Autumn term) 'Lost in space gameboard' and 'Lost in space recording sheet' for each group, an OHT of 'Find the way! gameboard', an A3 'Home we go!' (see General resources, Spring term), and a 'Target board 1''2' or '3' for each group; differentiated versions of 'Number bonds' less able, more able and templates versions of 'Keeping it whole' (Summer term, Unit 3) (see General resources).

Equipment
Whiteboards and pens; a class 100 square; an OHP; counters; Plasticine; paperclips; individual 100 square.

Lesson

Starter

Write a number up to 10 on the board. Time the children for two or three minutes (depending on the number) to see how many addition and subtraction facts they can write down on their whiteboards for that number. For example, possible facts for 3 are: $0 + 3 = 3$; $3 + 0 = 3$; $3 - 0 = 3$; $3 - 3 = 0$; $1 + 2 = 3$; $2 + 1 = 3$; $3 - 1 = 2$; $3 - 2 = 1$. Share facts, then repeat for another number.

Main teaching activities

Whole class: Explain that this week the children will practise mental strategies for adding and subtracting, using place value and partitioning and number facts that they already know. Ask them for addition and subtraction words; hold up the vocabulary cards as the children say them. Stick them on the board, then add any the children have forgotten.

Say that today the children will try keeping the first number of a calculation whole and adding or subtracting the other number by partitioning. Demonstrate this using a class 100 square. Write 24 + 15 on the board. Explain that we can keep 24 whole in our minds, but partition the 15 to add 10 (making 34) and then 5 (making 39). Show these stages on the 100 square. Record on the board: $24 + 10 + 5 = 34 + 5 = 39$. Repeat with four or five additions, showing what you are doing on the 100 square. Move on to a subtraction such as 53 – 24. Ask the children to keep 53 whole in their minds and take away 20 to leave 33, then 4 to leave 29. Record on the board: $53 - 20 - 4 = 33 - 4 = 29$. Repeat with four or five subtractions.

Group work: Distribute and demonstrate the 'Keeping it whole' activity sheet, which asks the children to practise what they have learned by generating calculations and working them out.

Differentiation

Less able: Fill in the template version of 'Keeping it whole' with numbers to 30 before copying it for the group. Allow the children to use 100 squares.
More able: Fill in the template version with numbers to 100.

Plenary & assessment

Link this lesson's work to money problems. For example: *Sally had 67p. She spent 23p. How much did she have left?* Ask the children to work it out on their whiteboards: 67p – 20p – 3p = 44p. Try a few similar problems.

Lesson 2

Starter

Ask the children to tell you what they know about odd and even numbers. If necessary, remind them that an odd number always has 1 left over when it is divided by 2, and an even number has nothing left over. Give them various two-digit starting numbers and ask them to count on and back in ones, clapping when they say an even number and stamping when they say an odd number. Repeat for counting in tens.

Main teaching activities

Whole class: Say that today, the children will use known number facts to help them add up other numbers. Go through the number bonds of 10, writing them on the board: 0 + 10 and 10 + 0; 1 + 9 and 9 + 1; 2 + 8 and 8 + 2; 3 + 7 and 7 + 3; 4 + 6 and 6 + 4; 5 + 5.

Write on the board some calculations that can be solved with these facts, and talk them through with the children. For example:

- 60 + 40: *We know that 6 + 4 = 10, so what must 60 + 40 equal? How about 30 + 70?*
- 12 + 8 + 6: *We know that 2 + 8 = 10, so this must be 10 + 10 + 6, which is 26.*
- 24 + 16: *4 + 6 = 10, so we could say 20 + 10 + 10, which equals 40.*

Work through several examples, asking the children to spot the number bonds.
Group work: Distribute and demonstrate the 'Number bonds' activity sheet.

Differentiation

Less able: Provide the version of 'Number bonds' with totals to 30, or use the template version to simplify the work further.
More able: Provide the version with totals to 100.

Plenary & assessment

Invite some children to share the calculation they found the most difficult and explain their method on the board. Play a class game of 'Find the way!' (as in Spring term, Unit 3, Lesson 2) using the OHT. Split the class into three teams, who take turns making the next move. You could add a further challenge by leaving counters on the numbers used, so no-one can use them again. Play the game two or three times.

Lesson 3

Starter

Use the 'Spider charts for multiplying' and 'Spider charts for dividing' to practise the 2 and 10 times-tables facts. Point to all the outside numbers on the multiplication charts in random order, and see how quickly the children can say the answers. Invite some children to do the pointing. Repeat with the division charts.

Main teaching activities

Whole class: Explain that today the children are going to think about bridging through 10. Check that they understand what that means: going through a tens boundary, as from 29 to 31. Write 26 + 8 on the board. Ask the children: what the next tens number is; how many units are needed to get to it; how they can break the 8 into two numbers, one to make 30 and the other left to add on to 30. Write what they say as a number sentence on the board, such as: $26 + 8 = 26 + 4 + 4 = 30 + 4 = 34$. Repeat with other 'two-digit add single-digit' additions.

Now move on to 'two-digit add two-digit' calculations, such as 28 + 16. Remind the children about the strategy of keeping the first number whole and partitioning the second. Following that idea, demonstrate how to add the tens number first and then add the units by making a 10 and adding what is left: $28 + 16 = 28 + 10 + 6 = 38 + 6 = 38 + 2 + 4 = 40 + 4 = 44$. Talk through the process. Do a few more examples.

Group work: Ask the children to practise this strategy using a game they played when they were learning about multiplication and division (Spring term, Unit 10). Demonstrate how to use the 'Home we go!' gameboard with 'Target board 1'. Ask the children to add the numbers on the gameboard to those on 'Target board 1', using the strategy for bridging through 10. After they have played once, ask them to record their work as you demonstrated in the lesson.

Differentiation
Less able: Provide 'Target board 2' with numbers to 10.
More able: Provide 'Target board 3' with two-digit numbers only.

Plenary & assessment

Invite some children from each group to demonstrate which numbers they chose, and to explain clearly how they worked out the calculation. Write 19 + 26 on the board and ask the children to think of as many different ways of calculating it as possible (e.g. $20 + 26 - 1$; $10 + 20 + 10 + 5$). Make sure they include today's strategy. Ask them which strategy they thought was the best.

Lesson 4

Starter

Give the children a lump of Plasticine each and remind them of the work they did making 3-D shapes in Autumn term, Unit 6. Ask them to name as many different 3-D shapes as they can. Ask them to make one 3-D shape with the Plasticine. When they have all done this, ask them to stand up if their shape has certain properties. For example: *Does your shape have six faces?… at least one triangle face?… no edges?… a square face?* Bring in as many different properties as you can. Ask the children to make another shape from the Plasticine. Repeat this a few times.

Main teaching activities

Whole class: Say that today the children will use doubles to help them with addition. Write some single-digit numbers, two-digit numbers to 20 and multiples of 10 to 100 on the board and ask the children to double them, writing the answers on their whiteboards to show you.

Write 30 + 40 on the board. Ask the children how doubling could help them to add these numbers. Look for the strategy: 30 + 40 = 30 + 30 + 10 = double 30 + 10. Repeat with these additions: 20 + 21, 7 + 8, 50 + 60, 20 + 31. In each case, record the reasoning used.

Group work: Model the group work. The children need to spread a set of 'Near doubles game cards' face up on the table, then find two numbers that come next to each other (such as 12 and 13), then add them together using the 'near doubles' method. Ask the children to work out and record the additions as you did in the main teaching session: 12 + 13 = 12 + 12 + 1 = 25.

Differentiation
Less able: Give this group the near doubles cards with numbers to 20.
More able: Challenge this group to use all the near doubles cards.

Plenary & assessment
Write some missing number addition sentences on the board, such as: 20 + □ = 41; 15 + □ = 29; 7 + □ = 13. Ask the children to work out which 'near double' number would go in each box to make the number sentence correct (21, 14, 6). Each time, ask the children to explain how they found the answer; target children whom you wish to assess. Look for speed and confidence in answering.

Lesson ⑤

Starter
Repeat the Starter from Lesson 4. (It has been a long time since the children thought about the properties of shapes, so two starters on this will be helpful.)

Main teaching activities
Whole class: Ask the children what is meant by 'finding the difference' between two numbers. Write some two-digit numbers up to 50 on the board. Ask the children to calculate the differences between pairs of these numbers using a number line. For example:

$34 - 29$ $+1$ $+4$

29   30   34   The difference is 5.

Group work: Ask the children to practise the subtraction strategy of finding the difference by counting up. Give them the 'Lost in space' gameboard and explain the rules for this lesson, keeping the number range 1 to 50.

Differentiation
Less able: The children can use number cards 1 to 12.
More able: The children can use number cards to 100.

Plenary & assessment
Divide the class into three teams. Play 'Lost in space' again together, using an OHT. During the game, choose children to demonstrate how to count along a number line on the board for their team. Ask these children: *What is the first thing you do? What is the next multiple of 10? How many units do you need to get to the next multiple of 10? What do you do next? How do you find the answer?*

Name		Date	

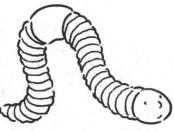

Keeping it whole

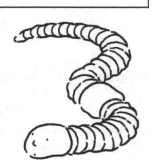

46	35	27	53	38	45

Use pairs of these numbers to make up some calculations.

For each pair of numbers, work out one addition and one subtraction.

Keep the larger number whole and add or subtract the smaller number.

For example:

Numbers: | 46 | 35 |

Addition: 46 + 30 = 76   Subtraction: 46 – 30 = 16
             76 + 5 = 81   16 – 5 = 11

Now you try:

Numbers: ☐ ☐   Addition: Subtraction:

Numbers: ☐ ☐   Addition: Subtraction:

Numbers: ☐ ☐   Addition: Subtraction:

Numbers: ☐ ☐   Addition: Subtraction:

Make up some more calculations, using the numbers above.

Write on the back of this sheet.

| Name | Date |

Number bonds

Answer these calculations by looking for number bonds of 10.
Use them to help you find the answer more quickly.

For example: 17 + 3	Find the bond: 7 + 3	Work it out! 10 + 10 = 20
Now you try: **1.** 21 + 19	Find the bond:	Work it out!
2. 23 + 27	Find the bond:	Work it out!
3. 12 + 7 + 8	Find the bond:	Work it out!
4. 14 + 26	Find the bond:	Work it out!
5. 26 + 24	Find the bond:	Work it out!
6. 21 + 29	Find the bond:	Work it out!
7. 17 + 18 + 2	Find the bond:	Work it out!
8. 15 + 19 + 11	Find the bond:	Work it out!

This unit concentrates on using the mental strategies that were learned in Unit 3 to solve 'real life' problems that involve money and measures. There is a recap of the stages that need to be thought about in order to solve a problem. The children will be solving one and two-step problems and investigations. They will be making up their own problems and visualising and acting some out.

LEARNING OBJECTIVES

		Topics	Starter	Main teaching activities
Lesson	1	Problems involving 'real life', money or measures	● Read the time to the hour, half hour or quarter hour on an analogue clock.	● Use mental addition and subtraction, simple multiplication and division to solve simple word problems, using one or two steps. ● Explain how the problem was solved. ● Recognise all coins and begin to use £.p notation for money. ● Find totals, give change, and work out which coins to pay.
Lesson	2	Problems involving 'real life', money or measures	● Order the months of the year.	As for Lesson 1.
Lesson	3	Problems involving 'real life', money or measures	● **State the subtraction corresponding to a given addition, and vice versa**.	As for Lesson 1.
Lesson	4	Problems involving 'real life', money or measures	As for Lesson 3.	As for Lesson 1.
Lesson	5	Problems involving 'real life', money or measures	● **Know by heart multiplication facts for the 2 and 10 times-tables**. ● Derive quickly division facts corresponding to the 2 and 10 times-tables.	As for Lesson 1.

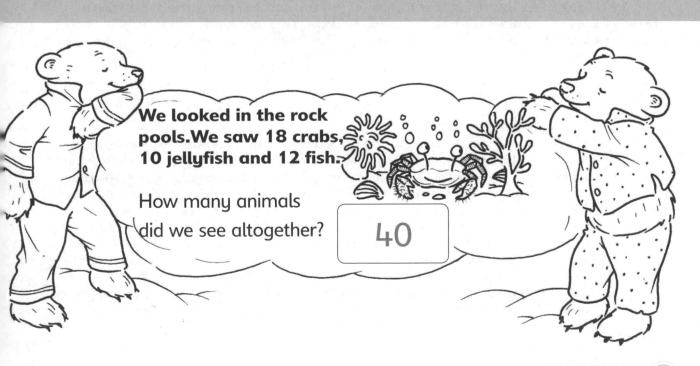

We looked in the rock pools. We saw 18 crabs, 10 jellyfish and 12 fish.

How many animals did we see altogether?

40

Lessons overview

Preparation

Copy 'How to solve a problem' onto A3 paper. Copy 'Small spider charts' onto A4 card and laminate, but keep as a whole sheet. Copy 'Making up problems' onto an OHT. Copy 'Addition and subtraction cards' and 'Months of the year cards' onto A3 card and cut out the cards. Copy 'Money problem cards' onto card and cut out the cards. Copy all three versions of 'Two steps' onto acetate.

Learning objectives

Starter
- Read the time to the hour, half hour or quarter hour on an analogue clock.
- Order the months of the year.
- **State the subtraction corresponding to a given addition, and vice versa.**
- **Know by heart multiplication facts for the 2 and 10 times-tables**.
- Derive quickly division facts corresponding to the 2 and 10 times-tables.

Main teaching activities
- Use mental addition and subtraction, simple multiplication and division to solve simple word problems, using one or two steps.
- Explain how the problem was solved.
- Recognise all coins and begin to use £.p notation for money.
- Find totals, give change, and work out which coins to pay.

Vocabulary

money, coin, penny, pence, pound, £, price, cost, buy, bought, spend, spent, pay, change, costs more, costs less, how much… ?, total, difference between, altogether

Throughout this unit, give all the children opportunities to use *The Toy Shop* from the NNS ICT CD.

You will need:

Photocopiable pages
'Down by the sea' (page 170), 'Beach maths' (page 171), 'Two steps' (page 172) and 'Here kitty, kitty…' (page 173) for each pair.

CD pages
'Months of the year cards', an A3 copy of 'How to solve a problem' and 'Small spider charts' for each pair (see General resources, Autumn term), 'Problems', 'Making up problems', 'Addition and subtraction cards' (see General resources, Spring term), 'Visualising problems 2', 'Money problem cards'; 'Down by the sea', 'Beach maths' and 'Two steps' less able, more able and template versions, OHTs of all versions of 'Two steps' (Summer term, Unit 4) (see General Resources).

Equipment
A card clock for each child; OHO; individual whiteboards and pens; counting apparatus; large sheets of paper; colouring pens and pencils; 5p, 10p and 20p coins, *The Toy Shop* CD.

Lesson

Starter

Give each child a card clock. Ask the children to show you various o'clock, half past, quarter to and quarter past times. Move on to questions such as: *My clock says 8 o'clock. It is one hour slow. Show me what time it really is. My clock says 9:30. It is two hours fast… My clock says 1 o'clock. It is half an hour slow… My clock says half past 3. It is 15 minutes fast…*

Main teaching activities

Whole class: Say that this week, the children will use the mental strategies they learned in Unit 3 to solve 'real-life' problems that involve money and measures. Display the 'How to solve a problem' poster, and talk through the steps needed to solve the first problem on the OHT of 'Making up problems'. *Can anyone remember what we need to do when we have a word problem to solve?* Direct their attention to the poster. When you reach Step 4, ask the children to think of a strategy to work out the answer. Remind them of the strategies they used in Unit 3: partitioning one of the numbers; looking for pairs that total 10; near doubling; counting on; bridging through 10. Ask them to decide which one is 'best' to help them solve this problem. Allow them to discuss with a partner and then feed back to the class. Solve the other three problems on the OHT in the same way.

Paired work: Organise the children into ability pairs. Give each pair the 'Down by the sea' activity sheet. Encourage the children to write down how they worked out these problems, using numbers rather than words.

Differentiation

Less able: Provide the version of the activity sheet with simpler numbers. Give support with reading and recording, and provide counting apparatus, if needed.

More able: Provide the version with more complex numbers. You could offer a challenge by asking the children to find two different methods of solving each problem.

Plenary & assessment

Write some information on the board, such as 1m, 80cm, string, how much? or £5, £1.50, how much altogether? Ask the children to talk to a partner and make up a problem from this information. For example: 'I had 1m of string. I cut off 80cm to tie up a parcel. How much did I have left?' or 'I had saved £5. My grandma gave me £1.50. How much have I got now?' Invite some pairs to share their problems and the rest of the class to solve them. Record the answers on the board. If there is a pounds and pence answer such as £6.50, write it as £650. Ask the children whether this is correct. Remind them to put the decimal point after the number of pounds in order to separate pounds from pence. Write up some pence amounts (such as 150p) and ask the children to write them using pounds and pence notation (£1.50). Repeat this a few times.

Lesson ②

Starter

Ask the children to say the months of the year in order together. Give 12 children a month card each and ask the others to order them by telling them where to stand. For each month, ask the children what the weather is like, what they may be doing and whether there are any significant dates (such as Diwali, Christmas or Hannukah).

Main teaching activities

Whole class: Remind the children of the Plenary in Lesson 1. Say that today they will be working with a partner to make up their own problems. They may remember doing this before (see Spring term, Unit 4). Using an OHT of 'Making up problems', talk through some possible one-step and two-step problems. For example, the information 5 kilograms, 3 and a half kilograms, flour could be used to generate: *The baker has 3 and a half kilograms of flour. He needs 5 kilograms to bake his bread. How much more flour does he need?* or *The baker had two bags of flour. One had 5 kilograms in and the other had 3 and a half kilograms. How much flour did he have altogether?* As you make up the problems, encourage the children to think visually and to use drawings in their recording when possible, rather than words. Model this idea simply.

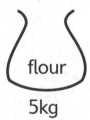

flour

5kg

flour

3.5kg

Paired work: The children should work in ability pairs. Give each pair a copy of the 'Beach maths' activity sheet, which gives them information to make into problems. Encourage them to jot their ideas down simply, or draw them when possible, so they don't waste time writing too many words.

Differentiation

Less able: Provide the version of 'Beach maths' with simpler information.

More able: Provide the version with more complex information and a final challenge.

Plenary & assessment

Invite the children to share their problems with the class. Ask the class to solve the problems. Each time, ask: *How did you solve the problem? Was there any information you didn't need? How many steps did you need to take?*

Write some information on the board that could involve multiplication and division, and ask the children to make up a problem from it.

Lesson

Starter

Hold up the 'Addition and subtraction cards' that have at least one single-digit number. For each one, ask the children to write on their whiteboards the corresponding addition or subtraction to show you. Ask someone to demonstrate, using a number line, why their answer matches the original calculation. For example: you hold up 12 + 7 = 19, they write down 19 – 7 = 12 and demonstrate:

$$12 + 7 = 19$$

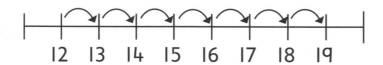

12 13 14 15 16 17 18 19

$$19 - 7 = 12$$

Main teaching activities

Whole class: Tell the children that today they will act out some problems to do with money. Ask whether they can remember what 'visualising' means. Ask them to shut their eyes and visualise what you say. *Imagine a tree. It is short and round with green leaves. Does your tree have lots of leaves or just a few? On the tree there are ten apples. They look very tasty. Pick half of them. How many have you picked? How many are left on the tree?* Repeat with a few scenarios that require the children to visualise amounts of money, using the 'Visualising problems 2' resource sheet.

Group work: Organise the children into mixed-ability groups. The children will be revisiting the idea of making up problems, but these are purely money and are at a level of difficulty appropriate to this part of the year. Give each group a card from 'Money problem cards'. They will need to be able to act out the problem in class, so that everyone knows what it is about and can work out the answer. They may use pens and paper to draw pictures, but they must try very hard not to use any words (written or spoken). Model an example from the sheet. Allow about 20 minutes for this preparation, telling the children at five-minute intervals how long they have left

Plenary & assessment

Extend this Plenary session. Give each group of children time to act out their problem, and the rest of the class time to solve it. Assess whether the performers understand the problem. Then assess the other children's responses: *Did they work out what was being asked? How did you solve the problem? Did they handle the information correctly? What strategies did they use?*

Lesson ④

Starter
Repeat the Starter from Lesson 3, but hold up the 'Addition and subtraction cards' with two-digit numbers only.

Main teaching activities
Whole class: Make sure the children understand that 'two-step' problems have two parts – that is, two things to work out in order to find the answer. Display the 'How to solve a problem' poster and talk through the steps necessary to solve a problem. Demonstrate this with a problem from the 'Two steps' activity sheet (use the version for the less able group).
Paired/individual work: Give 'Two steps' to pairs or individuals. Ask them to solve the problems as you have just demonstrated.

Differentiation
Less able: Provide the version of 'Two steps' with smaller numbers.
More able: Provide the version with larger numbers.

Plenary & assessment
Work through one problem from each version of the activity sheet. Display the problems on the OHP so everyone can participate. Ask questions such as: *What question is being asked? What information do we need? How can we solve the problem? How can we add/subtract these numbers? Is there another way?*

Lesson ⑤

Starter
Give each pair of children the 'Small spider charts' sheet. Count together in multiples of 2, using fingers. Stop at various points – for example, when they get to 10, ask: *How many fingers is that? How many lots of 2 make 10? We can say that 2 five times is 10.* Write on the board: $2 \times 5 = 10$. Repeat with multiples of 10. Now ask the children to look at their spider charts. Ask them to work with the 10 times-table chart first. One child should point at the numbers around the chart and the other should answer. Time them for two minutes. How many times can they go round the chart? Ask them to swap over and repeat for the 2 times-table chart.

Main teaching activities
Whole class: Say that today the children will look at another type of problem called an investigation. This doesn't always have just one correct answer. Go through an example with the children: *I bought a cola pop. It cost 6p. I paid for it with the exact money. Which coins did I use? I could have done it in five different ways. Write down on your whiteboard as many of the ways as you can. You can talk to a friend about the answers.* Ask questions such as: *What do you need to find out? How are you going to start? What coins can you use? Would a 10p be any good? Why not? What coins did you use?*
Paired work: Organise the children into mixed-ability pairs to work on the investigation on the 'Here kitty, kitty…' activity sheet. Give them 5p, 10p and 20p coins to help them if necessary.

Plenary & assessment
Invite some pairs of children to talk through their work and the answers they found. Assess how well they coped with the investigation.

Recap on the types of problem solving the children have been doing this week: one-step and two-step word problems and investigations.

Name	Date

Down by the sea

Work out the answers to these problems.

Show your strategies in the boxes.

We looked in the rock pools. We saw 18 crabs, 10 jellyfish and 12 fish. How many animals did we see altogether?	How I solved the problem:
I bought an ice cream. It cost £1.50. I gave the shop keeper £2. How much change did I get?	How I solved the problem:
I bought a bucket and spade and a fishing net. The bucket and spade cost 99p. The fishing net cost £1.50 How much did I spend altogether?	How I solved the problem:
My friend bought 5 ice lollies. They each cost 40p. How much did he spend?	How I solved the problem:
I saw 29 dolphins in the sea. My friend saw 9 more than I did. How many did she see?	How I solved the problem:

■ SCHOLASTIC

photocopiable

| Name | Date |

Beach maths

Make up problems using the information in the boxes.

You can draw pictures if you want.

14 jellyfish 16 crabs	Possible problem:
15 minutes half past 4	Possible problem:
4 ice creams 50p £5	Possible problem:
35 fish 15 dolphins 15 limpets	Possible problem:
15 sea horses 12 penguins 10	Possible problem:
subtract 43 37	Possible problem:

Name	Date

Two steps

Here are some two-step problems.

You need to work out the first part, then use that to work out the second part.

1. Sam bought eight oranges costing 10p each. How much change did he get from £1?	**Step 1**
	Step 2
2. Raz bought a comic for 50p and a bag of crisps for 10p. How much change did he get from £1?	**Step 1**
	Step 2
3. There are ten people on the bus. Five get off and six more get on. How many people are on the bus now?	**Step 1**
	Step 2
4. There are 25 apples. Kim takes 11 and Amil takes 9. How many apples are left?	**Step 1**
	Step 2
5. There are 30 children in the room. 12 of them are wearing shorts, 7 of them dresses and the rest trousers. How many are wearing trousers?	**Step 1**
	Step 2
6. There are two red sweets, three blue sweets and five orange sweets in a packet. How many sweets are there altogether in 10 packets?	**Step 1**
	Step 2

| Name | Date |

Here kitty, kitty...

Angie bought a toy kitten. It cost 45p.
She used only silver coins to pay for it.

There are nine different ways to pay 45p

if you use only silver coins.

How many can you find?

Record your answers in this box.

Hints...

What are the only coins you can use? Can you use a 50p coin? Put the

coins on front of you and try to make 45p using them. You could start

with a 20p coin.

If the kitten cost 50p, how many ways would there be to pay for it?

Work it out on the back of this sheet.

Children use and begin to read the vocabulary related to capacity. They estimate and measure capacities in litres and 100ml increments. They read metric scales for length, mass and capacity. They draw and measure lines in centimetres.

LEARNING OBJECTIVES

	Topics	Starter	Main teaching activities
Lesson 1	Measures	● **State the subtraction corresponding to a given addition and vice versa.**	● Use and begin to read the vocabulary related to capacity. ● **Estimate, measure then compare capacities, using standard units** (m, litre); **suggest suitable units and equipment for such measurements.** ● **Read a simple scale to the nearest labelled division.**
Lesson 2	Measures	● Derive quickly doubles of multiples of 5 to 50. ● Derive quickly halves of multiples of 10 to 100. ● Identify near doubles from doubles already known.	As for Lesson 1.
Lesson 3	Measures	● Read the time to the hour, half hour or quarter hour on an analogue clock.	As for Lesson 1.
Lesson 4	Measures	● **Read and write whole numbers to at least 100** in figures and words. ● Know what each digit in a two-digit number represents, including zero as a place holder.	● **Read a simple scale to the nearest labelled division, including using a ruler to draw and measure lines to the nearest centimetre.**

Lessons overview

Preparation
Enlarge and photocopy 'Measures vocabulary' for capacity for classroom use.

Learning objectives
Starter
● **State the subtraction corresponding to a given addition and vice versa.**
● Derive quickly doubles of multiples of 5 to 50.
● Derive quickly halves of multiples of 10 to 100.
● Identify near doubles from doubles already known.
● Read the time to the hour, half hour or quarter hour on an analogue clock.
Main teaching activity
● Use and begin to read the vocabulary related to capacity.
● **Estimate, measure then compare capacities, using standard units** (m, litre); **suggest suitable units and equipment for such measurements.**
● **Read a simple scale to the nearest labelled division, including using a ruler to draw and measure lines to the nearest centimetre**.

Vocabulary
litre, half-litre, millilitre, full, half full

You will need:
CD pages
0–9 number cards for each child, 'Measures vocabulary' for capacity, 'Addition and subtraction cards' (see General resources, Autumn term).

Equipment
Individual whiteboards; containers of different capacities; spoons, cups… as uniform non-standard units; container with an elastic band around it, approximately at the mid-point of the side; containers with scales in litres; containers with scales in 100ml; cardboard clock for each child, water or dry sand; marbles.

Lesson

Starter
Begin by holding up some of the 'Addition and subtraction cards' and ask the children to write the corresponding number sentence on their whiteboards and show you. Repeat this a few times. Move on to writing numbers on the board and asking the children to make up two corresponding number sentences for each, for example, you write 6 4 10, they write 6 + 4 = 10 and 10 – 4 = 6. Repeat this with different numbers.

Main teaching activities
Whole class: Say: *Today we are going to begin a series of lessons on capacity. What do I mean by 'capacity'?* Ask the children to give examples of words that they know for capacity and write these onto the board. For each word given, invite the children to give an example of how it could be used in a sentence. Pin up the capacity vocabulary cards as a reminder.

Now show the children two containers of different sizes and ask: *Which one holds more? Which holds less? Why do you think that? How can you check your estimate?* Explain that it is possible to check how much something will hold by filling the container with, for example, cupfuls or spoonfuls…. Ask: *Which unit do you think would be suitable? Why do you think that? Invite a child to check the capacity of each of the containers by filling using a suitable unit.*

Explain that the standard units for measuring capacity are litres and millilitres. On the board, write: *1 litre is the same as 1000 millilitres.* Ask if anyone can make a link with other measures; praise the response that 1kg is equivalent to 1000g. Show the children a container marked in litres. Invite a child to pour in water to the 1 litre mark. Now repeat this with a container marked in 100ml. Ask: *How many 100 millilitres will there be in a litre?* Invite a child to pour some water into this container to the 100ml mark. Write 100ml on the board.

Group work: The following activities are intended to be used during this and the following two lessons. The children should work in mixed-ability groups of three or four to tackle the activities. These instructions can be written on the board for the children.

1. Estimate the order of capacities for four different containers. Then choose an appropriate uniform non-standard unit and check the estimate by measuring. Decide how to record the estimate and results.

2. Use the container with an elastic band on it. Ask: *How many spoonfuls of water do you think will be needed to fill the container to the elastic band mark?* Check by pouring. Record the estimate and measure. Now move the elastic band to a different position and repeat the activity.

3. Use a container with a scale which is marked in 100ml. Fill the container to the 100ml mark. Say: *How many marbles do you think you will need to put into the container in order to move the level of the water to the 200ml mark? Write down your estimate. Now try it. Did you make a good estimate? Now how many marbles do you think you will need to add to the container to move the level of the water to the 500ml mark?*

4. Find some containers which you estimate will hold about 2 litres. Check by pouring water from these into a container with a scale marked in litres. Decide how to record your results.

5. Choose some containers. Decide for each one whether to measure its capacity in 100 millilitres or litres. Estimate then measure the capacity by filling and pouring. Ask: *Did you make a good estimate? Record your estimate and measure.*

Plenary & assessment
Invite children who tackled activities 1 and 2 to explain how they carried out the activities, and how they recorded their work. Ask the children to evaluate the effectiveness of their chosen recording. Ask, for activity 2: *How close was your estimate? What happened when you moved the band and tried again?* Discuss how the children can become more accurate in estimating by learning from previous experience.

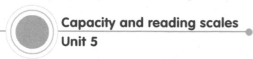
Lessons

Lesson 2 starter

The children will each need a set of 0–9 number cards for this activity. Call out numbers from one to 15 and ask the children to show you their doubles, e.g. you call out 12, they show you 24. Move on to multiples of five to 50, e.g. you call out 35 and they show you 70, and then tens to one hundred. Hold up some single-digit number cards for the children to add together, and expect them to work out the answer using near doubles, e.g. if you hold up 5 and 6, they need to show you 11 and then explain how they got that answer by doubling. Do this for numbers up to 20 and near multiples of 10.

Lesson 3 starter

Each child will need a clock. Ask them to find a selection of times: o'clock, half past, quarter past and quarter to. Ask problems such as: *My clock says half past seven. It is half an hour fast. What time is it really? My watch says 3 o'clock. It is 15 minutes slow. What time is it really?*

Main teaching activities

Whole class: Invite children from each group to recap on what they did in Lesson 1. Ask questions about the vocabulary for capacity, and invite individual children to use a vocabulary word in a sentence. Ask questions such as: *How many millilitres are there in a litre? So how many 100 millilitres are there in a litre? How much is half a litre in millilitres?*
Group work: Ask the children to continue with the activities from lesson 1.

Plenary & assessment

Review the activities 3–5 above during these two days. For activity 3, ask: *How many marbles did you need to move the water level to 200 ml? So how many do you think you would need to move the water level to 800 ml?… 1 litre? Why do you think that? How accurate do you think this is? Why do you think that?* For activity 4, ask how the children decided to record their results. Invite them to evaluate the effectiveness of their chosen recording. For activity 5, ask: *For this container, which units did you choose? Was this a good choice? How do you know that?* Invite the children to say where they have seen litres and millilitres used in everyday life. They may suggest, for example, when buying petrol it is sold by the litre, or on drink cans and bottles. You may wish to make a collection in the classroom of commercial packaging which shows measurements in litres and millilitres.

Lesson overview

Preparation
Enlarge and photocopy 'Measures vocabulary' for capacity for classroom use. Copy 'Reading scales' and 'Drawing scales' onto acetate.

Learning objectives
Starter
● **Read and write whole numbers to at least 100** in figures and words.
● **Know what each digit in a two-digit number represents, including zero as a place holder.**
Main teaching activity
● **Read a simple scale to the nearest labelled division, including using a ruler to draw and measure lines to the nearest centimetre.**

Vocabulary
length, weight, capacity, compare, measuring scales, guess, estimate, nearly, roughly, about, close to, about the same as, just over, just under, ruler, metre stick, tape measure, metre, centimetre, balance, scales, kilogram, half kilogram, gram, container, full, half-full, empty, litre, half-litre, millilitre

You will need:
Photocopiable pages
'Reading scales' (page 178) and 'Drawing scales' (page 179) for each pair.

CD pages
0–9 number cards,(see General resources, Autumn term).

Equipment
Individual whiteboards and pens; metre stick; rulers and paper for each child; weighing scales; measuring jug.

Lesson ④

Starter

Ask the children to write single-digit numbers on their whiteboards and give them instructions to follow, for example: *Write three, double it, add five, add nine. How did you do that? Double it, what is your number? What is the zero there for? Add four, add eleven. How did you do that?*

Main teaching activities

Whole class: Tell the children that today and tomorrow they will practise reading scales. Ask: *What do I mean by reading scales?* Show a ruler, weighing scales and a measuring jug. Ask: *Why do you think we need scales? Talk to a partner and chat about when in real life people would need to read scales.* Take feedback. Give some examples, such as making a cake, when you need specific amounts that are weighed out. Tell them that some of the scales they will be reading are similar to ones they have used this week and some are different.

Put the acetate of 'Reading scales' on the OHP. Show one picture at a time. Ask the children what they think the item is measuring – length, weight or capacity – and why. Then look at the units and ask whether this confirms their thoughts. Discuss how scales are used to work out measurements. Discuss the units. Can the children tell the size or amount by the unit?

Group work: The children will need to work in pairs or small groups on 'Reading scales' and 'Drawing scales'. Put a copy of 'Reading scales' on the OHP again and demonstrate what the children should do. Give them five minutes or so and then draw the class together and ask some children to come to the front and explain how they read two or three of the scales. Then explain 'Drawing scales', which asks the children to draw on the measurement according to the amount written.

Differentiation

This should be through peer support. Work with any groups of children that need your help.

Plenary & assessment

Put the two acetates of 'Reading scales and 'Drawing scales' on the OHP and work through each, asking the children to mark and correct their own work. Choose one measuring scale and make up a word problem that would include it, for example: *This measuring jug shows that there is 500ml of orange squash in it. There was a litre; some has been poured into a glass. How much has been poured into a glass?*

Name   Date

Reading scales

What do these scales say?

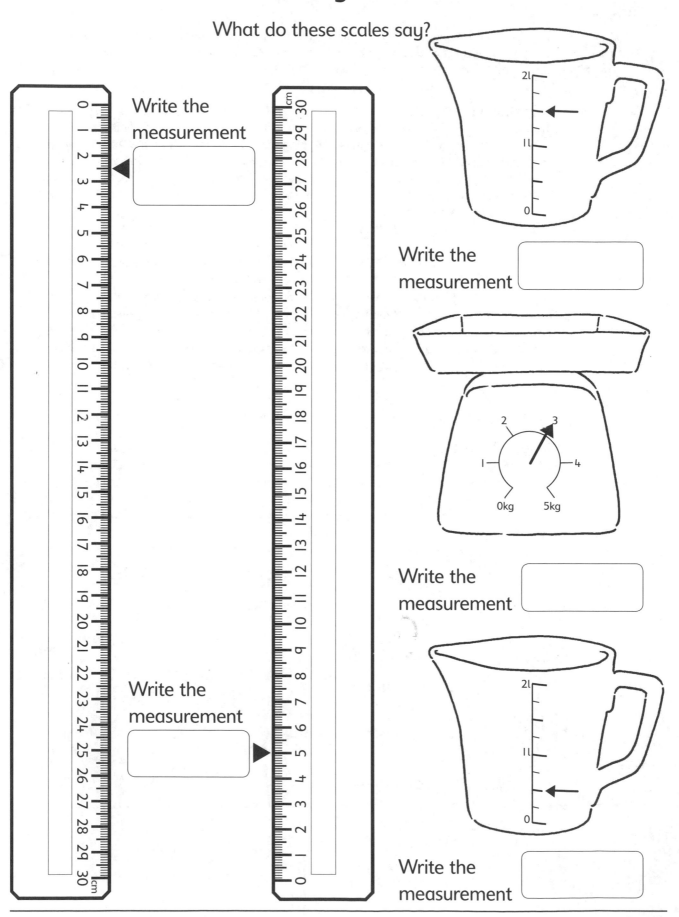

Write the measurement

Write the measurement

Write the measurement

Write the measurement

Write the measurement

Name

Date

Drawing scales

Draw an arrow
to show 20 cms

Draw an arrow
to show 15 cms

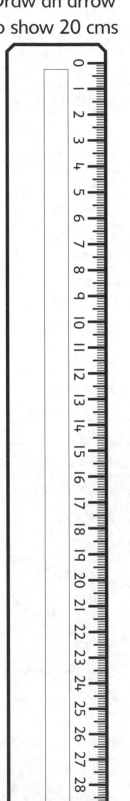

Draw an arrow to show
just less than $\frac{1}{2}$ litre

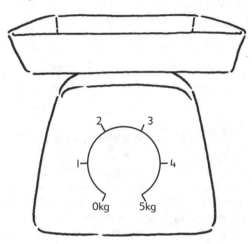

Draw an arrow to show
$2\frac{1}{2}$ kg

Draw an arrow to show
1 l 500ml

Shapes in pictures and making moves

Children use the vocabulary related to capacity. They estimate and measure capacities in litres and 100ml increments. They read metric scales for length, mass and capacity. They draw and measure lines in centimetres.

LEARNING OBJECTIVES

	Topics	Starter	Main teaching activity
Lesson 1	Shape and space Reasoning about numbers or shapes	● **Know by heart multiplication facts for the 2 and 10 times-tables.** ● Derive quickly division facts corresponding to the 2 and 10 times-tables.	● Relate solid shapes to pictures of them. ● Investigate a general statement about familiar numbers or shapes by finding examples that satisfy it.
Lesson 2	Shape and space	● **Use the mathematical names for common 3-D and 2-D shapes.** ● **Sort shapes and describe some of their features.**	● **Use mathematical vocabulary to describe position, direction and movement.** ● Know that a right angle is a measure of a quarter turn, and recognise right angles in squares and rectangles.
Lesson 3	Shape and space	● Count on in steps of 3, 4 or 5 to at least 30.	● **Use mathematical vocabulary to describe position, direction and movement.** ● Give instructions for moving along a route in straight lines and round right-angled corners.

Lessons   overview

Preparation
Laminate a copy of 'Function machine game' for each child; make laminated card shapes from 'Templates for irregular shapes' and 'Templates for regular shapes'; make vocabulary cards from '3-D shape vocabulary' and 'Position vocabulary' for each group. Make on OHT of 'Amazing maze'. Make copies of 'Treasure shapes' and 'Treasure shapes recording sheets'.

Learning objectives
Starter
● **Know by heart multiplication facts for the 2 and 10 times-tables.**
● Derive quickly division facts corresponding to the 2 and 10 times-tables.
● **Use the mathematical names for common 3-D and 2-D shapes.**
● **Sort shapes and describe some of their features.**
● Count on in steps of 3, 4 or 5 to at least 30.
Main teaching activities
● Relate solid shapes to pictures of them.
● Investigate a general statement about familiar numbers or shapes by finding examples that satisfy it.
● **Use mathematical vocabulary to describe position, direction and movement**.
● Know that a right angle is a measure of a quarter turn, and recognise right angles in squares and rectangles.
● Give instructions for moving along a route in straight lines and round right-angled corners.

Vocabulary
shape, flat, curved, straight, solid, corner, point ,face, side, edge, surface, cube, cuboid, pyramid, sphere, cone, cylinder, circle, triangle, square, rectangle, star, pentagon, hexagon, octagon, position, over, under, underneath, above, below, outside, inside, in front, behind, back, before, after, beside, next to, opposite, apart, middle, edge, centre, corner

You will need:
Photocopiable pages
A3 copy of 'Treasure shapes' (page 183) and 'Treasure shapes recording sheet' (see page 184), one for each child.

CD pages
'Function machine game' for each child, 'Templates for irregular shapes 1' and '2', and 'Templates for regular shapes', '3-D shape vocabulary' cards for each group, 'Position vocabulary' cards (see General resources, Autumn term), an OHT of 'Amazing maze' (see General resources).

Equipment
Plasticine; dry-wipe pens and cloths; coloured pencils; 3-D shapes; a teddy bear or similar toy; a card clock for each child; A3 paper; pens or coloured pencils; a toy car for each group; counters.

Lesson

Starter

Rehearse the 2 and 10 times-tables by chanting multiples together, counting on fingers. Ask the children at various points what finger they are on and what that means (for example, sixth finger when counting in twos means 6 lots of 2, which is 12). Reverse the activity for division facts: chant multiples and when you reach 12 (for example) ask what you get if you divide 12 by 2; the children look at their fingers. Give the children function machine sheets; ask them to write some numbers from 1–10 then, when you say *Go*, to multiply them by 2 or 10. Now ask them to write multiples of 2 and 10, then divide when you say *Go*.

Main teaching activities

Whole class: This lesson is about recognising 3-D shapes from 2-D pictures. Go over the vocabulary of 3-D shapes, using the cards. Hold up a sphere and ask the children to describe it. Show the 'Treasure shapes' picture and ask whether they can see any spheres in it. Discuss how they recognised the spheres: round, no edges and so on. Repeat with cubes, cuboids, cylinders, cones and pyramids.

Group work: The children should work in mixed-ability pairs or small groups, with an A3 copy of the picture and some Plasticine. Between them, they should make each of the 3-D shapes they have seen in the main teaching activity, and use these to identify the shapes in the picture. They should colour each type of shape with a different-coloured pencil, then record (on the recording sheet) how many of each shape they found.

Plenary & assessment

Discuss how many of each shape the children found and how they recognised them. Write this statement on the board: All 3-D shapes have faces. Ask the children to say whether this is true and explain how they know, using 'Treasure shapes' and real shapes. Expect such responses as: a face is a surface and all 3-D shapes have surfaces; we can see three faces on this picture of a cube, so we know it must have six really.

Lesson

Starter

Give each child a 3-D and a 2-D shape card. Hold up a shape vocabulary card and ask children with any shape that links to it to stand up. Ask a few children to explain why they are standing. Repeat for as many vocabulary cards as possible.

Main teaching activities

Whole class: Remind the children of previous work (Spring term, Unit 6) on placing, moving and turning things. Explore the words 'position', 'direction' and 'movement' with the children: *What does that word mean? What other words could we use to describe that? How could we show it?* Place a teddy in different positions and ask the children to say where it is. Now ask them to close their eyes and visualise themselves in different places. For example: *Imagine you are below something. Who can tell me where it is?* Let them make up their own scenarios for these words and phrases: higher than, lower than, further away from, on the edge of and at the corner of. They can share these with a partner, then describe some to the class.

Group work: The children should work in groups of three with a set of 'Position vocabulary' cards and three A3 sheets of paper headed 'position', 'direction' and 'movement'. They should sort the cards onto the correct sheets and then write (or stick) them down to make three posters. Give them 10 minutes, then bring the class together to check how they are getting on. Ask the children to use at least two words from each poster to make up a story they can tell the class.

Plenary & assessment

Look at the posters and check that the words are on the correct sheets. Talk through and correct any errors with position words, but leave direction and movement words for the next lesson. Invite each group to tell their story. Tell the children that the teddy wants to be placed in a certain position and give clues for them to tell you where – for example: further away from the table (put it next to the table); not here (move it further away); here! Repeat for a few positions.

Lesson ③

Starter

Hold up a triangle and ask how many sides it has. Ask a child to write the number on the board. Show two triangles and ask: *How many sides altogether?* Ask the child at the board to write that number. Repeat for up to ten triangles. Ask the children what they notice. (They are counting in threes.) Repeat for quadrilaterals. Can the children predict what will happen with pentagons? Try it and see.

Main teaching activities

Whole class: Revisit the vocabulary of direction and movement. Ask: *Who can tell me what a turn is? Can you show me? What is a quarter turn? What angle does a quarter turn make? Which direction is clockwise… anticlockwise?* Give the children card clocks. *Show me 12 o'clock. Move the minute hand a quarter turn clockwise. What time does that say?* Now move it a half turn clockwise. *What time is that?* Make a whole turn anticlockwise. *What time is that?* Repeat with the children moving: *Now everyone stand up. Turn clockwise for a quarter turn…* and so on.

Now project the OHT of 'Amazing maze' and ask the children to tell you how to move a counter through the maze.

Paired work: The children work in pairs to design a maze on A3 paper with right-angled turns (both clockwise and anticlockwise) and straight-on moves, then give each other instructions to steer a toy car through the maze.

Plenary & assessment

Ask the class to give directions through each of the mazes. Ask the children to make a right angle with their hands. Ask them to look around the room and point to right angles. Ask: *What shapes have right angles?* Discuss right angles in real life: in objects, shapes and turns.

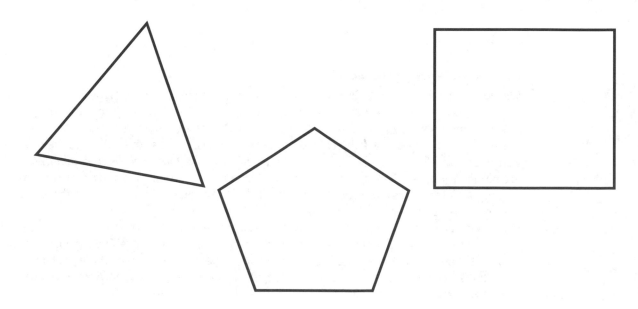

Name		Date	

Treasure shapes

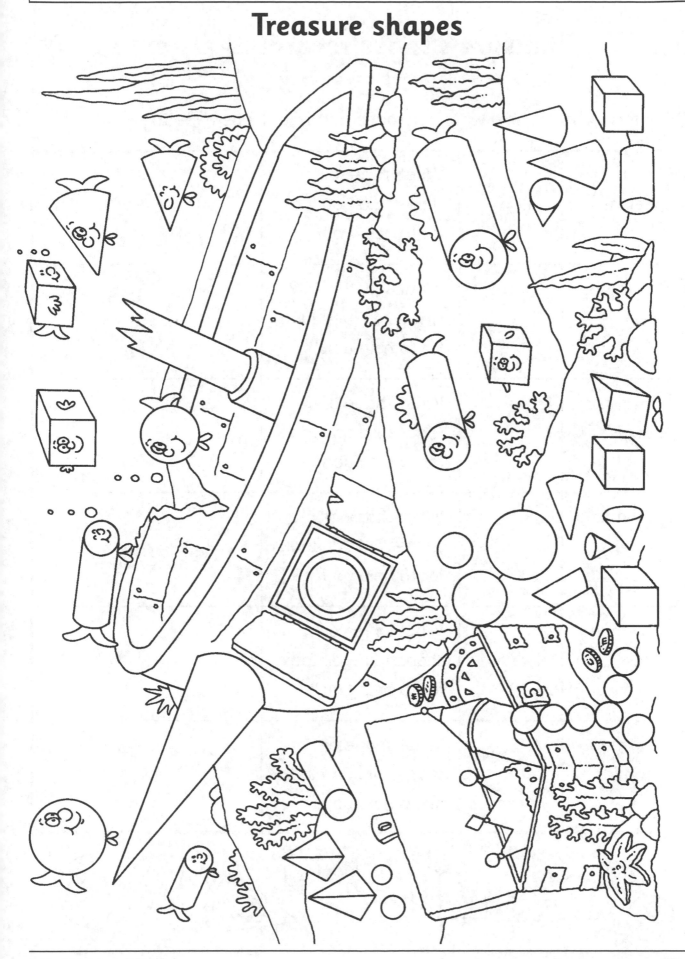

Name	Date

Treasure shapes recording sheet

Fill in this chart to show what you found and what helped you to find it.

How many spheres?		What shape or shapes did you look for to help you?	
How many cubes?		What shape or shapes did you look for to help you?	
How many cuboids?		What shape or shapes did you look for to help you?	
How many cylinders?		What shape or shapes did you look for to help you?	
How many cones?		What shape or shapes did you look for to help you?	
How many pyramids?		What shape or shapes did you look for to help you?	

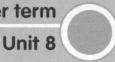 # Puzzles and investigations

This unit begins with counting sequences and asks the children to look for patterns in them to help them predict following numbers. The rest of the week entails solving puzzles and investigations. One lesson is a money investigation, then there are two number investigations with an emphasis on using prior knowledge to make different numbers in different ways. The final lesson involves number patterns and shapes.

LEARNING OBJECTIVES

	Topics	Starter	Main teaching activities
Lesson 1	Counting, properties of numbers and number sequences	● Add/subtract 9 or 11: add/subtract 10 and adjust by 1.	● **Describe and extend simple number sequences**: count on in steps of 3, 4 or 5 to at least 30, from and back to zero, then from and back to any given small number.
Lesson 2	Counting, properties of numbers and number sequences Reasoning about numbers or shapes	● As for Lesson 1.	● **Describe and extend simple number sequences**: count on in steps of 3, 4 or 5 to at least 30, from and back to zero, then from and back to any given small number. ● Solve mathematical problems or puzzles, recognise simple patterns and relationships, generalise and predict. ● **Explain how a problem was solved** orally and, where appropriate, in writing.
Lesson 3	Counting, properties of numbers and number sequences Reasoning about numbers or shapes	● **Read and write whole numbers to at least 100** in figures and words.	● As for Lesson 2.

Lesson ① overview

Preparation
If necessary, photocopy onto card and laminate enough copies of 'Count it!' (gameboard, instructions and cards) for each group of four children. Make an A3 copy of the gameboard.

Learning objectives
Starter
● Add/subtract 9 or 11: add/subtract 10 and adjust by 1.
Main teaching activities
● **Describe and extend simple number sequences**: count on in steps of 3, 4 or 5 to at least 30, from and back to zero, then from and back to any given small number.

Vocabulary
zero, one hundred, two hundred… one thousand, count on, count back, count on in ones/twos/tens, multiple of, sequence, continue, predict, pattern, rule, odd, even

You will need:
CD pages
'0–100 number cards' (see General resources, Autumn term), 'Count it!' instructions, cards and gameboard for each group, plus an A3 gameboard (see General resources, Spring term).

Equipment
A class 100 square; individual whiteboards and pens; individual 100 squares (if needed); coins; counters; an OHP.

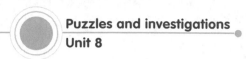

Lesson 1

Starter

Use a class 100 square to count together on and back in tens and ones: *Find 27. What is 10 more? What is 1 less?* Repeat. Now ask the children to imagine a 100 square. Say a number and ask them to look at it in their minds; ask them which number is below it, above it, one more, ten less and so on. Repeat. Now ask: *How can you add 9 onto 14 easily in your head?* (By adding 10 and taking away 1.) Ask them to add 9 to various two-digit numbers in this way, visualising the 100 square and writing on their whiteboards. Repeat for adding 11. Give any children who struggle a 100 square.

Main teaching activities

Whole class: This lesson is about counting in steps of 3, 4 and 5. Pick a single-digit number card and ask the children to count forwards and then backwards from it, first in threes, then in fours and finally in fives. Repeat a few times, including a few two-digit starting numbers (up to 30).

Say a starting number, then move your finger along a counting stick, asking the children to count in threes, fours or fives. Ask the children to predict what number you will point to and why. Write some counting sequences on the board. Ask the children whether each sequence has a pattern they can use to check that the numbers are correct. For example:

5 8 11 14 17 __ __ __ … (alternate odd/even numbers)
6 __ 16 21 26 31 __ __ … (alternate final digits the same)
47 43 39 35 31 27 __ __ 15 __ 7 … (groups of five numbers ending 7 3 9 5 1, all odd).

Group work: Put the children into mixed-ability groups of four. Model the 'Count it!' game using the instructions.

Differentiation

Less able: Provide a 100 square as a visual aid.
More able: Give this group the cards that ask them to count on in threes and fours.

Plenary & assessment

Play the 'Count it!' game as a class, using an A3 gameboard. Write the counting that you do on the board. Focus on any patterns you have looked at earlier in the lesson. Count the money together at the end, beginning with the highest-value coins.

Lessons 2 3 overview

Preparation

Make a set of regular shape templates for each pair of children. Display an A3 copy of 'Number words'. Use the A3 'Count it!' gameboard from Lesson 1. Prepare an OHT with the headings: Dice 1, Dice 2, Total, How many more do you need to make 12?, Number sentence.

Learning objectives

Starter
● Add/subtract 9 or 11: add/subtract 10 and adjust by 1.
● **Read and write whole numbers to at least 100** in figures and words.
Main teaching activities
● **Describe and extend simple number sequences**: count on in steps of 3, 4 or 5 to at least 30, from and back to zero, then from and back to any given small number.
● Solve mathematical problems or puzzles, recognise simple patterns and relationships, generalise and predict.
● **Explain how a problem was solved** orally and, where appropriate, in writing.

Vocabulary

zero, one hundred, two hundred… one thousand, count on, count back, count on in ones/ twos/tens, multiple of, sequence, continue, predict, pattern, rule, odd, even

You will need:

CD pages
'0–100 number cards', 'Regular shape templates' for each pair (see General resources, Autumn term); an A3 copy of 'Number words', 'Count it!' instructions, cards and A3 gameboard (see General resources, Spring term), 'Star number' (see General resources).

Equipment
Two dice for each pair; individual whiteboards and pens; counters.

Lesson ②

Starter

Repeat the Starter activity from Lesson 1. Encourage the children to visualise the 100 square. After some practice at adding 1, 10, 9 and 11, move on to taking away 1, 10 and 9 with the help of a 100 square.

Main teaching activities

Whole class: You will need the OHT you have prepared earlier with the headings Dice 1, Dice 2, Total, How many more do you need to make 12?, Number sentence, a marker pen and two dice. The aim is to find ways of making 12 by adding the two numbers thrown with the dice and working out what the third number (to make 12) must be. Invite various children to come to the front, throw two dice and write the numbers on the acetate. Ask: *What do these numbers total? How did you work that out? What do we need to add on to make 12? How did you work that out?* Write what they say as a number sentence. Write the numbers on the board in a different order and ask whether this makes a difference to the total. Make sure the children understand that it does not. Repeat with several more pairs of numbers.

Dice 1	Dice 2	Total	How many more do you need to make 12?	Number sentence

Paired work: Ask the children to work in pairs, finding as many other combinations to make 12 as they can. Give each pair two dice and a whiteboard and pen for recording. Tell the children to record their results in a table in the same way that you did (you can leave the OHT displayed for their reference).

Differentiation

Less able: Give these children 12 counters each. They can match the counters with the numbers on the dice and count how many are left over.

More able: These children can use their own methods to make 12 in as many ways as possible by adding three numbers. Also encourage them to think of ways to make 12 using subtraction, such as 20 – 4 – 4 or 24 – 20 + 8.

Plenary & assessment

Discuss the children's findings. Invite some pairs from the main and less able groups to explain their answers. Invite some pairs from the more able group to explain how they worked out the totals.

Lesson ③

Starter

Ask the children to write a two-digit number on their whiteboards. Give them instructions to follow, such as: *Write 18, add 2, double your number, subtract 10, add 3, add 8, swap the digits round, what is your number?* Repeat with more numbers. Ask the children to write some two-digit numbers in words, encouraging them to look at the 'Number words' poster for clues.

Main teaching activity

Whole class: This lesson is about making numbers in different ways. Write '10' on the board and ask the children to suggest some ways of making 10. Target the lower-ability children to answer first, when the easier methods have not yet been suggested. Encourage additions and subtractions, mixtures of both (such as $20 - 19 + 9$), multiplications (5×2), divisions ($20 \div 2$) and fractions ($\frac{1}{4}$ of 40). Write another number on the board; ask the children to work with a partner and come up with as many ways of making the number as they can, writing on their whiteboards. Take feedback, and find out which pair has the most unusual way.

Paired work: Give each pair some number cards to 50 and the 'Star number' activity sheet for recording.

Differentiation

Less able: Give these children some number cards to 20.
More able: Give these children some number cards to 100.

Plenary & assessment

Ask a pair from each ability group to give an example of their work, writing all the ways they found on the board. Ask the class to vote for the most interesting method, and then to think of another unusual way of making a number such as 15, 50 or 75.

Summer term
Unit 9

Finding appropriate strategies to solve problems

The first lesson in this unit is about ordering numbers to 100 using the context of money. The next two involve using appropriate strategies to solve addition and subtraction problems in the context of money and length.

LEARNING OBJECTIVES

		Topics	Starter	Main teaching activities
Lesson	1	Place value and ordering	● **Know by heart multiplication facts for the 2 and 10 times-tables.** ● Derive quickly division facts for the 2 and 10 times-tables.	● **Order whole numbers to at least 100,** and position them on a number line and 100 square.
Lesson	2	Understanding addition and subtraction Mental calculation strategies (+ and −) Making decisions Problems involving 'real life', money and measures	● **Know by heart all addition and subtraction facts for each number to at least 10.**	● Extend understanding of the operations of addition and subtraction. ● Add/subtract 19 or 21. ● **Choose and use appropriate operations and efficient calculation strategies.** ● Use mental addition and subtraction, simple multiplication and division to solve simple word problems, using one or two steps. ● Explain how the problem was solved.
Lesson	3	Rapid recall of addition and subtraction facts	● Know by heart all pairs of numbers with a total of 20.	As for Lesson 2.

Lesson overview

Preparation
If necessary, make A3 copies of 'Spider charts for multiplying' and 'Spider charts for dividing'. Copy and laminate 'Small spider charts' and cut out the charts.

Learning objectives
Starter
● **Know by heart multiplication facts for the 2 and 10 times-tables.**
● Derive quickly division facts corresponding to the 2 and 10 times-tables.
Main teaching activities
● **Order whole numbers** to at least 100, and position them on a number line or 100 square.

Vocabulary
order, compare, larger, largest, greater, greatest, smaller, smallest, less, least, size, halfway between

You will need:

Photocopiable pages
A copy of 'Ordering amounts of money' (page 193) for each child.

CD pages
'0–100 number cards', 'Blank number lines' for each child, A3 copies of 'Spider charts for multiplying' and 'Spider charts for dividing', 'Small spider charts' for each pair (see General resources, Autumn term).

Equipment
A selection of coins.

Lesson

Starter

Use the A3 spider charts to practise the 2 and 10 times-tables. Remind children to point to the numbers randomly. Ask the children to call out the number you point at divided by 2 or 10. Repeat.

Main teaching activities

Whole class: This lesson is about ordering numbers to 100 and finding numbers that go between them. Hold up two number cards and ask the children to point to the one that would go first on a 0–100 number line. Repeat. Invite five children to pick a number card each and ask the class where they should stand to be in order from smallest to largest. Repeat.

Show the children four coins: 1p, 5p, 10p and 20p. *Which is worth most? Least?* Draw a blank number line with 11 divisions; label the first one 0 and the last one £1. Ask where the coins should go. Invite a child to place them on the number line. Ask which amounts go on the division lines and which coins you would use to make them (for example, 30p goes on the next division to 20p and can be made with 10p and 20p). Ask: *My comic costs between 80p and 90p; what could it have cost?* Mark your choice on the number line. Repeat.

Paired work: Give each pair the 'Ordering amounts of money' sheet and model an example.

Differentiation

Less able: Provide the version of the activity sheet with totals that are multiples of 10p.
More able: Provide the version with some totals above £1. Supply coins if necessary.

Plenary & assessment

Invite children from each group to draw number lines on the board and say what numbers they plotted and why they put them where they did.

Lessons   overview

Preparation

Copy '+ and − 19 and 21 cards', 'Coin cards and labels', 'Price labels (pence)' and 'Price labels (£.p)' onto card and cut out one of each set of cards for each pair. Copy the 'Which strategy?' game onto A3 paper and cut out. Make an OHT of 'Problems'. Copy 'Home we go!' onto A3 card and laminate for each group of two to four children.

Learning objectives

Starter
● **Know by heart all addition and subtraction facts for each number to at least 10.**
● Know by heart all pairs of numbers with a total of 20.

Main teaching activities
● Extend understanding of the operations of addition and subtraction.
● Add/subtract 19 or 21.
● **Choose and use appropriate operations and efficient calculation strategies.**
● Use mental addition and subtraction, simple multiplication and division to solve simple word problems, using one or two steps.
● Explain how the problem was solved.

Vocabulary

money, coin, penny, pence, pound, £, spend, pay, change, total, addition, subtraction, difference, equal, count on, how much more?, bridging, nearest 10, next 10

You will need:

Photocopiable pages
'Solve me!' (page 194) for each child or pair.

CD pages
'0–100 number cards', 'Coin cards and labels', 'Price labels (pence)', 'Price labels (£.p)', 'How to solve a problem' poster, 'Addition and subtraction vocabulary' (see General resources, Autumn term); 'Problems', (see General resources, Spring term), '+ and − 19 and 21 cards', 'What did you do?', 'Which strategy?' game (Autumn term, Unit 3) and 'Solve me!', less able and more able versions (Summer term, Unit 9) (see General resources).

Equipment
Individual whiteboards; Blu-Tack; a class 100 square; individual 100 squares; plastic coins, real coins and large card coins; a pendulum; counters; counting apparatus.

Lesson

Starter

Write on the board: □ + △ = 10. Ask the children to write on their whiteboards number sentences that will fit this. Discuss what they have written. Find all the possible sentences. Use fingers to check, as well as jumps along a 0–10 number line. Repeat for a total below 10.

Main teaching activities

Whole class: The next two lessons are about adding and subtracting money and measures. Ask the children to tell you some words about addition and subtraction. As they do this, show the appropriate word cards and Blu-Tack them to the board. Discuss the strategies the children have learned for mental addition and subtraction.

Use the 'Which strategy?' board and cards: hold up a calculation and ask the children which box you should put it in. Repeat. Now write 36 + 19 on the board and ask them how they would work this out. (Add 20, then adjust.) Practise some similar examples, using a class 100 square to demonstrate. Ask the children to close their eyes and visualise a 100 square, find 13 and then add 19 (by adding 20 and taking away 1). Repeat a few times for + 21 and – 21. Let any children who need support use a small 100 square.

Ask the children which coins we use. As they say the coin names, hold up the coin label cards and real coins, plus large card coins for everyone to see. Attach these to a board. Give the children a money problem based on shopping, such as: *I went to the baker's and bought a roll for 35p and a doughnut for 19p. How much did I spend?* Ask them to estimate the answer roughly, then work it out together (using the same strategy as above). Repeat with a few similar problems.

Paired work: Give each pair a copy of 'What did you do?', a pile of pence price labels and a pile of '+ and – 19 and 21' cards. Model this activity. *Pick a card from each pile and follow their instructions. Try to visualise a 100 square when you are calculating. When you have an answer, record your work on the 'What did you do?' sheet. Now make up a money problem for your calculation. Do this five times.* The children should work in mixed-ability pairs.

Differentiation

Less able: Give these children an individual 100 square. If they really struggle, ask them to add and subtract 9 and 11.
More able: Ask these children to add and subtract 18 and 22 as well as 19 and 21.

Plenary & assessment

Invite a few children to tell the class one of their made-up money problems. Ask the class to solve these and explain what they did. Ask questions such as: *Did you add or subtract 1 when you added 19? Why? What about subtracting 19? Why? Can you show me using a number line?*

Lesson ③

Starter

Call out some numbers from zero to 20 and ask the children to write on their whiteboards the number that goes with each to make 20. After a few examples, use a pendulum to practise quick recall: as it swings one way, you call out a number; as it swings the other way, the children call out the number that goes with it to make 20.

Main teaching activities

Whole class: This lesson is about using the strategies from Lesson 2 to solve two-step problems that involve measures and money. Discuss the strategies for adding and subtracting that the children have learned. Ask them to remind each other what they must do to solve a problem; show the problem-solving poster and the OHT of 'Problems'. Talk through each problem: pick out the information that is needed; decide on the best strategy; estimate and then calculate the answer; check that the answer makes sense in context.

Individual work: Ask the children to solve some problems individually, choosing the best strategies to answer them. Model an example from the 'Solve me!' activity sheet.

Differentiation

Less able: Provide the version of 'Solve me!' with simpler measures and prices.
More able: Provide the version with more complex measures and prices.

Plenary & assessment

Invite some children to explain how they solved their problems. Use this for assessment. Question them carefully about the process and about why they chose the strategy they used. Ask how they could check their answers; encourage them to use inverses. Demonstrate this with an arrow diagram.

Name   Date

Ordering amounts of money

For each problem:
- **plot the amounts of money on the number line**
- **decide on three answers**
- **plot your answers on the number line.**

Here is an example:

My sweets cost between 20p and 40p. How much could they have cost?	My three costs: 25p 30p 35p

25p 30p 35p

0   20p ↓ ↓ ↓ 40p   £1

1. My ice cream cost between 55p and 65p. How much could it have cost?	My three costs:

0   55p   65p   £1

2. My comic cost between 50p and 75p. How much could it have cost?	My three costs:

0   £1

3. My book cost between 85p and 98p. How much could it have cost?	My three costs:

0   £1

On the back of this sheet, make up some more problems for your partner to work on.

Name	Date

Solve me!

Here are some problems to solve. Remember to:

1. look for the question

2. look for the information

3. decide what to do

4. estimate the answer

5. work out the answer

6. check!

1. Lucy's gran needs 2m of material to make Lucy a dress.

Each metre costs £1.50.

How much does she spend? ☐

She gives the shopkeeper £5. ☐

How much change is she given?

How I worked out my answer: _____

2. Kiefa needs to buy 3m of string for school.

The string costs 21p a metre. ☐

How much money will he need?

He has 50p. ☐

How much more does he need?

How I worked out my answer: _____

3. Sanjay needs 5m of rope.

Each metre costs £2. ☐

How much money does he need?

He has four £1 coins. ☐

How much more does he need?

How I worked out my answer: _____

4. Kanar needs to buy 2m of ribbon.

The ribbon costs 35p a metre. ☐

How much does she need to pay?

She pays the shopkeeper £1. ☐

How much change does she receive?

How I worked out my answer: _____

× and ÷ strategies, and real life problem solving with money

The first three lessons focus on mental strategies to solve multiplication and division, including doubling and halving, using tables facts and counting in steps to help answer calculations, and partitioning. The final two lessons are about solving 'real life' problems to do with money involving both pounds and pence.

LEARNING OBJECTIVES

		Topics	Starter	Main teaching activities
Lesson	1	Understanding multiplication and division	● Begin to know multiplication facts for the 5 times-table.	● **Know and use halving as the inverse of doubling.**
Lesson	2	Mental calculation strategies (× and ÷)	● Derive quickly: – doubles of all numbers to at least 15 (e.g. 11 + 11 or 11 × 2) – doubles of multiples of 5 to 50 (e.g. 20 × 2 or 35 × 2) – halves of multiples of 10 to 100 (e.g. half of 70).	● Use known number facts and place value to carry out mentally simple multiplications and divisions.
Lesson	3	Mental calculation strategies (× and ÷)	As for Lesson 2.	As for Lesson 2.
Lesson	4	Problems involving 'real life', money or measures Reasoning about numbers and shapes	● Know by heart all pairs of numbers with a total of 20 (e.g. 13 + 7, 6 + 14). ● Know by heart all pairs of multiples of 10 with a total of 100 (e.g. 30 + 70).	● Recognise all coins and begin to use £.p notation for money. ● Find totals, give change, and work out which coins to pay. ● **Explain how a problem was solved** orally and in writing.
Lesson	5	As for Lesson 4.	As for Lesson 4.	As for Lesson 4.

Lessons   overview

Preparation
Make cards from 'Multiplication and division vocabulary' and 'Doubles and halves "Follow me" cards'. Make cards for each group of three children from 'What we know 1' and 'What we know 2'. Photocopy 'Dartboard doubles' onto card, laminate and cut up for each group.

Learning objectives
Starter
● Begin to know multiplication facts for the 5 times-table.
● Derive quickly: doubles of all numbers to at least 15 (e.g. 11 + 11 or 11 × 2); doubles of multiples of 5 to 50 (e.g. 20 × 2 or 35 × 2); halves of multiples of 10 to 100 (e.g. half of 70).
Main teaching activities
● Know and use halving as the inverse of doubling.
● Use known number facts and place value to carry out mentally simple multiplications and divisions.

Vocabulary
lots of, groups of, times, multiplied by, multiple of, repeated addition, array, row, column, equal, repeated subtraction, divided by, plus, left, left over, times, group in

You will need:
CD pages
'0–100 number cards', 'Multiplication and division vocabulary' cards, 'Dartboard doubles' game, spinner and gameboard (see General resources, Autumn term) for each group, 'Doubles and halves "Follow me" cards', (see General resources, Spring term), 'What we know 1' cards and 'What we know 2' cards for each group, an A3 copy of 'Spider charts for ×5 and ÷5' (see General resources).

Equipment
Blue-Tack; individual whiteboards and pens; counting apparatus; counters.

Lesson ①

Starter

Show the A3 spider chart for ×5 and ask the children to count in fives slowly as you point to the numbers 1–10 in order. Repeat, but stop at certain places and ask how many lots of five make the number they have just said. Repeat with the children using their fingers, as in previous lessons. Point to random numbers and ask the children for the answer when 5 is multiplied by that number.

Main teaching activities

Whole class: This unit is about multiplication and division. Ask: *What do we mean by 'multiply' and 'divide'? What vocabulary do we use for these operations?* Show the vocabulary cards as the children say the words, and stick them to the board; add any that the children don't say. Group the cards into multiplying and dividing words.

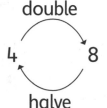

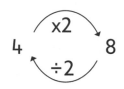

Say that today's lesson is about doubling and halving. *What do we mean by 'doubling'? What can we do to double 4?* (Add 4 + 4 or multiply 4 × 2.) Write 4 + 4 and 4 × 2 on the board. *What do we mean by 'halving'?* Use an arrow diagram to demonstrate that halving is the inverse of doubling.

Write some more numbers on the board and ask for volunteers to draw the arrow diagrams. Say: *Doubling is the inverse of halving, as multiplication is the inverse of division. So if we know that double 12 is 24, we know that half of 24 is 12.* Say a few examples for the children to answer on their whiteboards, such as: *Double 18 is 36, write down half of 36; double 11 is 22, write down half of 22; half of 28 is 14, write down double 14.*

Ask the children to write 6 on their whiteboards, then draw an arrow diagram to double it and halve the double. They could do this in either of the ways shown above, perhaps using 'D' and 'H' to stand for 'double' and 'half'. Now ask them to write 10, then draw an arrow diagram to halve it and double the half:

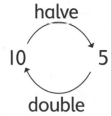
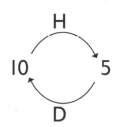
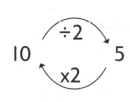

Repeat with a variety of numbers until most (if not all) of the class are confident.
Group work: Ask the children to play 'Dartboard doubles' in pairs or groups of three. Use the instructions to demonstrate. The children have played this game before (see Autumn term, Unit 11); this time, they should record their work using arrow diagrams. Model this.

Differentiation

Less able: These children should use only numbers to 20, with counting apparatus.
More able: Write extra numbers on the blank cards provided, such as 34, 45, 16 and 150.

Plenary & assessment

Play the doubles and halves 'Follow me' game as a class. Give a few cards to each group or pair. This is more effective than giving each child a card, for two reasons: it gives support to any children who are liable to become anxious; and it keeps the children involved throughout the game.

Lesson ②

Starter

The children will need single-digit number cards. Call out numbers to 15 (except 11, which can't be answered using one set of single-digit number cards) and ask the children to double them, then show you the answers. Call out their doubles for the children to halve. Ask the children what double 11 is. Repeat for multiples of 5 to 50 and 10 to 100, giving instructions such as: *Double 7, double 40, halve 80, double 35, halve 16, halve 30, double 30, double 45.* Ask the children what double 50 is.

Main teaching activities

Whole class: Today's lesson is about using what we know to multiply and divide mentally. The children know the 2 and 10 times-tables, know that a number ×1 is the same number, are learning the 5 times-table and can count in threes and fours. Write these number sentences on the board: $1 \times \square = 7$; $\square \times 10 = 60$; $2 \times \square = 20$; $15 = 3 \times \square$; $\square \times 2 = 50$; $\square \div 2 = 20$; $5 \div \square = 5$; $80 \div \square = 8$; $\square \div 3 = 10$. Ask the children to write on their whiteboards what they think should go in each box. Discuss what information they knew that helped them to find the answers.

Group work: Put the children in mixed-ability groups of three or four. The children in each group should work together to solve calculations. Demonstrate how to use the 'What we know 1' cards.

Plenary & assessment

Go through the cards used. Ask the children to tell you the answers and explain what information they knew that helped them to find the answers. For example, ask: *What multiplied by 9 gives 9? How do we know that? What is the rule that helps us? Can that help us to work out what number divided by 9 gives 1?*

Lesson ③

Starter

Repeat the Starter from Lesson 2, but ask the children to write the answers on their whiteboards. During the activity, ask questions such as: *Write down double 5, now double that, double it again, halve it, halve it again, what have you got? Can you explain why?*

Main teaching activities

Whole class: Write some calculations on the board as in Lesson 2; ask the children to solve them and to explain what information they knew that helped them to find the answers. Explain that today the children will look at partitioning numbers as a way of multiplying and dividing. Write 23 × 2 on the board. *How can we use partitioning and doubling to help us solve this?* (We can partition 23 into 20 and 3, double these and add the answers.) Write up 36 ÷ 2 and ask the children to answer it, using partitioning and halving. Repeat for various similar calculations.

Group work: Repeat the activity from Lesson 2, using the 'What we know 2' cards.

Plenary & assessment

Go through the cards used. Ask the children to give you the answers and explain how partitioning helped them to use what they knew. For example, look at 22 × 2 and ask: *What do you get if you partition 22? What are you doing when you multiply by 2? How can you double 20?*

Lessons   overview

Preparation
Copy 'How much change?' onto an OHT.

Learning objectives

Starter
- Know by heart all pairs of numbers with a total of 20 (e.g. 13 + 7, 6 + 14).
- Know by heart all pairs of multiples of 10 with a total of 100 (e.g. 30 + 70).

Main teaching activities
- Recognise all coins and begin to use £.p notation for money
- Find totals, give change, and work out which coins to pay.
- **Explain how a problem was solved** orally and in writing.

Vocabulary
lots of, groups of, times, multiply, multiplied by, multiple of, repeated addition, array, row, column, equal groups of, repeated subtraction, divide, divided by.

You will need:

Photocopiable pages
An OHT of 'How much change?' (page 200) 'Change problems' (page 201) for each child.

CD pages
An A3 copy of 'Flip-flap for 20', 'Price labels (pence)' and 'Price labels (£.p)' for each group, 'How to solve a problem' poster, (see General resources, Autumn term) 'Flip-flap for 10' for each child (see General resources, Spring term); 'Change problems', less able, more able and template versions (Summer term, Unit 10) (see General resources).

Equipment
Individual whiteboards and pens; coins; an OHP.

Lesson

Starter
Show the children your A3 'Flip-flap for 20' unfolded and ask how many ladybirds they can see. Fold it so that when you hold it up, they can see one ladybird. Ask: *If you can only see one and there are 20 altogether, how many can see? Fold it so that they can see 12: Now how many can you see? How many can I see?* Repeat several times. Give each child a copy of 'Flip-flap for 10'. Ask the children to imagine that each snail means ten snails. Ask them to show you 40, 60, 20 and so on. Now ask questions such as: *If I can see 70, show me how many you can see.*

Main teaching activities

Whole class: The next two lessons are about solving money problems. Show the coins we use; ask the children to identify them and say what each is worth. Hold up some of the 'pence' price label cards and ask the children which coins they could use to make each amount. Ask a child to explain, for example, how you could swap three pennies for one 2p coin and a penny. After a couple of goes with the children calling out or raising hands, ask them to write the answers on their whiteboards. Move on to doing the same thing with the '£.p' labels. Remind the children that the number after the £ sign is the pounds and the number after the decimal point is the pence.

Tell the children that you have £1. Choose a volunteer to be the shopkeeper, who picks a 'pence' card and tells you what it is. Say: *That is the amount I have spent. I am going to give my pound to the shopkeeper. What change does s/he need to give me?* Allow some thinking time, then check the children's answers by counting up on a number line on the board. Ask the children which coins you should use. Repeat for a different card.

Group work: Ask the children to work in groups of three or four. Each group needs a pile of price label cards ('pence' and '£.p') face down, and a container with coins including £1 and £2. They take turns to pick a card, read the amount they will spend and decide how many whole pounds to give the shopkeeper; then the group work out the change together using a number line.

Differentiation

Less able: Provide price label cards with amounts to £1, and real coins for the children to use. If possible, move them on to finding change from £2.

More able: Encourage the children to find change from £5 and £10.

Plenary & assessment

Invite a few children, particularly any whom you wish to assess, to show what they did in the group activity. Ask questions such as: *How are you going to find out the change? What amount will you count on from? What is the first amount you will count to? What next? What is the total change?* You or a more able child could draw the answers on a number line.

Lesson ⑤

Starter

Repeat the Starter from Lesson 4, but spend longer on using the 'Flip-flap for 10' to explore the multiples of 10.

Main teaching activities

Whole class: This lesson is about real-life money problems. Ask: *When do we have problems to solve that involve money?* Talk about shopping and how we might ask ourselves: 'Can I afford both of those?' Recap on what we need to do when solving a problem. Write the stages of problem solving (see the 'How to solve a problem' poster) on the board. Stick the problem-solving poster on the wall. Work through the three problems on the OHT of 'How much change?' Ask questions about the process as you go along. For example, when considering the first problem, ask questions such as: (1) *What is the problem asking us to find? Which words tell us that?* (2) *What information do we need to find the answer? Do we need to know which shop I was in? Do we need to know how much the mango cost?* (3) *What do we have to do? Would it help to count on from 59p to £1?* (4) *What is the answer? Does that make sense? How can we check it? Would it help to add our answer to the cost of the mango and see if that makes £1?*
Group work: Ask the children to work in pairs on the 'Change problems' activity sheet. Talk it through with them first.

Differentiation

Less able: Provide the version of 'Change problems' with smaller totals.
More able: Provide the version with larger totals.

Plenary & assessment

Invite a few children, particularly any whom you wish to assess, to show what they did to find the answers to the problems. Ask questions similar to those suggested above.

Name	Date

How much change?

I was in the greengrocer's and I saw a nice-looking mango.

I asked my mum if she would buy it for me.

She gave me a pound. It cost 59p.

How much change should I get?

Which three coins could I be given as change?

I was in the corner shop and I decided to buy a bag of crisps and a bottle of water.

The crisps were 45p.

The water was 65p.

I gave the shopkeeper £2.

How much change should I get?

Which three coins could I be given?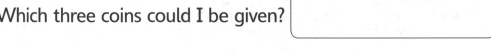

I was in the newsagent's and I bought two comics.

One was £1.20 and the other was £1.10.

I gave the shopkeeper £3.

How much change should I get?

Which two coins could I be given?

Name

Date

Change problems

Find the answers to these problems.

Write down the steps you took.

I was in the corner shop and I bought a bag of crisps and a drink.
The crisps were 45p. The drink was 55p. I gave the shopkeeper £2.

How much change should I get?

Which coin could I be given?

How I worked it out:

I was in the toy shop and I bought a bag of marbles and a bag of dice.
The marbles were 57p a bag. The dice were 68p a bag. I gave the shopkeeper £2.

How much change should I get?

Which three coins could I be given?

How I worked it out:

I was in the florist's and I bought two flowers.
They cost 29p each. I gave the florist £1.

How much change should I get?

Which three coins could I be given?

How I worked it out:

I was in the newsagent's and I bought three birthday cards.
One was 25p, another was 26p and the third was 50p. I gave the shopkeeper £1.

Was that enough?

How I worked it out:

Summer term
Unit 11 Fractions

This unit focuses on fractions. It begins by concentrating on halves and quarters of different numbers. It then moves on to link to time and movement, when the children focus on the use of clocks for fraction work. In the last two lessons the children use and apply their work by putting fractions into a problem-solving context.

LEARNING OBJECTIVES

		Topics	Starter	Main teaching activities
Lesson	1	Fractions	● **State the subtraction corresponding to a given addition and vice versa.**	● Begin to recognise and find one half and one quarter of shapes and small numbers of objects.
Lesson	2	Fractions	As for Lesson 2.	● Begin to recognise that two halves or four quarters make one whole and that two quarters and one half are equal.
Lesson	3	Fractions	● Begin to know multiplication facts for the 5 times-table.	As for Lesson 2.
Lesson	4	Making decisions	● Derive quickly: – doubles of all numbers to at least 15. – doubles of multiples of 5 to 50. – halves of multiples of 10 to 100.	● **Choose and use appropriate operations and efficient calculation strategies to solve problems.**.
Lesson	5	Making decisions	As for Lesson 4.	As for Lesson 4.

Lessons overview

Preparation
Copy 'Fraction strips' onto acetate and cut out. Copy 'Fraction number line and cards' onto A3 paper and laminate, then cut out the cards. Remove the hands from one of the card clocks and copy it onto acetate. Cut out three card circles the same size as the clock; keep one whole, halve the second and quarter the third. Adapt the 'Number spinners' and 'Fraction spinners' (see Lesson 3 Plenary). Make five Multilink towers: 1) five red, five green; 2) three red, three yellow, three blue, three green; 3) six red, three yellow, three green; 4) four red, four yellow, four blue, four green; 5) eight red, four yellow, four green.

Learning objectives
Starter
● **State the subtraction corresponding to a given addition, and vice versa.**
● Begin to know multiplication facts for the 5 times-table.
Main teaching activities
● Begin to recognise and find one half and one quarter of shapes and small numbers of objects.
● Begin to recognise that two halves or four quarters make one whole and that two quarters and one half are equivalent.

Vocabulary
part, equal parts, fraction, one whole, one half, two halves, one quarter, two… three… four quarters

You will need:
Photocopiable pages
'Clock fractions', (page 207), A3 copy and one per child.

CD pages
0–100 number cards, (see General resources, Autumn term) 'Fraction strips', 'Spin a fraction', 'Fraction number line and cards', 'Addition and subtraction cards', 'Pennies game' and 'Recording sheet' 3 (see General resources, Spring term) 'Spider charts for ×5', (see General resources).

Equipment
Multilink; individual whiteboards and pens; counters; pennies; card clocks.

Lesson ①

Starter

Show some of the addition cards from 'Addition and subtraction cards' and ask the children to write the corresponding subtraction on their whiteboards.

Main teaching activities

Whole class: This week's lessons are about using fractions. Ask: *Who can tell me something about a fraction?* Write down responses on the board. As in Spring term, Unit 11, aim for these statements (prompting if necessary): *A fraction is part of a whole thing. Half is when you divide something into two equal parts. 4 is half of 8. A quarter is when you divide something into four equal pieces. Two halves make a whole. Four quarters make a whole. A quarter is half of a half.* Remind the children that finding a fraction such as a half or a quarter is the same as dividing, because you are taking a whole number of things and sharing them out equally.

Ask whether the children remember the fraction strips and what they demonstrate (see Spring term, Unit 11). Use the strips to demonstrate that one whole is equal to two halves and four quarters, two quarters is equal to one half, and three quarters is equal to one half and one quarter. Put 12 counters on the whole strip. Give another 12 to a volunteer to put correctly on the halves strip (six in each section) and 12 to another volunteer to put on the quarters strip. Ask how many would go in each section if you had 16, 20 and 24 counters; then what would happen if you had 14 counters and then 15, and why. Agree that only even numbers can be halved, and that the half can only be halved again (to make quarters) if it is even.

Group work: Ask the children to practise finding fractions of numbers by playing the 'Pennies game'. Ask whether they remember the game. Briefly model the instructions using up to 50 pennies. This time, they need to use recording sheet 3, which asks them to identify whether the number of pennies they picked is odd or even.

Differentation

Less able: Work with this group and encourage them to find quarters as well as halves, using up to 30 counters.

More able: This group could use number cards to generate numbers from 30 to 100.

Plenary & assessment

Use the Multilink towers to make true and false statements. Ask the children to respond by holding their thumbs up/down or writing T/F on their whiteboards, and to explain their decisions. Reinforce the fact that any number that can be halved is even. Make statements such as: 1. *Half of this tower is green.* (T) *A quarter of it is green.* (F) *You can find a quarter of 10 cubes.* (F) *Why not?* 2. *Half of this tower is red.* (F) *The red and the green make up half.* (T) *If I add the yellow to the red and green, I will have $\frac{3}{4}$.* (T) 3. *Half of this tower is yellow.* (F) *A quarter is green.* (T) *The green and the yellow make half.* (T) 4. *The yellow, blue and green cubes make half of this tower.* (F) *The red make a quarter.* (T) *Any three of the colours together make $\frac{3}{4}$.* (T) 5. *The red and yellow cubes make $\frac{3}{4}$.* (T) *The green and yellow cubes also make $\frac{3}{4}$.* (F) *The green and the yellow make half.* (T)

Lesson ②

Starter

Show some of the subtraction cards from 'Addition and subtraction cards' and ask the children to write the corresponding addition on their whiteboards.

Main teaching activities

Whole class: Ask the children to tell you the 'fraction facts' they learned yesterday. Say that today they will be linking fractions with time. Ask: *Can anyone tell me when we use fractions to talk about time?* (Quarter past, half past and quarter to.) Show the clock OHT and say: *This is a whole clock. How many minutes are there all the way round it? So how many minutes are there in an hour?* Cover half the clock with the half card circle. *How much of the clock can you see now? How much of it can't you see? How many minutes are showing? How did you work that out? Did anyone halve 60? If I put this other half on the clock, how much is covered now?* Take off the card halves and cover the first quarter (from 12 to 3), and ask similar questions. Invite children to come to the front to cover different quarters: 3 to 6, 6 to 9, 9 to 12 and other quarters such as 2 to 5. Ask for a volunteer to cover three quarters.
Paired work: Using an A3 copy of 'Clock fractions', make and label some halves and quarters of the clock faces. Give each pair a copy of the sheet. Encourage the children to make halves and quarters in various ways. (Keep the second copy for Lesson 3.)

Differentiation

Less able: Provide pre-cut half and quarter circle shapes. Ask the children to find up to four different ways of making half and then a quarter.
More able: Ask this group to find three-quarters as well as halves and quarters.

Plenary & assessment

Ask a few pairs to show some of the ways they covered fractions of their clocks. Ask questions such as: (cover from 4 to 10) *How do we know this is half?* (Cover from 2 to 5, then 8 to 11) *What fraction is covered here? And here? How do you know? Are two quarters the same as a half?* Show the children the fraction number line and ask them to place some of the fraction cards on the line. Discuss where each card should go, and what clues are on the number line.

Lesson ③

Starter

Practise recall of 5 times-table facts by counting in multiples with fingers, then using the ×5 spider chart.

Main teaching activities

Whole class: The children will need a card clock each. Ask them to find 12 o'clock. Now ask them to move the minute hand around in fractions of an hour, and tell you the new time. For example: *Move clockwise a quarter of an hour, clockwise half an hour, anticlockwise a quarter of an hour.* If necessary, remind them to move the hour hand as well. Spend 5 minutes or so doing this.
Group work: Remind the children of yesterday's task. Give them the second copy of 'Clock fractions'. Ask them to find different ways of making half and three-quarters, using quarter pieces only. The halves should be different from those made the day before.

Differentiation

Less able: Ask these children to make quarters and halves, using the quarter piece.
More able: Encourage this group to look for other fractions, perhaps thirds or twelfths.

Plenary & assessment

Play 'Spin a fraction' as a class team game. Adapt the number spinner to give six larger even numbers to 50 and the fraction spinner to include $\frac{3}{4}$. When the $\frac{3}{4}$ comes up, ask the children how they can find this amount. If necessary, prompt them by saying: *If we know $\frac{1}{4}$ is… then $\frac{3}{4}$ is three times…*

Lessons   overview

Preparation

If necessary: make an A3 poster of 'How to solve a problem'; copy the 'Dartboard doubles' game onto card, then laminate the gameboard and cut out the spinners and cards. Make an OHT of 'Fraction problems'. Make enough copies of 'Fraction cards' to cut out three or four cards for each pair of children.

Learning objectives

Starter
● Derive quickly:
  – doubles of all numbers to at least 15.
  – doubles of multiples of 5 to 50.
  – halves of multiples of 10 to 100.

Main teaching activities
● **Choose and use appropriate operations and efficient calculation strategies to solve problems**.

Vocabulary

calculate, calculation, mental calculation, jotting answer, correct, number sentence, sign, operation, symbol

You will need:

Photocopiable pages
'Fraction problems' (page 208) for each pair.

CD pages

An A3 copy of 'How to solve a problem', 'Dartboard doubles', game, spinnder and gameboard, 'Fraction cards', 'Fraction problems', less able, more able and template versions (Summer term, Unit 11) (see General resources).

Equipment

Individual whiteboards and pens; counters; counting equipment.

Lesson

Starter

Call out some numbers in the ranges specified by the learning objectives (see above) and ask the children to double and halve them, writing on their whiteboards. Play 'Dartboard doubles', adapting the instructions so the whole class can play in two or three teams.

Main teaching activities

Whole class: The next two lessons are about solving problems that involve fractions. Ask: *What do we need to do when we are working out the answer to a problem?* Write the children's responses on the board. Display the 'How to solve a problem' poster as a reminder. Work through the problems on the OHT of 'Fraction problems' together, inviting children to come to the OHP and underline the relevant information in each problem. Talk about the strategies that can be used to solve these problems, such as: partitioning and halving or quartering each number, then recombining; putting counters into two or four groups. Discuss which strategy is the most efficient for each problem, and why.

Paired work: Ask the children to work in pairs to complete 'Fraction problems'.

Differentiation

Less able: Provide the less able version of 'Fraction problems'. Give help with reading. Let the children use counting equipment.

More able: Provide the more able version of 'Fraction problems'.

Plenary & assessment

Invite some pairs from each ability group to explain how they solved one of their problems. Include those children whom you wish to assess. Ask questions such as: *How did you find a quarter? What would three quarters of that number be?*

Lesson  5

Starter

Repeat the Starter from Lesson 4, but use numbers to 20. Ask the children to double and double again, and to halve and halve again where appropriate.

Main teaching activities

Whole class: Explain that today the children will make up their own problems for the rest of the class to solve. Write some information on the board, such as: $\frac{1}{4}$, 20 apples, Granny Smith. Make up a problem from these: *Granny Smith picked 20 apples from her apple tree. She needed a quarter of these to make apple sauce, and she gave the rest to me. How many did she use for her sauce?* Show the problem on the board, using simple pictures, words and numbers. Ask the children to solve it. Ask the children to turn to a partner and together make up a similar problem, using the same information. Give them a few minutes, then take feedback. Write some more information on the board and repeat the process.

Paired work: Give each pair of children three or four fraction cards; ask them to make up one problem for each card.

Differentiation

Less able: Provide cards with numbers to 20, quarters and halves.
More able: Provide cards with $\frac{3}{4}$ and higher numbers. Write information (with numbers to 100) on the blank cards for these children to use.

Plenary & assessment

Invite pairs from each ability group to describe one of their problems and invite the other children to solve it. Include those children whom you wish to assess. As they begin to solve the problems, ask: *What do you need to know? How are you going to use this information? What do you need to know before you can work out $\frac{3}{4}$?*

Name   Date

Clock fractions

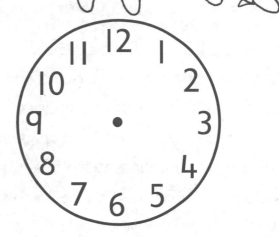

Cut out the two circles at the bottom of the page.

Colour the fractions you make on the clocks.
Fill in the sentence to say what the fraction is.

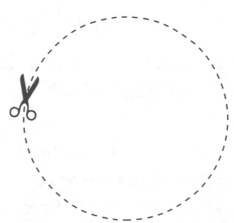

I've covered _____ of my clock.   I've covered _____ of my clock.

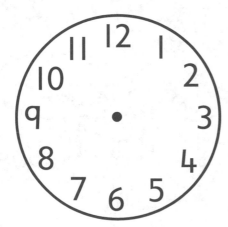

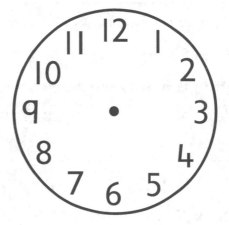

I've covered _____ of my clock.   I've covered _____ of my clock.

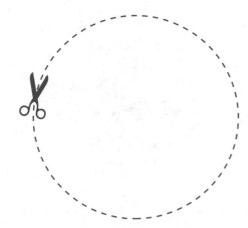

Cut this one in half.   **Cut this one into quarters.**

| Name | Date |

Fraction problems

I had a car collection. There were 30 cars in it.

I gave half of my collection to my best friend.

How many cars did I have left?

My answer and how I worked it out:

_____

My teacher was baking biscuits for our class.

There are 20 children in our class.

She baked a biscuit for each child.

A quarter of our class were missing when she brought them in.

How many biscuits did she have left over?

My answer and how I worked it out:

_____

Juan counted his toy farm animals. He had 50.

He gave half of them to his little sister.

How many animals did he have left?

My answer and how I worked it out:

_____

Sakina had 14 pairs of shoes.

She wanted to give a quarter of them away.

Could she? Why or why not?

My answer and how I worked it out: _____

_____

Marcia bought a packet of sweets.

There were 40 in the packet.

She gave a quarter to her mum.

How many did they each have?

My answer and how I worked it out: _____

_____

Children suggest units for estimating and measuring time in everyday situations. They read analogue and digital clocks to read time to the hour, half and quarter hour. They find answers to time-related word problems.

LEARNING OBJECTIVES

	Topics	Starter	Main teaching activities
Lesson 1	Measures	● Suggest suitable units to estimate or measure time. ● Know by heart all pairs of multiples of 10 with a total of 100.	● Suggest suitable units to estimate or measure time.
Lesson 2	Measures	● **Use the mathematical names for common 2-D shapes and describe some of their features.**	As for Lesson 1.
Lesson 3	Measures	As for Lesson 2.	● Read the time to the hour, half hour or quarter hour on an analogue clock and a 12-hour digital clock, and understand the notation 7:30.
Lesson 4	Measures	● **Know by heart all addition and subtraction facts for each number to at least 10.**	As for Lesson 3.
Lesson 5	Measures	● Add/subtract 9 or 11: add/subtract 10 and adjust by 1. ● Add/subtract 19 or 21: add/ subtract 20 and adjust by 1.	As for Lesson 3.

Lessons overview

Preparation
If you haven't already done this, copy the 'Up the mountain' gameboard onto A3 paper for whole-class use. Enlarge and photocopy 'Measures vocabulary' for time, 'Months of the year cards' and 'More time vocabulary' onto card. Group the time vocabulary cards into days of the week, months, seasons, general words and comparisons.

Learning objectives
Starter
● Suggest suitable units to estimate or measure time.
● Know by heart all pairs of multiples 10 with a total of 100.
● **Use the mathematical names for common 2-D shapes and describe some of their features.**
Main teaching activity
● Suggest suitable units to estimate or measure time.

Vocabulary
Monday, Tuesday… Sunday, January, February… December, spring, summer, autumn, winter, day, week, fortnight, month, year, weekend, birthday, holiday, morning, afternoon, evening, night, midnight, bedtime, dinnertime, playtime, today, yesterday, tomorrow, before, after, next, last, now, soon, early, late, quick, quicker, quickest, quickly, fast, faster, fastest, slow, slower, slowest, slowly, old, older, oldest, new, newer, newest, takes longer, takes less time

You will need:
CD pages
'0–100 number cards', 'Up the mountain gameboard', 'Measures vocabulary' for time, 'Months of the year cards', 'Templates for irregular shapes 1' and '2' and 'Templates for regular shapes' (see General resources, Autumn term); 'More time vocabulary' (see General resources).

Equipment
Three or four counters; dice; individual whiteboards, pens and cloths; tape recorder.

Lesson ①

Starter

You will need the number cards to 20, the cards with multiples of ten to 100, and the 'Up the mountain' gameboard. Divide the children into three or four teams. Pick a number card, show it to the class and expect all the children to write on their whiteboards the number that goes with it to make 20 or, if a multiple of 10, 100. The children can support each other in this activity. When everyone has written their answer and they are all correct, throw the dice and whichever number thrown matches the team number, i.e. one for Team 1, two for Team 2 etc, they move a place up the mountain. If you throw a five or six everyone moves up either five or six spaces.

Main teaching activities

Whole class: Say: *This week you will be thinking about time. Today and tomorrow we are concentrating on how we measure time. Let's start by thinking about the words that we know that are to do with time. What vocabulary would we use for this topic?* Listen to the children's suggestions and talk about when they would use each one. Don't show the vocabulary cards just yet.

Say: *I'm going to hold up a vocabulary card now and I would like you to think about the other words that would go with it.* Show one of the days of the week cards. After the children have told you that this is a day and what the others are, give one card to each of seven children and ask the class to order them. Ask them to tell you something that happens on each day of the week, either in their home life or their school life. Repeat this with the months of the year, bringing in birthdays, seasons and holidays.

Show the cards that say: 'day', 'week', 'fortnight', 'month', 'year', 'weekend', 'morning', 'afternoon', 'evening', 'night', 'midnight', 'bedtime', 'dinnertime', 'playtime', 'today', 'yesterday', 'tomorrow' and ask the children what they think is meant by these words.

Mix up all the vocabulary words that you have shown and randomly choose four of them. Show them to the children and ask them to turn to a partner and make up a short story that uses all four words correctly. Give them an example: words: *week, evening, tomorrow, bedtime. My mum said that tomorrow my bedtime can be later than normal, because in the evening we are going to the circus. The circus came to town last week and will be going in a few days. I'm very excited about seeing it.*

Group work: The children should work in pairs or small groups. Give four vocabulary cards to each group and ask them to make up a story to include each word. They can jot their ideas down on paper or a whiteboard, or simply remember them.

Plenary & assessment

Ask each group to share their stories. If you have any facilities for doing so, you could make audio recordings for the future. Discuss whether any of the vocabulary words were difficult to use, and invite all of the children to think about ways in which these could be incorporated into sentences.

Lesson ②

Starter

Give each child a shape cut from 'Templates for irregular shapes' and 'Templates for regular shapes'. Call out the properties of shapes to do with number of sides, corners and lines of symmetry, and their names. Ask the children to stand if their shape matches the properties or names that you are calling out.

Main teaching activity

Whole class: This is a continuation of yesterday's work. Today, recap on the vocabulary that the children thought about yesterday and then show them the comparison and measure type words: 'before', 'after', 'next', 'last', 'now', 'soon', 'early', 'late', 'quick', 'quicker', 'quickest', 'quickly', 'fast', 'faster', 'fastest', 'slow', 'slower', 'slowest', 'slowly', 'old', 'older', 'oldest', 'new', 'newer', 'newest', 'takes longer', 'takes less time'. Ask the children to work with a partner. Give each pair one of the first eight words and ask them to make up a sentence using it. Listen to each pair's ideas.

Group work: Show the five sets of cards that have got the three or four linked words (e.g. 'quick', 'quicker', 'quickest', 'quickly'). Give each pair one of these and ask them to make up a story which uses each word. Give them an example first: *My friend is a fast runner. She ran a race and was faster than anyone else. She is the fastest runner in our class.*

Plenary & assessment

Listen to each pair's story. Recap the vocabularu used during the lesson. Finish by asking questoins such as: *What have you learnt today? What did you find difficult/easy?*

Lessons overview

Preparation
Copy the 'Up the mountain' gameboard onto A3 paper for whole-class use. Copy and cut out the 'Analogue and digital time cards' and the 'Time "follow me" cards'. Copy 'Race against time' onto card. Cut out the problem cards and laminate the game board if possible.

Learning objectives
Starter
● **Use the mathematical names for common 2-D shapes and describe some of their features.**
● **Know by heart all addition and subtraction facts for each number to at least 10.**
● Add/subtract 9 or 11: add/subtract 10 and adjust by 1.
● Add/subject 19 or 21: add/subtract 20 and adjust by 1.
Main teaching activity
● Read the time to the hour, half hour or quarter hour on an analogue clock and a 12-hour digital clock, and understand the notation 7:30

Vocabulary
hour, minute, second, o'clock, half past, quarter to, quarter past, clock, watch, hands, digital/analogue clock/watch, timer

You will need:
CD pages
'Analogue and digital time cards', an 'Up the mountain gameboard' (see General resources, Autumn term) for each group, 'Time "follow me" cards', 'Race against time' instructions, gameboard and cards (see General resources).

Equipment
Individual whiteboards, pens and cloths; dice; counters; clocks; paper; hundred squares; small cubes and dice.

Lesson ③

Starter

Give each child a piece of paper and ask them to fold it. Give criteria as yesterday to do with the properties of the shapes. If they fit your criteria, ask the children to stand up. Ask them to fold their paper again and repeat what you have just done.

Main teaching activity

Introduce this series of three lessons by looking at the vocabulary of clock times from 'Analogue and digital time cards'. Ask the children to try to give you a sentence using each word. Next, give each child a clock. As you did last term, ask them to look at it and give you some facts about it. Look for answers like: *The numbers go round from one to 12. Those numbers show us what the hour is. If the minute hand is on the 12, it is something o'clock. If the minute hand is on the six, it is half past something. If the minute hand is on the three, it is quarter past something. If the minute hand is on the nine, it is quarter to something. The little marks in between the numbers are minutes. There are five minutes from one number to the next.*

Focus on the last two points. Ask the children to put a finger on the 12, then move to the 1. Ask how many minutes that is. Then repeat, with a finger on the 2, and so on so that the children are counting in fives from zero to 60. Use the clock as a sort of spider chart. Count round in fives again, and when you get to the 3 ask how many minutes past the o'clock position that is. Make the link with it being three lots of 5. Also make the link between saying, for example, *12:15 and quarter past 12.* Do the same at 6 and 9. Each time, link with how many minutes, lots of 5 and the digital and analogue ways of representing them. Finally, go to the 12 and ask the children how many minutes, making the link to: *12 lots of 5, which is 60, the number of minutes in an hour; 1:00, which is where you will be 60 minutes after 12 o'clock; its analogue version of 1 o'clock.*

Call out some times for the children to find on their clocks. Make these a mixture of analogue and digital times, e.g. *3:45, quarter past 6, 2:30.* Remind the children of the game they played last term, called 'Up the mountain'. Divide the class into two teams, one 'even' and the other 'odd'. Call out a time, wait until everyone has found it (the children can help each other) and then throw a dice. If an even number is thrown the even team moves up the mountain, if an odd number is thrown the odd team moves. The winning team is the one that gets to the top of the mountain first.

Plenary & assessment

Ask the children how this game has helped them in their learning about time. Give the children a clock each, and finish the session by asking them some problems, such as: *My clock says 3 o'clock; it is one hour slow. Show me what time it is really. My clock says half past seven; it is half an hour fast. What time is it really?*

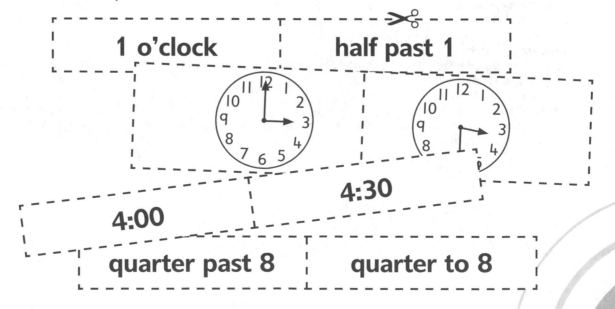

Lesson

Starter

Write this statement on the board: □ + □ = 3. Ask the children to write on their whiteboards four number sentences to make the statement true. Give them about a minute and then ask them to show you. Write on the board their answers beginning with 0 + 3 = 3 and then 3 + 0 = 3 beside it, 1 + 2 = 3 and 2 + 1 = 3 beside it. Repeat this with □ + □ = 4 and then 5, 6 and 7. Again, write what they have and any they have missed on the board systematically. Ask them what they notice. Aim for using the same numbers twice but in a different order. Move on to subtraction: 3 − □ = □. Write these on the board beside the corresponding additions. Again repeat with 4, 5, 6 and 7. Ask what they notice, aiming towards the inversion aspect and also the fact that the numbers can't be swapped to give the same answer.

Main teaching activity

Whole class: Call out various o'clock, quarter past, half past and quarter to times for the children to find on their clocks. Mix these analogue times with digital. For each time, after they have found it, invite some children to write the analogue and digital times on the board. After they have had lots of practice, tell the children that they will be playing a matching game similar to one they did last term. They will practise matching digital and analogue times and clock faces. Demonstrate the 'Up the mountain' game, as played in Term 2, Unit 11, Lesson 4 but using 'Analogue and digital time cards'.

Plenary & assessment

Play the 'follow me' game using 'Time "follow me" cards'. Give pairs or small groups of children a few cards. Play once and then talk through the sequence, then play again.

Lesson

Starter

Give each child a 100 square. Say a starting number for them to put their fingers on. Then ask them to add 9, add 11, add 19 take away 21, add 9 and then tell you where they are. Repeat this a few times with different starting numbers and instructions. Next, ask them to do the same thing but visualise the 100 square in their heads.

Main teaching activity

Whole class: Begin by asking the children to find different times on their clocks; ask some problems similar to those random ones in Lesson 3's Plenary. Choose a theme, such as sport's day, and make up problems: *It is now 2 o'clock. The race starts in an hour. What time does it start? The race started at half past 1. It took Sam one and a half hours to finish. At what time did he finish?*
Group work: Tell the children that they will be playing another game. This time they have to solve problems to get across the board. Demonstrate the 'Race against time' game. Encourage the children to work in mixed-ability groups in which at least one child is a good reader. Provide clocks for each group.

Plenary & assessment

Discuss the problems, inviting children to come to the front to explain how they solved them. Ask the children to talk to each other about some of the things they have learned to do with time. Take some whole-class feedback.

Handling data

In this unit the children will be solving given problems by sorting, classifying and organising information in pictograms and block graphs. They will also be discussing and explaining their results. As well as revision of graphs, there is the opportunity to test a hypothesis, draw, label and interpret their own graphs and identify errors on given examples to consolidate their ability to make up graphs.

LEARNING OBJECTIVES

		Topics	Starter	Main teaching activities
Lesson	1	Organising and using data	● Read the time to the hour, half hour or quarter hour on an analogue clock.	● Solve a given problem by sorting, classifying and organising information in simple ways, such as: in a list or simple table; in a pictogram; in a block graph. ● Discuss and explain results.
Lesson	2	Organising and using data	● **Read and write whole numbers to at least 100** in figures.	As for Lesson 1.
Lesson	3	Organising and using data	● Find one half and one quarter of small numbers.	As for Lesson 1.
Lesson	4	Organising and using data	● **Know by heart all addition and subtraction facts for each number to at least 10.**	As for Lesson 1.
Lesson	5	Measures	● **Know by heart multiplication facts for the 2 and 10 times-tables.** ● Derive quickly division facts for the 2 and 10 times-tables. ● Begin to know multiplication facts for the 5 times-table.	As for Lesson 1.

Lessons overview

Preparation

If necessary: copy the 'Up the mountain' gameboard onto A3 paper; make and laminate a copy of the 'Function machine game' for each child; make enlarged 'Organising data vocabulary cards'; make OHTs of Ways to organise data', 'Pictograms' and 'Sports block graph'. Draw vertical and horizontal axes on a sheet of A1 paper, and make separate labels on paper with Blu-Tack on the back: 'Number of children', 'Countries', the numbers 1–20 (shown vertically) and 'Block graph to show where we want to go on holiday'. Make OHTs of 'We need help!', 'Empty pictogram', 'Spot the mistakes 1', 'Spot the mistakes 2' (both versions), 'Unfinished graphs 1' and 'Unfinished graphs 2', and cut out the acetate smiley faces on 'Empty pictogram'.

Learning objectives

Starter

- Read the time to the hour, half hour or quarter hour on an analogue clock.
- **Read and write whole numbers to at least 100** in figures.
- Find one half and one quarter of small numbers.
- **Know by heart all addition and subtraction facts for each number to at least 10.**
- **Know by heart multiplication facts for the 2 and 10 times-tables.**
- Derive quickly division facts for the 2 and 10 times-tables.
- Begin to know multiplication facts for the 5 times-table.

Main teaching activities

- Solve a given problem by sorting, classifying and organising information in simple ways, such as; in a list or simple table; in a pictogram; in a block graph.
- Discuss and explain results.

Vocabulary

count, tally, sort, vote, graph, block graph, pictogram, represent, group, set, list, label, title, most popular, least popular, most common, least common

You will need:

Photocopiable pages

'We need help!' (page 220), 'Empty pictogram' (page 221), 'Spot the mistakes 1' (page 222), 'Spot the mistakes 2' (page 223) and 'Unfinished graphs 2' (page 224) for each child, plus OHT versions.

CD pages

'0–100 number cards', 'Up the mountain' gameboard, 'Function machine game' for each child, 'Organising data vocabulary cards', an OHT of 'Ways to organise data', 'Pictograms' and 'Sports block graph' (see General resources, Autumn term) an OHT of 'Empty pictogram'; OHTs of 'Spot the mistakes 1' and 'Unfinished graphs 1', 'We need help!' less able and more able versions 'Spot the mistakes 2' and 'Unfinished graphs 2', less able version (see Summer term, Unit 13) (see General resources).

Equipment

A card clock for each child; dice; two counters; individual whiteboards, pens and cloths; an OHT sheet of squared paper; an OHP and OHP pen; Post-it Notes; A1 paper; Blu-Tack; squared paper; scissors; adhesive.

Lesson

Starter

Stick the A3 'Up the mountain' gameboard to the board. Give each child a card clock. Divide the class into two teams: 'even' and 'odd'. Call out simple clock times for the children to show on their card clocks and hold up. When all the clocks are showing the time, throw the dice: the 'even' team moves up the mountain one place if an even number is thrown and the 'odd' team if an odd number is thrown. The first team to reach the top wins. As well as asking directly for times such as four o'clock, half past seven or quarter to six, say: *Find half past 3; now find one hour after that time, now find half an hour earlier…*

Main teaching activities

Whole class and group work: This week the children will be learning how to organise and use data. Ask: *What do we mean by 'data'? How might we 'organise and use' it? Can you tell me some words that we use for this topic?* Match the words the children say with the vocabulary cards, and remind them of any they have not mentioned. Discuss what the words mean. Remind the children of their work on organising data in the Spring term. *Can anyone remember any of the ways we used?* (counting, tallying, sorting, voting and making block graphs and pictograms). Ask them to explain what each way looks like, perhaps drawing an example on the board. Sum up by saying: *These are ways to represent, group, set or list information. When we do this, it saves us writing lots of words and helps us to see information easily. It also helps us to answer questions about the information.*

Project the OHPs of 'Ways to organise data', 'Pictograms' and 'Sports block graph'. These show different ways of organising information. For each way, ask questions such as: *How is the information shown? What does this show us? What four things can you tell me from this… ? What is the most popular/least popular… ? What is the most common/least common… ? How many people were asked/involved?* Ask the children to tell a friend one piece of information from each example. Take feedback.

Introduce the idea of using data to test a hypothesis. Say: *Do you remember last term, when we made a block graph using Post-it Notes? What did it show? Today, we are going to make a block graph about holidays. My travel agent has run out of brochures for different summer holiday places. He needs to order some, but he is only allowed them for six different countries. He is also only allowed to order lots of brochures for one country; the rest of the countries can only have one brochure each. He thinks most people will want to go to Spain. Can we help him see whether Spain is the right choice? Can we help him decide which other countries to choose?*

Encourage the children to suggest voting for the country they would most like to visit. The six most popular countries will go on the graph. Collect the names of about ten countries, including Spain. Do a tally vote to find the six most popular. Give the children a Post-it Note each; ask them to write their choice (from the six) and draw a sun on it. Prepare six 'country' labels on Post-it Notes. Gather the class together. Show them the labels you prepared earlier and the new ones, and invite some children to stick these onto your skeleton graph and explain why they are putting them there. Check that the other children agree. Invite everyone to come to the front and add their Post-it Note to the graph.

Differentiation

Pair children who may need support with writing with children who can help them.

Plenary & assessment

Discuss what information the graph shows. Ask questions, particularly of the How many more/ less… ? type. Target less able children with easier questions such as: *Which is the most popular country?* Encourage the children to ask each other questions, or to talk to a friend and make up a question for the class. Find out whether the data supports the travel agent's hypothesis. Discuss why the graph is more useful than the list of votes. Keep the graph on display.

Lesson

Starter

Call out single-digit and two-digit numbers for the children to write down on their whiteboards. Now ask them to write a two-digit number and then add numbers that you call out. Call out numbers from 1–10 and multiples of 10 to 100. Use this to practise bridging through 10. For example: *Write down 24, add 7, take away 10, add 9. What do you have? Write down 48, add 9, add 20, take away 7, take away another 7. What do you have?*

Main teaching activities

Whole class: Show the Post-it Note graph from yesterday and recap what it was about. Ask the children why the labels are important. Explain that in today's lesson they will draw and label their own graphs. Project the OHT of 'We need help!' Discuss the problem and agree that the children have to find out which is the most popular place. Model the process of making a block graph on an OHT sheet of squared paper: ask the children what to do first (draw the graph axes), then repeat for the labels and the blocks.

Group work: The children should work in groups of four to make their own block graph of the data on squared paper. Remind them to write the labels and title. Then ask them to think of some questions to ask each other.

Differentiation

Less able: Provide the version of 'We need help!' with simpler data. Provide a skeleton graph and suggest that the children draw blocks for the circus, theme park and seaside only.
More able: Provide the version with more complex data.

Plenary & assessment

Ask the groups to show their graphs and feed back some questions for the class to answer. Find out what everyone concluded. The graph should have helped them to see that the most popular choice is the theme park. Ask: *Why is drawing a graph a good way to solve this problem? Why are the labels important?* Cover the labels on the OHT version and ask the children questions similar to those they made up: this will show them that a graph is harder to interpret without labels.

Lesson ③

Starter

Give each child number cards 0–9. Call out some even numbers to 30 and multiples of 10 to 100 and ask the children to show you half of each number. Call out some more (using multiples of 4) and ask the children to show you a quarter. Encourage them to find a quarter by halving and halving again.

Main teaching activities

Whole class: Ask the children what a pictogram is. Explain that today they will make up and use their own pictograms. Show the OHT of 'Empty pictogram'. Ask them to suggest what the title and axis labels could be. Stress that the title is necessary to explain what the pictogram is about. Agree that this title could be 'Children's pets', 'Pets in a zoo' or 'Children's favourite animals'. Invite some children to place acetate smiley faces on each section of the pictogram. Talk about what information this provides. Move the faces around and ask how that alters the graph.

Tell the children that they will now collect data to make their own pictograms. Write these headings on the board: 'Favourite fruit', 'Favourite animals', 'Favourite colours'. Take suggestions and list five fruits, animals and colours. Ask the children to decide which of each list is their favourite. From a show of hands, write the votes beside each option.
Paired work: The children should work in pairs to choose one set of data and make a pictogram on 'Our pictogram'. Demonstrate how to do this, using the instructions on the sheet.

Differentiation

Less able: Write the labels for children who have writing difficulties. Provide cut-out smiley faces.
More able: Show this group how to make a pictogram where one smiley face represents two children.

Plenary & assessment

Invite some pairs to show and explain their pictograms. Ask the other pairs to ask each other questions about their pictograms (such as: 'Which is the least popular fruit?', 'How many children are in our class today?', 'How many more children like red than green?'). Assess the children's ability to make up and answer such questions. Briefly share with the class the more able group's pictogram, and ask how the number of smiley faces in each column was found (by halving the number of children).

Lesson ④

Starter

Write on the board: □ + □ = 8. Ask the children to write on their whiteboards four number sentences that make this statement true. Give them about 1 minute, then ask them to show you. Write their answers on the board. Add any answers they have not found. Repeat with totals of 9 and 10. Now write 8 − □ = □ on the board beside the corresponding addition. Repeat with totals of 9 and 10. Ask what the children notice; look for the idea of inverse operations.

Main teaching activities

Whole class: In the next two lessons, the children will consolidate their work on constructing, labelling and interpreting graphs. Show the OHT of 'Spot the mistakes 1'. The two graphs each have six mistakes. Ask the children to spot the mistakes and tell you what should be there. Mark corrections on the OHT. Prompt if necessary (for example: *What do you notice about the numbers?*).
Paired work: Ask the children to work in pairs on 'Spot the mistakes 2'. They have to spot and correct the mistakes on the graph.

Differentiation

Less able: Provide the version of 'Spot the mistakes 2' with four mistakes.
More able: Give this group about 10 minutes to spot and correct the mistakes, so that they have more time to write down facts from the corrected graph.

Plenary & assessment

Show an OHT of the 'less able' version of the sheet and ask the less able group what mistakes they found. Repeat for the 'main' version, asking anyone to contribute. Focus on the labelling of the vertical axis: stress the importance of writing a zero at the bottom. Ask the children to tell each other facts from the corrected graph (such as: *Yellow was the most popular colour; four more children liked pink than orange*). Assess their ability to find information.

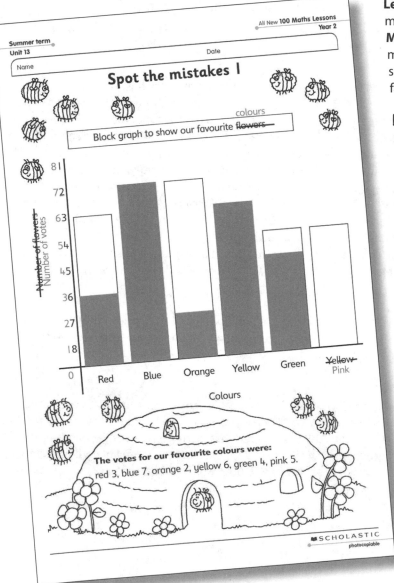

Lesson ⑤

Starter

Recite the 2 and 10 times-tables together. Count in multiples of 2 and 10, using fingers. Stop the children at various points, asking which finger they have got to and how many lots of 2 or 10 that is. Give each child a function machine, pen and cloth. Ask them to write any numbers from 1 to 10 on the input side and write ×2 in the middle. When you say *Go!* they should fill in the output side as quickly as possible. Now ask them to rub out the answers and ×2, then write ×10 and the new answers. Repeat for ×5. Repeat for division: ask the children to use multiples of 2 and ÷2, then multiples of 10 and ÷10.

Main teaching activities

Whole class: Today the children will continue to consolidate their understanding of graphs by trying to complete unfinished graphs. The graphs may have missing labels, blocks, pictures or other features. Show the OHT of 'Unfinished graphs 1'. Ask for volunteers to fill in the missing parts of each graph. Give hints if necessary (for example: *Do you know what each smiley face stands for?*).

Paired work: Encourage the children to work with the same partner as in Lesson 4 to finish the graph on 'Unfinished graphs 2'.

Differentiation

Less able: Provide the version of 'Unfinished graphs 2' with four things missing.

More able: Give this group about 10 minutes to complete the graph, so that they have more time to write down facts from the completed graph.

Plenary & assessment

Show an OHT of 'Unfinished graphs 2'. Ask the children to tell you how to complete the graph. Recap on the purpose of a graph by asking them why it needs to have a title, axis labels, blocks and so on. Repeat the questions you asked in Lesson 1: *What does 'data' mean? What do we mean by 'organising and using data'? Why are graphs and other ways of organising data useful?* Ask questions such as: *What must we always write on a graph? Why are labels important?* Target children whom you wish to assess.

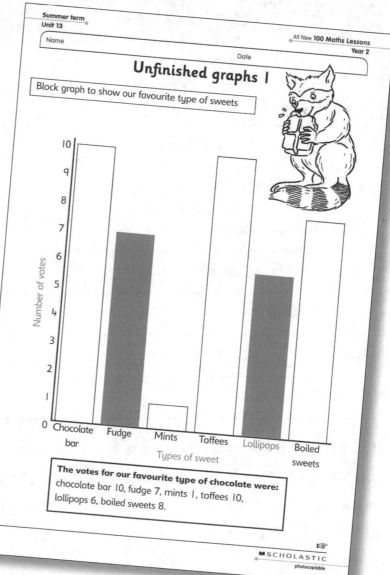

Summer term
Unit 13

Name

All New **100 Maths Lessons**
Year 2

Date

Unfinished graphs 1

Block graph to show our favourite type of sweets

Number of votes / Types of sweet

Chocolate bar, Fudge, Mints, Toffees, Lollipops, Boiled sweets

The votes for our favourite type of chocolate were:
chocolate bar 10, fudge 7, mints 1, toffees 10, lollipops 6, boiled sweets 8.

SCHOLASTIC
photocopiable

Name	Date

We need help!

Class 5 at Butterscotch School have been asked to choose where they will go for their summer trip.

They can't agree! Some of them want to do one thing, and some want to do something else.

Can you help them make up their minds?

Here is a list of the children and where they would like to go.

Children	Want to go to
Sam, Pat, Peter, Raj and Samir	the circus
Robert, Lucy, Annabel, Kanar, Suzi and Leticia	the seaside
Patrice, Rah, Becky and Theo	London
Wanda and Emil	the zoo
Paul, Ryan and Robin	a museum
Adam, Lafita, Hyatt and Laura	a theme park
Amy and Sue	the woods
Caroline, Marissa and Tim	the seaside and a theme park
Ricky, Carla and Macy	the circus and a theme park

Put all this information into a block graph.

Use the graph to help them decide where they will go.

Remember to write a title for the graph and label the axes.

When you have made your graph, think up some questions to ask each other about it.

If you have time, think of some more questions to ask during the Plenary.

Name	Date

Empty pictogram

by [   ]

1. Choose which pictogram to do.

2. Make up a title for it.

3. Fill in the label boxes.

4. Draw a symbol on each square.

Cut them out and put them where you want them to go.

When you are sure they are in the right places, stick them down.

Title: [   ]

Each [   ] **stands for one child.** [   ] **= 1 child**

Write down as many facts from your graph as you can on the back of this sheet.

Name   Date

Spot the mistakes 1

Block graph to show the times that we go to bed

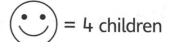

Half past 7   = 4 children

8 o'clock

Our bed times

Half past 7

8 o'clock

Half past 6

Our bed times

Our bed times are:

Half past six 2, seven o'clock 4, half past seven 6
eight o'clock 7, half past eight 2.

Name	Date

Spot the mistakes 2

There are eight mistakes on this graph.

Can you find them all? When you find them, put them right!

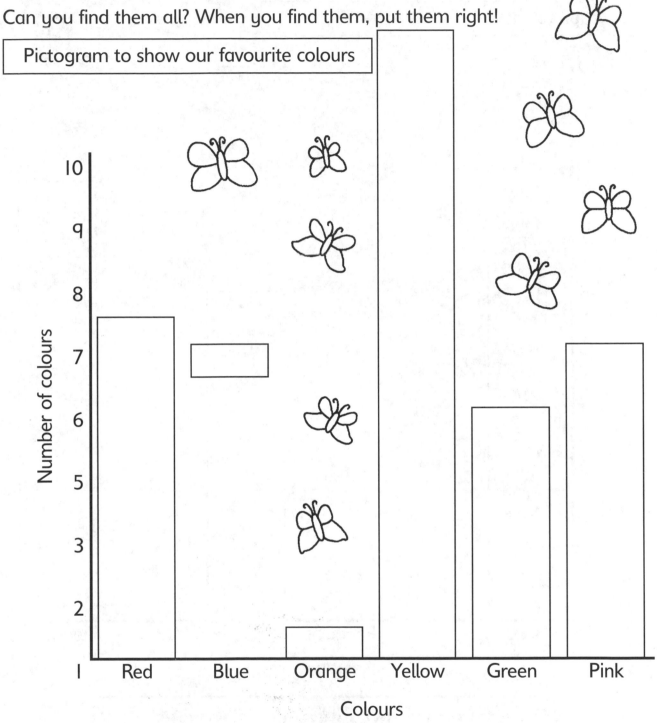

Pictogram to show our favourite colours

The votes for our favourite colours were:

red 8, blue 7, orange 1, yellow 10, green 6, pink 5.

When you have corrected the graph, write down as many facts from it as you can on the back of the sheet.

Name	Date

Unfinished graphs 2

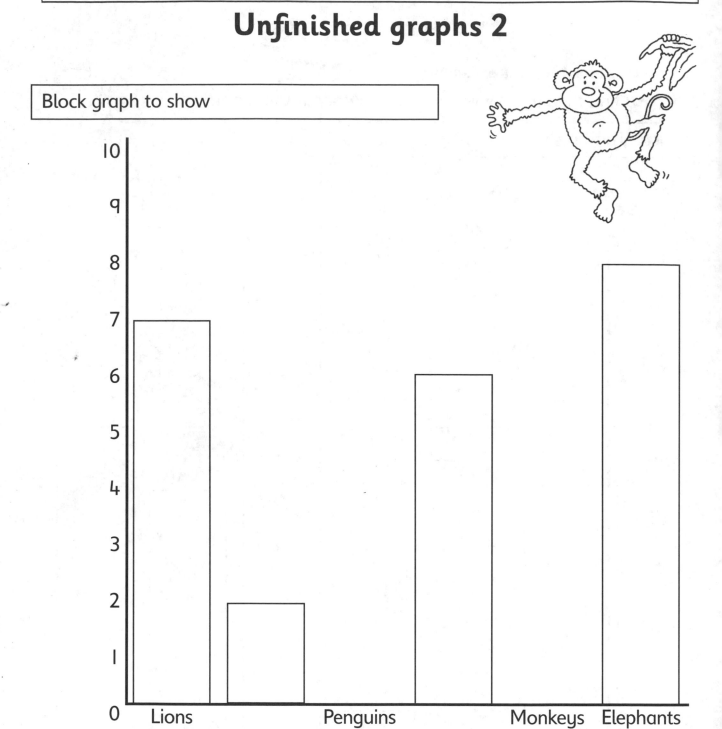

Block graph to show

The votes for our favourite zoo animals were:

lions   , penguins 9, monkeys 10, camels 2, rhinos 6,
elephants   .

When you have corrected the graph, write down as many facts from it as you can on the back of the sheet.

◀ S C H O L A S T I C
photocopiable